A student teacher's guide to primary school placement

Learning to survive and prosper

Denis Hayes

RoutledgeFalmer
Taylor & Francis Group

LONDON AND NEW YORK

First published 2003
by RoutledgeFalmer
11 New Fetter Lane, London EC4P 4EE

Simultaneously published in the USA and Canada
by RoutledgeFalmer
29 West 35th Street, New York, NY 10001

RoutledgeFalmer is an imprint of the Taylor & Francis Group

© 2003 Denis Hayes

Typeset in Palatino by Keystroke, Jacaranda Lodge, Wolverhampton
Printed and bound in Great Britain by St Edmundsbury Press, Bury St Edmunds, Suffolk

British Library Cataloguing in Publication Data
A catalogue record for this book is available from the British Library

Library of Congress Cataloging in Publication Data
A catalog record has been requested

ISBN 0–415–28783–9

A student teacher's guide to primary school placement

THE LONDON BOROUGH

School
be the r
walk in
to some

It hel
coped.
teacher
strategi
you suc

- Prin
  of in
- Plac
  plac
- Prac
  teac
  envi
- Prog
  teac

This te
embarl
mento1

Denis
Plymo1

t can also
1unting to
ve lessons

eople have
nt (trainee)
ice, he offers
ement to help

ses a variety
ok.
1g in, school

planning,
classroom

qualified

about to
r teacher

ersity of

DEDICATION

I dedicate this book to my surviving children, Stephen and Kerensa, with deep thankfulness to God for who they are, what they believe and how they live their lives.

CONTENTS

FIGURES

ACKNOWLEDGEMENTS

Every book consists of knowledge, information and wisdom gleaned from many different sources. This book is no exception. Over the past thirty years or so it has been my privilege and pleasure to meet thousands of pupils, students, teachers and people with an interest in education, all of whom, in small ways or large, have contributed to my own understanding. I have attended lectures, participated in discussions, picked up snippets of an idea, read books and articles, witnessed situations and, through these varied influences, tried to make sense of the mysterious process of teaching and learning. I have also been on the receiving end of government policies, sometimes being horrified at the ineptness and lack of sensitivity they have shown and sometimes grateful for their insight and initiative. I have spoken to many heads, teachers and mentors about the stresses and strains as well as the joys of the job, and been heartened by the fact that without exception they are passionate to help children and young people grow and develop. Their commitment, selfless acts of service and determination to promote the best interests of the child has been humbling and inspiring. Most of all, I have learned from the children themselves, with their sense of fun, enthusiasm, unpredictability and ability to turn a grey, cheerless Monday morning into a kaleidoscope of colour. To all these unnamed people I give my humble thanks.

I have attempted to the best of my ability to give credit to every person whose work I have used or whose ideas I have incorporated in the text, and to honestly represent their views. If I have failed in any measure, then I apologize and resolve to make amends in future editions. My earnest thanks are extended to my colleagues at the University of Plymouth, unsung heroes all, who strive so earnestly to support and train aspiring teachers. Finally, to Anna Clarkson of RoutledgeFalmer for her encouragement, guidance and expertise.

INTRODUCTION

This book has been written to help trainee teachers prosper during the time they spend on school placement (sometimes referred to as *school experience* or *teaching practice*). It contains advice, strategies and suggestions that will assist them in finding a way through the complex world of school and classroom life, and to think deeply about the issues and practicalities that relate to the job of becoming a teacher.

Teachers in training are able to take a variety of routes into the profession, including school-based training where they are attached to one school. The majority of them, however, follow the traditional route of a three- or four-year undergraduate degree or a one-year postgraduate course (PGCE) to achieve qualified teacher status (QTS). For the purpose of this book, the institution or provider responsible for the training will simply be referred to as 'the college'. A sizeable proportion of the book is based on research that draws on trainee primary teachers' accounts of their school experience, the emotional demands placed on them and the way that they coped with a variety of relational and practical challenges. The final chapter uses interview evidence from newly qualified teachers about their experiences during the first six months of teaching.

There are no easy solutions to the complex issues that characterize the average classroom, yet this is exactly what some people demand. 'Never mind that theory stuff,' they mutter, 'just tell us what to do.' If only life were that simple! The truth is that although there are many specific things that trainees need to learn throughout their training course, effective teachers must be willing to engage with a range of problems, dilemmas and decisions that defy simple resolution and to press on with knowledgeable determination. Reading this book will not, of course, magically transform someone into a good classroom practitioner, but it will provide a solid platform for achieving such a goal. It provides explanations about school life, the challenges faced by trainee teachers and strategies for enhancing the likelihood of success in classroom teaching. Case study material, including numerous narratives, is used throughout the book to exemplify key points and assist in solving some of the dilemmas faced by practitioners.

Part 1, Principles, is a summary of the tenets that underpin successful teaching and raises a variety of issues that are explored more fully in the remainder of the book. Part 2, Placement, offers detailed advice about preparing for, and prospering in, school placements, including a number of accounts written by trainee teachers about their experiences. The accounts expose the situations with which they grappled, their heightened emotions, and the ways in which they learned to cope with the many challenges and opportunities that they encountered in school.

Part 3, Practice, focuses on the practical skills that affect classroom practice and prospering as a trainee teacher on school placement, including children's learning needs, lesson planning, teaching skills, maintaining order and assessment.

Part 4, Progress, deals with preparation for the first post, application letters, interview strategies and extracts of writings from newly qualified teachers that expose the reality of the first months in post and strategies for coping.

The text also contains a number of 'Teaching principles' to stimulate thoughtful reflection about the implications of seminal points raised in the text.

Teaching has had a mixed press over recent years, yet it provides one of the most interesting and worthwhile vocations imaginable. It is never likely to be the easiest of jobs because teachers are dealing with immature young lives and the high expectations of parents and the community. Times of discouragement and frustration, however, are amply compensated for by the many occasions when teachers walk with a spring in their step because they have been able to make a positive difference to children's lives. Aspiring teachers should never lose sight of the fact that this was the principal reason they made their career decision in the first place.

PART 1

Principles

CHAPTER 1

Learning to be a teacher

The expectations that society holds of teachers are high and extensive. The general public insists that they set a good example and behave professionally. Head teachers and governors are anxious that they should improve test results as this is one of the main factors taken into account when judging the school's success. Parents are interested in the way their children are treated, whether they are happy and what they achieve. Prospective parents may select a school on the basis of its national ratings in performance tables. Children expect teachers to maintain order and give them interesting and occasionally exciting work to do. Much is therefore expected of teachers and their sphere of accountability is wide (see Figure 1.1).

At the start of your training course it is possible to imagine that being a teacher is principally about the delivery of a curriculum to a passive audience of eager children, who are waiting on your every word. In fact, although imparting information is very

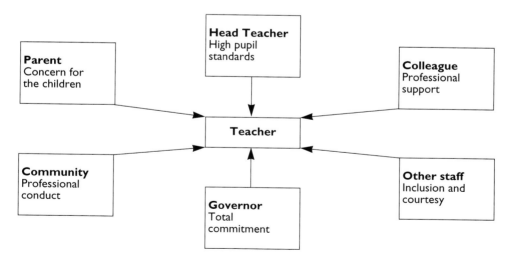

Figure 1.1 *Expectations made of teachers*

important, it is only part of providing a broad education for children. A full education will incorporate a range of practical and social skills, and will promote in children an appetite for learning, the ability to get along with other people, independence in thinking and confidence to act appropriately. A head full of knowledge is useful but of little value if it cannot be utilized.

All trainee teachers have to spend a lot of their time on school placement to gain experience of teaching and to become familiar with the teacher's wider role outside the classroom. These additional responsibilities include the need to collaborate with colleagues and carry out regular duties such as taking the register, helping with playground patrols and completing pupil records. Being a good classroom practitioner, though of central importance, is not the only task of a teacher in twenty-first century schools. As well as in-school duties, there are numerous external agencies (e.g. social services) to which teachers must relate and with whom they are required to co-operate.

It is important to become familiar with the many different things that you need to do as a teacher, and there is certainly no shortage of them (see TTA 2002a). For instance, you need to have a grasp of the areas of the curriculum that must be covered for each year group during each term and what children ought to be learning while they are at a particular stage of their schooling. You also need to know about different forms of assessment, formal testing and target setting that take place in school. There will be records to keep about children's progress and decisions to make about what information to write down and what to store in your head. However, in the process of 'doing' it is important to bear in mind *why* you are doing it. For instance, classroom activities are not just to keep children occupied, they are to help them to understand better or gain an opportunity to practise skills and clarify issues. Similarly, keeping records of children's progress is not for the purpose of proving that you are capable of writing something down but to assist in shaping future lessons for helping children to learn more effectively and for transmitting information to colleagues and parents.

Whatever else teaching may be, it is rarely tedious! Even teachers who deal successfully with the variety of learning and emotional needs that exist within every group of children are hard-pressed to cope with the many other demands that the job requires outside the classroom. The fact that so many do so is testament to the commitment and dedication that the vast majority of the profession exhibit, day in day out. Hargreaves and Fullan (1998) identify an important point when they argue that keeping the flames of passion alive in teaching is a challenge for all teachers and yet, amazingly, so many teachers succeed in doing exactly this.

Most people can think back to teachers they had when they were pupils, some who made learning exciting, some that were fun to be with and others who were uninspiring. Perhaps certain teachers transformed their lives, or damaged them. Others may have given them a love for a subject, or destroyed any semblance of interest they had in it. One way and another, teachers make a difference to children's lives, but it is hard to understand the mysterious way in which the various ingredients of character, knowledge, teaching skills and relationships combine within a particular school context to produce an effective teacher and motivated learner. Engaging with these elements is a key component of the stimulating prospect that lies ahead for every aspiring practitioner.

Qualifying as a teacher

Students working towards Qualified Teacher Status (QTS) whether undergraduates or postgraduates, are normally referred to as 'trainee teachers' or 'trainees' in government literature. Other documentation often uses the term 'student teacher' to emphasize the importance of viewing the pre-service time as an educational endeavour rather than a rigid apprenticeship. However, for simplicity, the term 'trainee teacher' or 'trainee' will be used throughout the remainder of the book.

Learning to be a teacher is a lengthy and involved process. The first stage involves training at pre-service level to reach the point where you are sufficiently competent to be 'let loose' on a class of children by yourself. For people taking a PGCE, this process has to be completed within ten months and provides a considerable but not unattainable challenge. Even by the end of the training course, however, there is a lot more learning to be done when you are a qualified teacher with a class of your own. Qualified teachers are now expected to be active in plotting their career and enhancing their skills and expertise. This development process is referred to as *continuing professional development* (CPD).

It is important to note that the best teachers are invariably *thinking* people who constantly evaluate their teaching and try to improve their effectiveness. Regardless of the route they take every trainee teacher must reach a minimum standard of competence before being awarded qualified teacher status. Studies show that the majority of trainees are motivated by similar factors, including:

◆ The satisfaction that is gained from working with children
◆ The prospect of making a real contribution to the development of young minds
◆ The pleasure of working in a classroom and school environment
◆ The job security that teaching offers.

A large element of motivation is rooted in *altruistic* factors. That is, people want to be teachers because they feel that it is a useful and worthwhile way to spend their time and make a positive contribution to the well-being of society. This does not mean that good working conditions, a decent salary and opportunities for promotion are not important. It is simply saying that nothing can compensate for the satisfaction that comes from doing a job that makes a significant difference to children's lives. An old slogan about teaching – No-one forgets a good teacher – has the ring of truth about it, though it is worth remembering that no-one forgets a poor one, either!

During your pre-service training there may be occasions when you wonder whether it is worthwhile. You may be discouraged by what seems like a never-ending pile of documentation, requirements and expectations. You may well say to yourself that *I did not come into teaching for this, I came to teach children*. At such times, it is essential that you hold on to your beliefs about education, for it is possible to concentrate so hard on 'doing the course' that you forget exactly why you decided to become a teacher in the first place. You won't go far wrong if you learn to trust your tutors, assist your fellow travellers and steadfastly remain as positive as you can, even when it feels as if you are wading through treacle.

Comment

Spear *et al.* (2000, p. 52) carried out a study into motivation for teaching. A comparison of fifteen studies about teachers' job satisfaction found that the following were relevant (the most significant are listed first):

◆ Working with children
◆ Good relationships with colleagues
◆ Development of warm personal relationships with pupils
◆ Intellectual challenge/use of subject knowledge
◆ Autonomy/independence
◆ Opportunities to be creative or innovative
◆ School organization and management
◆ Pupils' achievements and progress
◆ Additional roles and responsibilities held
◆ Job security
◆ Career prospects, pay and conditions
◆ Long holidays

As you grapple with the challenges to develop and improve your practice, the four issues explored below will act as a guide in your quest for effectiveness:

◆ Your attitude to life
◆ Your view of learning
◆ Your personality and presence
◆ Your teaching approach.

Your attitude to life

All practitioners bring with them a lifetime of different experiences that impact upon the way that they behave and respond in the classroom. For example, some people are naturally cheerful and easy-going, while others are more tentative and hesitant; some people are tolerant, others tend to be irritable. However, it is important to bear in mind that host teachers on a school placement make rapid decisions about trainees based upon their responsiveness, willingness to co-operate and personality. Impressions are therefore important and can be enhanced by the following:

Take a positive view of life

A cheerful person with an optimistic attitude is more likely to attract and inspire others. Trainee teachers who see the worst side of everything that happens need to change their outlook. There are enough pressures on teachers already without them having to put up with a miserable student. All teachers need to let off steam occasionally and express their disappointment and frustration, but this is different from being constantly pessimistic and aggrieved about trivial things rather than buckling down and doing something about it. Dickens wrote about Scrooge in *A Christmas Carol* that 'he carried his own low temperature about with him'. Burn brightly instead!

Speak openly yet courteously

One important aspect of being confident and assertive (as opposed to arrogant and self-opinionated) is to feel at liberty to speak openly but to do so with humility. This does not mean that trainees should bite their tongues and say nothing. On the contrary, the more you can articulate your ideas plainly and openly, the better impression you will create. However, it is essential to get a full picture of the situation first, think carefully about the implications and ask questions to clarify the position before offering a firm opinion. It may surprise you to know that one of the reasons that teachers enjoy having trainees is to gain a fresh perspective on classroom life and hear their well-considered viewpoints.

Suspend judgement

You may feel uncertain about the suggestions that teachers and tutors make to you and their sense of priorities. Before jumping to conclusions, however, it pays to find out about the way a school operates, why things are done in a particular way and the constraints under which they are operating. There are many aspects of school life dictated by external pressures that may not be immediately obvious to a newcomer.

It usually takes a week or two before these underlying factors become more apparent. Only then should you begin to make serious judgements.

Learn from others

Teachers are always pleased when trainees show a genuine interest in what they say and make every effort to respond wholeheartedly. It is sensible to get into the habit of telling the teacher that a particular suggestion that she or he has made has been helpful (assuming it has been). If you are uncertain about the appropriateness of the advice, simply say that you will need time to absorb what has been said and think about its practical implications. Continue the discussion when, and only when, you have reflected on the issues. Do not ignore the advice, or the teacher/tutor may conclude that you are being dismissive of their views.

Use time productively

Productive time necessitates being punctual, meeting deadlines and taking care to get your priorities well ordered. It is essential to gain a reputation as someone who can be relied upon to get a job done efficiently and on time. For instance, lessons need to be prepared thoroughly and resources organized in advance. During the times when you are not directly involved in teaching, there are always plenty of tasks awaiting attention, so make good use of every spare moment. Develop a 'do it now' mentality, rather than 'it can wait'.

Take an interest in the welfare of others

As a trainee teacher you may feel that you are the only person under pressure and with too much to do. This is far from true! Teachers, mentors and tutors are all grappling with a variety of demands, some of which are emotionally draining, some of which are intellectually stretching. Your sympathetic ear and caring attitude can make a big difference to the way they feel about themselves and carry out their responsibilities.

Value the children

Valuing children means accepting them as they are, while striving to help them become mature and fulfil their potential. The great majority of people who work in primary school do so because they enjoy being with children, most of whom are responsive and eager to learn. Of course, even co-operative children sometimes test your patience, but the worst behaved child has some redeeming features. Many children who fail to conform or exhibit anti-social behaviour have been poorly parented and need someone like you to be a good steady role model. Make every effort to convey the fact that you consider every child to be special.

Value support staff

Teachers get paid a lot more than the support staff, many of whom are extremely capable and conscientious. If you make up your mind to treat everyone with the utmost courtesy and be cordial towards them, regardless of status, you will always have allies in school. Many assistants willingly give their time over and above their hours, but it is important not to take what they do for granted or to be patronizing. Quite reasonably, they ask only to be informed about what is happening and included in decisions where it affects their working lives.

Value parents

To you as a teacher, parents can be a great source of strength or a thorn in your side. If you make up your mind to be pleasant, communicative and realistically positive about their offspring, you can expect them to respond in like manner. A cheery hello and a bright smile as you pass them helps to seal your relationship and create a good impression. It can be a bit frightening at first to talk to parents about their children in case you say the wrong thing or upset them, but this fear is greatly reduced once you see them as partners rather than predators.

Comment

Woods and Jeffrey (1996, p. 72) explore the real heart of effective teaching:

> Teaching is a matter of communicating and connecting, through the emotions, through care, trust, respect, rapport. It features a great deal of fun, excitement and enthusiasm.

Your view of learning

Trainee teachers do not initially make a significant difference to the learning environment of the classrooms within which they are placed, but over time their impact becomes increasingly important and influential. There are at least seven ways in which you can contribute helpfully:

1   *Promote purposeful learning.* This aim is largely accomplished by having a positive attitude to your work, being well prepared for lessons, looking smart and efficient, and adopting a strongly affirmative approach in the classroom and around the school. If you remain well focused on the task in hand and upbeat about learning, the children will respond appropriately. Then watch things sparkle!

2   *Speak warmly to children whenever possible.* Some children are not used to being spoken to kindly by adults outside school. Other children are nervous about doing things wrong and getting told off by the teacher. If you make it your aim to speak pleasantly to children, even when you need to be firm, you will gain their respect much more quickly than if you adopt a fierce manner. Children quickly form a judgement as to whether the teacher is for them or against them. Speaking warmly is not, of course, the same as speaking feebly.

3   *Value children's efforts and encourage further achievement.* Children like their efforts to be valued but have little time for teachers who become falsely enthusiastic about work of modest quality. They are also reluctant to receive accolades from teachers with whom they have yet to seal a relationship. There is a fine balance to be struck between praising a child for genuine effort and encouraging the child to do better. Teachers can unintentionally discourage children by implying that they can improve by trying harder when maximum effort has already been expended on the task. It is sometimes the *teacher* and not the child who is at fault, failing to explain the work carefully enough or setting tasks that are poorly matched to the child's ability and potential.

4   *Promote mutual support.* You will want to contribute to a classroom environment in which there is a spirit of mutual support and encouragement. Part of this process involves being resolute in refuting mockery or sarcasm from the children. Some children enjoy making hurtful remarks because it gives them a sense of superiority and power over the victim. This is a form of bullying and wholly unacceptable. Although most children enjoy being gently teased by a friendly teacher with whom they have a close relationship, they may misinterpret your hasty attempts at humour until they have got your measure and you have got theirs.

5   *Strive for equality of opportunity.* One of children's main complaints about school life is that things are not fair. Although this dissatisfaction sometimes stems from their lack of understanding of the situation and the constraints that teachers work under, it is sometimes justified. Take care that while you reward the diligent and co-operative children, you do not give the impression that you have favourites. Maintaining lists of which children have had a turn doing popular activities allows you to monitor anyone who is regularly missing out on learning opportunities. Watch out, too, for children who are supposed to be working collaboratively with their peers but are being excluded by other members of the group from doing the exciting tasks.

6 *Consider children's emotional and social needs.* In today's competitive age, it is possible to forget that in our attempts to raise the standard of children's achievements we also need to consider their emotional and social needs. Children come to school as 'little people' with a kaleidoscope of ideas, hopes and fears that characterize the young. You have a unique opportunity to influence their growth positively and prepare them to play their full role as citizens by influencing their tolerance, compassion and sense of justice. Children glean many of these attributes from imitating the way that the adults around them behave, especially their parents and teachers.

7 *Help children to value their physical environment.* An orderly classroom (as opposed to one that resembles a hospital waiting room) helps to promote good behaviour and concentrated effort. This is not only due to the calming effect it has on the children but the ease of access to resources and movement around the room that helps to reduce frustration and the potential for disorder. The regular use of the phrase 'our classroom' helps to emphasize the joint responsibility of children and adults.

Teaching principle

Personal and educational values, rather than the circumstances of the moment, should dictate actions.

Your personality and presence

Every head teacher and class teacher hopes that the next group of trainees will be well motivated, pleasant to work with, good with children and adults, and responsive to advice. Make sure that you don't disappoint them! There are numerous factors to consider.

Dress appropriately

Some school head teachers have expectations about the suitability of clothing. The majority of them, however, do not worry too much about the way teachers dress, providing it is suitable and smart. Children respond well to teachers who wear bright clothing, but don't be too trendy. During the first few days it is safer to dress conservatively. Later, you can adjust to the dress norm of the majority of staff if you judge that this will assist in becoming accepted. Either way, avoid being too casual or 'student-like' in appearance.

Speak normally

Some trainees imagine that they have to put on an artificial voice when they talk to children. In fact, it is important to speak naturally but clearly and with authority. Apart from anything else, using an unnatural voice often leads to throat problems. It pays to spend time improving the way you speak to children. Your voice tone should be relaxed and pleasant, inviting dialogue. Talking at children in a scolding and detached manner should rarely, if ever, be used, even when dealing with a blatant transgression of the rules. See Chapter 8 for more information about use of the voice.

Attend to body language

Body language refers to the impression that your physical appearance gives to others about your competence, confidence and ability to handle a given situation (Robertson 1996). It has been estimated that body language contributes about 70 per cent towards effective communication, compared with about one-quarter from tone of voice and a relatively small amount from the actual words that are spoken. When adults enter a classroom, the way in which they conduct themselves sends a message to children. Those who are tentative and ill at ease unintentionally invite the children to treat them with less respect than those who appear self-assured. Once in the classroom, there are at least four ways in which body language can work to a teacher's advantage. First, to stand upright but relaxed. Second, to maintain eye contact with individuals. Third, to stand in a space rather than behind a desk or against a wall. Fourth, to face a child 'square on' rather than 'side on' when speaking to him or her. In addition, the best way to ensure a positive impression is to be well-informed about what you are doing and confident in your ability to do it.

Show an interest in what children say

In their busy schedules, teachers are usually hard pressed to give every child attention. It is a good principle, however, to listen as carefully as possible to what children have to say. Your positive response and obvious interest can make a critical difference to children's self-esteem and cement your relationship with them. Children view the extent of your interest as a signal about how much you value them as individuals.

Stress positive behaviour

No teacher starts out intending to be negative but in the pressure of classroom life it is surprisingly easy to fall into the habit of focusing on every small misdemeanour, while ignoring the many positive things that are happening. The more you can promote a purposeful learning environment by acknowledging successes and appropriate behaviour, the more you and the children will enjoy the lessons. See Chapter 10 for further details.

Avoid the temptation to nag

Children hate to be moaned or shouted at. If you need to admonish a child, concentrate on the facts of the event and resist dragging up past behaviour or browbeating the transgressor. Some trainees appear to think that nagging a child will impress a tutor or teacher who is observing the lesson, but nothing could be further from the truth. The best approach is fourfold:

1   State the nature of the problem to the child involved
2   Specify what s/he has to do
3   Insist on and expect obedience
4   Move on quickly to the next phase of the lesson.

Learn to be flexible

However good your planning, preparation and teaching, there will be occasions when things do not go in the way you expect, either because of your inexperience or the children's reactions or events beyond your control. It is also possible for the class teacher to make last minute changes to the timetable or for unexpected factors to shorten the available teaching time. In such circumstances, it is best to accept the situation, make the best of things, demonstrate your flexibility, swallow your disappointment and get on with the job. You will be surprised how much you will grow in the teacher's estimation as a result.

Comment

Petty (1998, p. 84) warns against trying to be too popular with pupils and notes that the best pupil-teacher relationships are based on mutual respect. Thus:

> Don't try too hard with rapport. Be patient. You will be disliked if you are desperate to be liked. And don't expect too much. Your (pupils) don't want you to become a best friend or confidant. They have these already. All they want is that you should be effective in your teaching and classroom management, that you should be approachable, and that you should have a genuine interest in their learning.

Teaching principle

Persevere to be friendly, open and responsive, sufficiently modest so as not to appear arrogant, yet sufficiently bold so as not to seem vague.

Your teaching approach

The most significant element of your training course is to prepare you for classroom teaching (see Part 2). If you are in the early stages of your course, you will not yet have determined which style suits you best. Indeed, it is better to experiment with different approaches rather than to settle into a fixed approach too soon. However, take note of the following:

Effective learning is the priority

Lessons are not just about how well you teach but about how well the children learn. Sometimes a lesson seems to go well, yet the children learn little. Sometimes it seems to go badly and the children make unexpected advances in their understanding. Although skilful teaching is an important factor in assisting children's learning, other issues such as motivation, expectation and relevance of task are also significant.

Ensure that children are clear about your expectations of them

In a league table of reasons why children become unsettled and unco-operative, lack of clarity over teachers' expectations would come close to the top. Although there will always be a few children who use the fact that they did not understand what to do as an excuse for slackness, the majority want to do their best but need you to help them by being explicit about what you expect. Some children do not listen to what is said. Other children listen but do not hear, yet others hear but misunderstand the meaning. It is important to get into the habit of checking that you are clear in your own mind first about your expectations of the children, and then able to transmit your intentions unambiguously. Further checking and repetition of the request is often necessary, as some children forget or become confused. Be aware that a small number may claim that they have understood when they have not done, for fear of being scolded.

Involve the children

It is good practice to tell children what the lesson is about at the start of the session, give a brief outline of the structure and explain where it fits into the overall programme. When you do so, try to be imaginative in the way that you express yourself. A dry, bland description of the lesson objective is hardly likely to inspire or enthuse the children, so look for ways to make sure that your introduction and explanation engages their interest. Although you will have prepared your lesson in advance and elucidated its purpose and direction, there are occasional opportunities for the children to contribute their ideas and express opinions about possible variations and alternative ways of doing things. It is important to make the status of their contributions precise, as children become frustrated if they think that the teacher has canvassed their views, only to ignore what they say.

Pace the lesson suitably

A prompt and positive start should set the tone for the rest of the lesson. However, there is a difference between maintaining a good pace and accelerating so that only the most capable children can keep up. Although every lesson needs to move along with the minimum number of pauses, there should be opportunities for children to think, reflect and consider issues. In particular, if you are asking them questions that invite a variety of responses ('open questions'), it is essential to provide them with adequate time to consider what they say rather than accepting the first hand to shoot into the air. Make sure that the children are alert and listening before you begin, but once you start speaking, the crisp tone of your voice and vibrant body language should indicate that the lesson is going to be worthwhile. A balance has to be struck, however, between being lively and racing along at such a speed that you leave the children breathless and confused. This balance of pace and clarity is not easily achieved and will take considerable practice. One helpful tip is to discipline yourself to take 'five second pauses' about once every minute, slowly counting to five in your head with your lips tightly sealed!

Check that children have the necessary skills

Although it is important to set high expectations of children, there is little point in making the work unreasonably difficult so that they become disillusioned and restless. It is far better to build up the demands that you make of them from relatively straightforward tasks in the first instance (thereby guaranteeing success) towards more involved ones that provide a challenge for the more able children. Whatever the work set, children must have the conceptual, practical and study skills to cope with it and sufficient time to complete it.

Ensure that resources are available and sufficient

A shortage of resources will often lead to disputes that could otherwise have been avoided. The more that resources can be in place before the lesson commences, the less potential for disruption, though it is better to put items out of immediate reach if you intend to address the class first, as children will be tempted to fiddle with them. If you have to spend time running around sorting out practicalities during the lesson, you are inviting trouble.

Enthuse about effort and achievement

Nearly everyone enjoys praise and an acknowledgement of their efforts, but it is unwise to offer it when children are underachieving in the hope of inspiring them to try harder. Encouragement takes many forms, but is generally reserved for children who are struggling to complete tasks or are close to finishing. It is important to remember that your praise will be most effective with children who respect and like you. Self-satisfaction with a job well done and getting children to take pride in doing their very best is preferable to a teacher's praise or extrinsic forms of motivation (such as team points). Jones and Jones (1986) explain the difference between effective and ineffective praise. Effective praise is specific about the accomplishment and provides feedback to the child. By contrast, ineffective praise is random, bland and does not provide any specific information to the child. Furthermore, effective praise uses children's prior accomplishments as the context for describing present achievements and gives due recognition of the demands that the task makes of the child. Ineffective praise attributes success to external factors and is given without reference to the child's previous learning experiences.

Insist upon careful work and attitude

Most children do their best and only a few are deliberately careless or casual. A balance needs to be struck between ensuring that children take care with what they do, and being so fussy that it suppresses their creativity. Some younger children, in particular, become anxious and agitated because their work is imperfect. Part of the your role when setting tasks is to clarify the status of the finished product and explain to the children whether it is a draft or the final version.

A helpful description of the principles of effective teaching that are relevant to practitioners at all levels is provided by Edgington (1998, p. 176):

> Sometimes she initiates experiences with a view to stimulating, supporting or extending interest. Sometimes she acts as a role model for the children to encourage particular kinds of dispositions or skills. Sometimes she demonstrates skills or imparts knowledge. Often she uses a combination of these strategies. Whichever approach she uses, she keeps the needs of the children in her mind to help her determine the optimum moment for learning – the moment when the child wants to, or needs to, learn.

A teacher's ideal attitude towards children is summarized in Figure 1.2.

- Courteous but not fawning
- Fair in all circumstances
- Open and straightforward in approach
- Willing to discuss and share issues of common concern
- Praising genuine effort
- Patient and understanding
- Cool under pressure
- Listening carefully to what is said
- Treating children's ideas seriously
- Admitting to uncertainty
- Displaying a sense of humour
- Friendly but standing no nonsense
- Appreciating the qualities of individual children
- Inviting questions
- Offering opportunity to grapple with dilemmas
- Lending support and encouragement
- Promoting self-confidence and independence of mind

Figure 1.2 *The ideal attitude towards children*

Children's views about effective teachers

Studies have shown that children are very observant and sensitive to teachers' moods, behaviour and preferences. They know when the teacher is feeling grumpy. They sense the occasions when it is wise to tread carefully and when it is safe to share a joke. A small number of children choose to ignore their instincts or are insensitive to adult moods. In such cases, you may feel that they are being deliberately awkward and stirring your emotions quite calculatingly. You may find yourself reacting temperamentally and blaming the child for undermining your authority. Nevertheless, teachers who are predictable in their responses and do not resort to sanctions are the most popular with children. Your willingness to explain the work clearly, avoid complaining and offer straightforward advice without fuss or carping will endear you to the class. If you become irritable because children do not catch on straight away, many of them will pretend to know rather than face your scorn. The adult–child relationship is therefore at least as important as the teaching methods employed in promoting sound learning and discipline.

Many teachers have attractive personalities and use jokes and humour to 'oil the wheels' of a lesson and keep the children involved. However, if taken to extremes this strategy can be counterproductive and lead to overexcitement. A lively manner is

Comment

The most effective teaching approaches are those in which the needs of the individual are central to the process. Wallace (2000, p. 22) stresses the importance of recognizing the unique contribution and potential of every child:

> Flexibility in the classroom is both the keynote and the product of teachers' approaches to education. The classroom atmosphere is equally important. If each child is valued and praised for whatever contribution s/he can make to the community, or for each small step of progress, then it is easier to allow individual differences to emerge.

important, but having fun in lessons can be achieved without becoming a clown. Holmes (2000) comments on the use of humour in classrooms. She encourages new teachers to introduce lighter moments into lessons, yet to ensure that the majority of the time is spent purposefully:

> There is no government circular stating that classrooms must be devoid of laughter and, in fact, some teachers work laughter breaks into their lesson plans. The key here is balance. Use too much humour and you risk appearing to need adulation and affection from your pupils. Aim to throw in occasional high points of humour but it is possible to get carried away and become so delighted with your own wittiness that you fail to notice that the lesson is deteriorating as a result, so:
>
> - be sure not to waste time
> - be aware that any jokes or funny tales you tell will be repeated outside the lesson, so keep them tasteful and inoffensive
> - never employ humour at the expense of pupils, however well you know them.
>
> (Holmes 2000, p. 51)

Thoughtful children would probably describe the desirable qualities in teachers in these terms:

> To be a good teacher you need to be very patient, clever, well organized, quite humorous, able to maintain order, set a good example to everybody and fair at all times.

The intimate relationship that builds between a teacher and child is precious. It takes time for you, as a stranger to the classroom, to achieve such a privileged position. Nevertheless, taking account of the child's perspective will give you helpful insights in your quest to gain the status you desire.

Achieving high standards

Every child has the potential to learn, though some children have a poor attitude or have lost heart and it then becomes difficult for any teacher to make headway. Many children who underachieve are poorly motivated. Although the worth of children does not depend on their academic achievements, success can quickly transform their frame of mind and give them hope, which in turn leads to higher self-esteem and optimum progress. Ten principles underpin the quest for high levels of attainment:

1 *Find out what children already know.* Before teachers can set targets for learning, they have to be aware of what the children know. This knowledge can only be gained through having an intimate working relationship with children over a period of time and familiarity with test results and other forms of evidence. It is little wonder that trainee teachers' first few lessons with a new class tend to be poorly matched to ability.

2 *Make links with previous knowledge.* Children have had many previous learning opportunities and, other than in the unlikely event that the topic is completely new, they will already have some understanding of the concepts involved. It is standard practice at the start of a fresh series of lessons to remind children of what they have learned or ask them questions to elicit this information. The younger the children, the longer this extraction process takes, as they tend to forget quickly and take time to recall and articulate their thoughts. However, rooting learning in familiar situations and experiences is an important teaching strategy.

3 *Take account of individual potential.* It is self-evident that learning should be relevant to all children and correspond to their differing abilities as closely as possible, bearing in mind that nearly every child excels at certain things and struggles with others. Children should be helped to establish their own targets for learning and not be unduly concerned about what other members of the class are doing. A modest achievement for a less able child probably requires far more effort and determination than a high achievement for a very capable one.

4 *Allow for individual speed of working.* Some children tend to work too quickly and have to be encouraged to become more thoughtful and pay attention to detail. Other children work ponderously (perhaps through a lack of confidence) and need additional support and encouragement. It is easy for an inexperienced teacher to confuse a lack of ability in children with a lack of application, where

the former relates to brainpower and the latter to level of determination. Deep learning is a lengthy and complex process and cannot be neatly packaged in a meticulously timed lesson plan.

5   *Use direct and indirect methods.* Children can learn by being told directly, and it is often appropriate for teachers to employ a straightforward 'telling' approach, especially when basic information is being transmitted. However, children also benefit from indirect forms of learning, such as engaging in discussion, practical activities and tasks that require them to think and explore for themselves. Under these circumstances they need time to investigate, play, absorb the learning and discuss its implications with the teacher and one another. Most lessons include both direct and indirect forms of learning.

6   *Ensure that children have the skills to collaborate.* A lot has been written about the importance of children co-operating and collaborating on tasks. Consequently, it is quite common for children to sit together around tables when they are carrying out tasks and activities. Sometimes the seating arrangement is to facilitate social co-operation where the children learn to 'get along' together and sometimes for the children to collaborate on a task or project. Collaboration requires children to co-operate, but also to listen to other opinions, consider different perspectives, compromise over strategies and contribute to a group decision about the right options. Collaborative skills do not come naturally to most children and require a considerable amount of direction and guidance from the teacher.

7   *Ask interesting questions and encourage children to do the same.* Questions may require a single correct answer, several possible answers or a host of different possible answers. If questions are *factual*, they usually involve a single correct reply. If questions are a matter of *opinion*, they invite a variety of replies. Whatever sort of question is used, it is important for children to have opportunity to think, respond and (where appropriate) raise their own questions. One way in which the learning climate can be enhanced is to promote a thoughtfully questioning attitude among the children by using rhetorical questions of the type 'I wonder what would happen if . . .?' or 'Imagine a situation where . . .'. Further discussion of questioning techniques can be found in Chapter 8.

8   *Provide opportunities for enquiry.* Practical work in subjects like science often involves children discovering more about different phenomena. Sometimes there is a fixed outcome and the children are guided through the learning stages until they can reach the correct conclusion. Such fixed outcome enquiries are often referred to as *problem-solving*. By contrast, enquiries that have the potential to reach a variety of conclusions are known as *investigations*, in which children work together in groups of about four or five. Less experienced and younger pupils will normally require a lot of adult guidance in the form of suggestions about decisions and ensuring that every child gets a fair chance to participate fully.

9   *Clarify the extent of children's autonomy.* Teachers need to explain to children the

extent of their rights and responsibilities during sessions. During less structured lessons, in particular, it is important to spell out the limits of the children's entitlement to help themselves to resources, move around the room looking at what their peers are doing and try out their own ideas. Inexperienced teachers tend to maintain a tight rein over everything that happens for fear that things might get out of control. More experienced teachers recognize that giving children a degree of independence not only promotes self-confidence but ultimately a more harmonious classroom climate and positive working environment. Bird (1990) emphasized the importance of developing a child's independence in an active environment in order to reduce 'learned helplessness', arguing that passive learners are not effective thinkers. It is only effective thinkers that have the capacity to increase their own learning (see Chapter 6).

10   *Change a lesson's direction if necessary.* Even with thorough preparation and ideal conditions, there are occasions when a lesson lacks effectiveness, either because it is inappropriate to children's learning needs or for some unaccountable reason. If the lesson is failing to grip the children, you may need to inject more pace and enthusiasm into it. If a single aspect of the lesson captivates the children you have to decide whether to stick rigidly with your original plan or allow the lesson to be diverted into this fruitful area. If, for no obvious reason, the lesson is ragged and hard-going, it is best to persevere with it as planned, put the situation down to being 'one of those days' and take time to review the lesson closely afterwards. If children are restless, it may be appropriate to shorten the time that they have to sit still and listen to you talking or to curtail collaboration and insist that children work independently. This type of decision requires fine judgement and decisive action but it is important to ensure that it is you, and not the children, who ultimately determine the lesson pattern (see Chapter 7).

Promote success but view sincere failure positively

It is difficult to structure lessons in such a way that all children gain some success, while setting challenges that stretch the more able. While lessons need to be differentiated so that every child is engaging with work of an appropriate level of difficulty, it is also important to allow children to grapple with ideas and concepts that make them think hard. Some children enjoy experimenting and trying innovative approaches to learning that, while ending in apparent failure, teach them far more than the traditional approach that guarantees a correct end result. Whatever the outcome, you should value and commend genuine effort.

Consider assessment criteria when you plan lessons

As the intention of a lesson is that the children learn something to their advantage, it is obviously important that teachers discern the extent to which this has been achieved. Children will not always learn what teachers intend, but they should at least be aware of how they can discover what it is the children *have* achieved. Some lessons have objectives that are easily measurable, such as mastering a technical skill or spelling a list of key words. However, most learning requires repetition, practice, discussion and transferring skills to new situations. Although single lesson assessment criteria are important, it is often over a period of several sessions that a child's grasp of the skills or concept becomes apparent. Assessment issues are explored in Chapter 11.

Offer opportunities for feedback and reinforcement

Feedback should not only help children to improve the work that they are immediately engaged in, but encourage them to think more widely and better understand its implications. Knowing when to tell children and when to encourage them to find out for themselves is not easy to judge. It is often better for children to seek their own answers or collaborate with a friend unless they need to know the answer urgently, on which occasions you can provide it or direct them to a source. Having successfully completed a task once, a child will usually not yet have a thorough grasp of the skill or concept, so rehearsing ideas, asking interesting questions, suggesting alternatives, speculating on possibilities and trying different approaches are necessary to reinforce and extend learning.

Invite children to be constructively self-critical

Children are sometimes their own worst critics and it is important not to reinforce their self-doubts and negativity. However, children benefit from evaluating the quality of their own work and suggesting ways that it might be improved. This evaluative process is an integral part of individual target setting, whereby a child discusses with the teacher the direction of her or his learning. Some teachers formalize the process by keeping written records of the targets and when they appear to have been met. Children have to be taught how to be constructive in their evaluations, as initially many will interpret the process purely as fault finding rather than building on achievement. During the evaluative process, it is important not to give children the impression that however hard they try, their best is never good enough. Children love teachers who are willing to give advice, offer helpful comments, give specific guidance and provide opportunities for them to use their initiative. In surveys that have been carried out about the characteristics of teachers that children associate with success, a willingness to offer unconditional support and approachability rank highly.

All teachers want to improve their teaching, but it does not happen without a lot of hard work, advice, setbacks and times of unexpectedly rapid progress. When you stand in awe of the way that an experienced practitioner makes everything look easy,

Comment

Schools are happy places. A visitor to a school might witness the joie de vivre of youthful spirits, the merry camaraderie of the staff room, the affectionate banter in teacher-pupil relationships, laughter ringing along corridors and around playgrounds, the sheer fun of pupils associating together.

(Woods 1990, p. vii)

Woods also makes the point that not all schools are like this comforting description, and no school is constantly in a state of euphoria. Schools can also be miserable places, so the challenge for every adult is to persevere to create a happy and creative working atmosphere.

Teaching principle

Children need to be geared up for success.

remind yourself that it has taken a lot of determination to reach the high standards they now enjoy. The best teachers are those who are constantly examining their practice and seeking ways to improve it.

This chapter has focused on the principles that underpin the work of a teacher. In Part 2 we examine the practicalities associated with undertaking a school placement: the key issues in preparing for, and coping effectively with, time spent on school experience.

Further reading

Brighouse, T. and Woods, D. (2003) *The Joy of Teaching*, London: RoutledgeFalmer.
Clark, C. M. (1995) *Thoughtful Teaching*, London: Cassell.

Placement

CHAPTER 2

On the threshold of school experience

Commencing the placement

Success on school experience is a fundamental requirement for everyone who aspires to be a teacher. Regardless of academic excellence, sparkling personality and knowledge of educational theories, an inability to relate to children and colleagues will deal a fatal blow to every career aspiration. The time on placement therefore requires the utmost dedication and commitment from trainee teachers. Preparation for school experience that takes place in college is intended to give you sufficient knowledge and insight to enhance your chances of success. However, trainees discover that it isn't until they come to test their educational principles in the furnace of classroom life that they are able to translate theory into practice and use the practical experience to modify existing beliefs. You are unlikely to have much choice about the placement school, though every effort is made by those who allocate places to make allowance for your particular circumstances. In truth, the majority of trainees have to make the most out of the school to which they are sent. You may also have to make your own arrangements for finding lodgings if the placement is at a distance.

Before the placement begins in earnest, it is essential to spend time becoming familiar with the school, mentally rehearsing your ideas and strategies, and adjusting your approach to fit in with the prevailing situation as you find it. On a practical level, it is also important for you to clarify your travel arrangements and take into account issues such as parking and the distance you may have to carry teaching materials and books.

Time in school can affect your energy levels, quality of sleep and general health. As you commence your placement, it will be necessary to adjust your daily routine, taking particular care to monitor your time and commitments outside school. If you have parental or other family responsibilities, give careful thought to the way you intend to manage the situation. Some trainees who are parents become guilty about being so busy with schoolwork that they are unable to spend time with their own children. It is not unknown for busy teachers with young families to find that they have time and patience for all the children in their lives, except for those who live in the same house as them! Regrettably, some neglect of immediate family and friends is a cost that many trainee teachers have to pay during school experience.

Qualified teachers also have to grapple with time demands and find ways of coping. Some teachers like to arrive very early and leave promptly, or vice versa. Others seem to arrive early and stay late. Many teachers with families try to leave school at a reasonable time and do their preparation and marking at home once their children have gone to bed in the evening. You will not be expected to follow the class teacher's routine slavishly, but it will inevitably influence the way you organize your working day. For instance, teachers who rush off after school cannot spend time talking to you about your teaching. Consequently, it is important to agree times with the teacher and mentor for feedback and discussion, and stick to the schedule as closely as possible.

Although the school experience documentation from the college will indicate the level of support you can expect from staff in school, the situation varies slightly from place to place. Some older trainees get exasperated when more is expected of them by the staff simply because they are mature. At the other extreme, youthful looking trainees might be embarrassed by being mistaken for someone on work experience from the local High School, or in extreme cases, for one of the pupils! Such minor irritations can normally be sorted out and are not worth losing sleep over. Mature trainees can quietly explain to the host teachers that although they are older, they are still inexperienced and need the same support and advice as their junior colleagues. Younger trainees can compensate for their fresh looks by dressing a little more formally than would normally be necessary and demonstrating their professional commitment and reliability.

What is the school like?

Although schools look superficially similar, they vary considerably in their design, priorities, use of space and personnel, staff relationships and structure of the day, so what is appropriate in one situation may not be elsewhere. During the *preliminary visit* to a school, teachers and mentors do their best to give you a sufficient amount of information and guidance such that you can go away and prepare your lessons and make or acquire resources. Occasionally, the process does not work smoothly and you can find yourself with too much information to absorb or (more often) with an insufficiently clear view of what is expected of you. The following list indicates the sorts of variations that it is useful to take note of during your preliminary visits:

◆ The size and layout of the buildings
◆ The age range of the children
◆ The schemes of work used throughout the school

◆ The facilities in the Information and Communication Technology (ICT) suite
◆ The size and availability of a school hall
◆ Whether there are any specialist areas or rooms
◆ The amount of space in the staff room
◆ The availability of resources for teaching.

You must be familiar with procedures and routines if you are to assist the class teacher in the smooth running of the classroom. For instance, you need to know the time and place of assemblies and acts of worship, the systems for taking library books home and for choosing children to perform regular tasks (such as watering the plants, tidying shelves, running messages). You must pay attention to the way in which the attendance register is taken, dinner money is collected, absence letters dealt with, and late children managed. Take careful note, too, of the way that the children are welcomed and dismissed by the teacher at the beginning and end of the day.

Nearly all primary schools have timetabled lessons and specific occasions for using specialist spaces, such as the hall, ICT suite and play areas. Occasionally, a school is short of space and has to utilize the hall as an additional teaching area. In the run-up to special occasions, the hall may be out of action owing to rehearsals or a special event. It is obviously better to know about such changes in advance than to find out on the day, so it is essential to check the staff notice board regularly and monitor the situation. If the class has PE in the hall either side of lunch, you may discover that the session has to be curtailed due to the need for setting up or clearing away. If you have responsibility for games outside, find out the procedures for inclement weather and what happens to muddy shoes.

Of course, not everything that happens during the day can be predicted. School life takes many twists and turns and cannot be slotted into neat categories. Observe the way that the teacher deals with unusual and unexpected occurrences. Imagine the way that you would cope if you were in charge.

All schools are safety conscious and carry out fire drills regularly, so make sure that you have a clear idea of how to go about evacuating the children. Check the fire regulations and mentally rehearse the way in which you would supervise the children in an emergency. Each lesson should be assessed for risk, especially if there is equipment with moving parts and large space activities. Children sometimes put themselves in peril through exuberance or lack of experience. Proper training in the use of tools, adequate supervision during physical activities and high standards of behaviour, combine to reduce the likelihood of accidents. If there are children with allergies or prone to having fits (convulsions) it is important to know what to do and who to contact. Although you are unlikely to take the major responsibility for health and safety issues, ignorance is no excuse for inaction.

Your own safety is also important. High heels are particularly unsuitable for school. If you have to spend time outside with children, be careful to avoid excesses of heat or cold that might contribute to an illness. Never climb onto furniture or ascend a ladder. Take great care when you use a stapler. Teaching has enough challenges without compromising your health and well-being through carelessness. In addition, you are more likely to prosper on your placement if you maintain a regular sleep pattern. There is little merit in staying up late to complete a task if it leaves you feeling jaded and grumpy in the morning.

The better informed you are about all aspects of school and classroom life, the greater will be your confidence to respond appropriately to them. The most daunting part of any new situation is the unknown, so time taken to pinpoint details in advance of commencing your school placement is time well spent. The following is a useful guide for ascertaining the way in which the school and classroom operates.

General

There are a number of basic things to discover:

◆ The roles and responsibilities of different adults
◆ The location of the classroom with reference to other key areas such as entrance points, toilets, hall
◆ Where the children have lunch and what happens to food boxes
◆ The behaviour code and sanctions used throughout the school and classroom
◆ The use of rewards in school.

The classroom

In terms of the specific learning environment, make mental note of:

◆ The roles of assistants, parents, students
◆ Where frequently-used resources are stored
◆ Special areas inside the classroom (e.g. reading area)
◆ Special areas outside the classroom (e.g. messy area)
◆ Class rules and regulations
◆ The way that the teacher organizes activities.

The children

Information about pupils cannot be absorbed quickly but you can make a start on finding out:

◆ The number of boys and girls in the class
◆ The number of left-handed children
◆ The nature of children with exceptional learning difficulties
◆ The academic range

- The physical/mobility range
- The way children are grouped for learning
- Regular routines children have to follow.

The teacher

The teacher is your most important ally. Although it is unwise to try and replicate what the teacher does, it pays to take account of:

- The variety of tones of voice used when speaking to the children
- The way a lesson/session is introduced
- The use of questions during an interactive phase
- The standard of work demanded from the children
- The ways in which inappropriate behaviour is dealt with
- The level of independence that is fostered in children.

Working practices

By the time you arrive in school, routines and practices will normally be well established, so look out for:

- Classroom rules
- Procedures if children are unsure what to do
- Procedures if a child finishes early
- The extent that the children are encouraged to collaborate in learning
- Additional support offered to children who underachieve in literacy and numeracy
- The implementation of equal opportunities
- The availability and use of computers
- Parental involvement in the classroom.

The use of teaching strategies

The effective use of teaching skills is dealt with in depth in Chapters 8 and 9. It is worth observing closely the strategies used by the teacher in:

- Settling the children
- Introducing the lesson
- Moving the lesson along with a sense of purpose
- Explaining things to the children
- Using direct and speculative forms of questioning
- Using resources as a means of enhancing learning
- Allocating tasks

◆ Giving instructions about work and standards of behaviour
◆ Demonstrating skills to children
◆ Monitoring children's progress
◆ Intervening and guiding children during activities
◆ Keeping children on task
◆ Coping with interruptions
◆ Dealing with children's questions
◆ Handling disorder
◆ Offering feedback to pupils about their progress
◆ Concluding the lesson
◆ Sharing ideas and outcomes with the whole group or class
◆ Encouraging and rewarding effort and achievement.

During your preliminary visits and early days on placement, it is helpful to jot down details of specific events, such as when children go to the hall for PE, the maintenance of homework diaries and opportunities for children to select what they do (e.g. during free play activities). As you absorb information, use it to help you understand better what the child's experience of classroom life must be like. The points listed above are explored in depth in Part 3 of the book, Practice.

Comment

Alsop and Dock (1999, p. 33) point out that every school has a unique atmosphere, often referred to as the 'hidden curriculum' that is rooted in its prevailing attitudes and values:

> The hidden curriculum is a commonly used term to refer to the politics, attitudes and values promoted by school experiences. Much is learned in school that has nothing directly to do with the curriculum content of lessons, but is implied by school structures, procedures and organization.

Teaching principle

Be systematically observant during your preliminary visit and approach it as a prospective tenant rather than as a tourist.

What is the classroom like?

Classrooms vary in size and shape, but they nearly all contain similar basic resources. It pays to take careful account of the acoustics, visibility and accessibility, as this may influence the speed at which you speak, the place that you stand or sit, and the way that you organize resources. The classroom often serves multiple functions: workplace, quiet area, common room and even a place to eat, so it should be viewed as a flexible resource rather than a permanent fixture. The following factors are significant:

Physical characteristics

Waters (1996) suggests that rooms should be arranged in such a way that both teacher and children have an understanding of what is required at different times of day and minimize the disruption caused by movement. Familiarity with room shape and layout allow you to consider factors such as how loudly you need to speak, how many children can be accommodated in the available spaces and where equipment is stored. For instance, a long narrow room and one built in an 'L' shape requires a different teaching style from a conventional oblong style. The long, narrow room allows you to address the children without the need for extensive scanning, whereas the L-shaped room may require you to pay particular attention to your location so that you can see and be seen. Some rooms are of inadequate size to allow storage of equipment, which has to be fetched from other places. Other rooms are very large for the number of children and, although allowing for ease of storage and movement, present challenges in terms of classroom management and tidiness.

Number of children in the class

Larger numbers of children do not necessarily mean that teaching will be harder. However, there will be more names to learn, personalities to understand, resources to create and work to administer. All these factors need to be taken into account when planning lessons and creating learning opportunities for children. Sometimes, classes are heavily weighted in terms of gender, with a high percentage of one sex and few of the other. Under such circumstances you need to be sensitive to the possibility that the 'minority population' can be disadvantaged or they may seek to behave assertively to protect their interests.

Equipment available

Although classrooms contain the basic resources needed for regular teaching, they vary in the amount of equipment that is readily available without the need to go to a central resource area. Regardless of how much equipment the classroom contains, it is inevitable that for practical subjects, such as enquiry-based science, you will need to have access to resources stored elsewhere. The time and effort required for organizing equipment and returning it safely afterwards are significant factors to take into account in your lesson planning.

The number of computers in the classrooms

Although classroom computers are an important learning resource, they present challenges in three ways: (a) the space they occupy, (b) the level of adult support they require, (c) ensuring that every child is given fair access. A lot of classroom computers are either underused or children are left to fend for themselves for too long and make limited use of their opportunities. The availability of teaching assistants to support this aspect of learning is a key consideration for you when planning activities that make use of the computer.

How children gain access to their personal property

Schools have their own general regulations about children bringing items into school, but the class teacher will probably have a system for safeguarding them and making them available. It is important for you to become familiar with the procedures to save any misunderstanding about property rights. Although theft is not common in primary schools, it creates a lot of distress and unease when it happens, so every effort should be made to protect property without engendering an atmosphere of suspicion.

How much display space is available and how is it used

Classrooms vary in the amount of wall space available for displays. Some teachers prefer to keep display to a minimum, others view it as an opportunity to celebrate pupils' achievements publicly. The composition and prominence of display work therefore varies considerably. If display work is languishing, you may be able to breathe fresh life into it. If it is superbly presented and a major feature of the room, it is wise to confine your attention to a small area and concentrate on achieving high quality, rather than to attempt too much and do it badly.

Flexibility in the teaching programme

Except with the youngest children, most primary schools adhere to a rigid timetable. It is likely that core subjects taught in the mornings will be more highly structured than the foundation subjects that are commonly taught in the afternoon. In the morning it is quite common for there to be some 'setting' of children from a number of different classes into ability groups for mathematics and English. It is obviously necessary to adhere to the specific times allocated for use of the hall, music room or computer suite. You also need to clarify with the class teacher the degree of flexibility permitted for you to develop areas of learning such as creative writing and investigative science.

What are the school staff like?

Do not jump to conclusions about the teachers. When you first arrive in a school they are often busy and may not have much time to attend to you. Their distracted behaviour might give the impression that they are supercilious or indifferent, but this is rarely true despite the fact that they may have forgotten you are coming! Some schools have numerous visitors and until the staff know your status and significance it is not unusual to be looked at blankly or ignored by some people, so don't be alarmed if this happens to you. Schools vary considerably in size and composition, and every set of teachers and assistants is unique, so the following questions help you in gauging the staff situation.

How experienced are the teachers?

Experience is not only gained through years of practice but by thinking hard about the job and extending the frontiers of knowledge and methods of teaching. Long-serving teachers have discovered most of the hazards and shortcuts associated with the job; a new teacher may have considerable expertise in a subject such as ICT. Most teachers are more than willing to give advice if asked. It is useful to know the breadth and range of expertise that exists within the school, not least so that you know whom to ask about what. In a very small school, each teacher has to take responsibility for several curriculum areas.

When are teachers available?

All teachers are busy, but some seem to thrive on it. For others, pressure of work can become overwhelming. It is sensible to spend a few days considering the situation before approaching teachers for help, advice and information. And when you do so, it is essential to choose the right moment and avoid times when they are busy. Mentors have a responsibility to assist you through your school experience, induct you into good classroom practice and offer feedback about your progress. To do this satisfactorily requires the allocation of specific times for discussions. Squeezing your meetings into an odd five minutes during break time is no substitute for a sustained, in-depth briefing, so get the first one arranged as soon as possible.

How much is expected of you?

Most teachers and assistants are only too willing to give a trainee every help possible. However, they need to hear from you about the things that will be useful and the responsibilities that you feel you can handle. Don't assume that a teacher knows instinctively what you need, because she does not. Remember, too, that s/he will almost certainly have worked with other trainees, some of whom will have been very different in attitude, temperament and capability from you. On talking to your friends in other placements, you may discover that their experience is different from yours in a variety of ways. Don't dwell on these differences or imagine that you are in a worse situation than they are. Each school placement carries with it a minimum expectation for all trainees, but if you are capable of exceeding this basic requirement, all well and good. It is vital that you maintain an open dialogue with the class teacher to avoid any misunderstandings about your teaching commitments. The general rule is to be cautiously eager in responding to the teacher's suggestions but not to bite off more than you can chew.

What is the head teacher's attitude?

Head teachers are normally delighted to have trainees in the school. However, they are charged with numerous responsibilities and cannot always afford to spend as much time with you as they would ideally like. When a head teacher seems to be neglecting you, it is nearly always due to pressure of work. It does not mean that they are not receiving regular updates from the host teachers about you! However they behave towards you, head teachers hope and expect that trainee teachers will engage them with a cheery hello and smile when they pass in the corridor.

Teaching principle

Trainees are not the only concern of busy teachers.

What is the class teacher like?

Class teachers are almost invariably busy, dedicated and anxious that you are happy working with them. They also want to help you to fit in to the situation comfortably and get the most out of your school placement. On the other hand, teachers have clear ideas about the most effective teaching methods and classroom procedures, which may occasionally lead to difficulties if you have different priorities. For example, your enthusiasm for group work and discussion opportunities will not be easy to satisfy if the class teacher prefers an individualized style of learning. Variations in preference about teaching and learning raise issues relating to the extent to which you are willing to adjust and adapt your own approach to align with the teacher's expectations without sacrificing fundamental beliefs and principles. In extreme cases, the class teacher's teaching may conflict markedly with your own. In such situations you are faced with a choice. Either you can grin and bear it and do everything possible to adjust your teaching appropriately, or you can speak openly to the teacher about your anxieties and reach an agreement about the best way forward. It is worth taking advice from your mentor or tutor before proceeding. Rehearse what you intend to say and how you are going to say it, so that there are no misunderstandings and the discussion is a professional dialogue rather than a confrontation.

Teaching approach

An example of a way in which your approach may be different from that of the class teacher is that you may be convinced that giving children the opportunity to talk together and discuss issues will help to promote and deepen pupils' understanding. By contrast, the class teacher's approach may be far more direct and didactic. The teacher's lesson may involve spending time following set procedures that, in your eyes, create a static environment and are detrimental to learning. However, teachers normally have good reason for using a particular approach. For instance, they may use a formal approach because they found that the children took advantage when offered more freedom or were too noisy when collaborating. To a large extent you will want to maintain the sort of teaching approach used by the class teacher as the children will be used to it and may initially balk at a different method. However, most teachers will allow you to 'have a go' with your preferred approach to see whether your actions are as convincing as your arguments!

Relating to trainee teachers

School experience can never be quite like having your own class, but it is best to take a positive view of the opportunities it affords and accept its limitations. Not all teachers are experienced in dealing with trainee teachers, so it may take some time for them to be at ease with you. By contrast, many teachers treat you like a long lost cousin! Trainee teachers are agreed that their relationships with class teachers are the

Teaching principle

The class teacher should be your closest ally.

single most important factor influencing success on school placement, so make it a priority and do everything reasonable to support, respond to, and assist the teacher. This should not be done in a fawning way, of course, but in the firm belief that it is better for all concerned if teacher and trainee work in harmony.

What are the children like?

You cannot pick and choose the children in the class. You can, however, take advantage of the positive characteristics and develop strategies to cope with the less desirable ones. The more you know about the pupils' abilities and potential, the more you will be able to plan and teach effectively, and encourage positive values (Farrer 2000). In particular note the following:

Their enthusiasm to learn

If the children are keen, take careful note of the way that the teacher motivates them and provides them with a variety of stimulating tasks. If they are unresponsive, demonstrate to them by your tone of voice, interested comments and evident sense of purpose that learning can be interesting and fun, but don't expect an immediate transformation. Children with low self-confidence will need to be given a lot of encouragement and tasks that offer the chance for immediate success. If children relate to one another easily you can organize group work, co-operative tasks and enquiry-based investigations with reasonable confidence that the children will be able to cope with the tasks. If not, then you must spend time helping the children to develop these skills, beginning with work in friendship pairs and gradually introducing small group work.

The ability range

If there is a wide range, then the work will have to be differentiated in terms of the vocabulary that you use, the work you set for them to complete individually and your own expectations of the quality they will achieve. Whatever their ability, it is important to have a realistic but positive attitude and ensure that they can find success in their work. Natural ability impinges upon attainment but even children of modest proficiency can be inspired to reach greater heights of achievement.

Their responses to new adults

If they respond positively, try not to get too excited about it. It is better to remain slightly aloof at first until you know the class better, even when the children are openly welcoming. If they respond badly, it may be that they are shy or suspicious of you, or very attached to their class teacher. It is wise to take your time and allow yourself to grow on the children, rather than making an effort to be chummy. As you provide support and help for the children, their attitude will gradually change, though there may be some children who never fully accept you as a teacher.

It is often the case that children are initially very curious and ask searching questions about you. While you will want to be pleasant and responsive, if the questions are too personal it is best to deflect them with a polite but terse: 'I may tell you one day' or 'that is just for me to know'. Children do not have access to details about your background, of course, so the only way they can discover things about you is to ask questions, watch your responses and evaluate you on that evidence. Some trainees find it helpful to share something about themselves early on with the children. If you decide that this is a useful strategy, strictly limit the detail you supply and don't invite questions. You may be taken aback to discover that it never occurs to some children that you have an existence outside school.

Early encounters with a new class are rarely smooth. As a trainee teacher you do not have a reputation going ahead of you into the classroom, so a period of orientation and adjustment is unavoidable. You must be patient and persevere during this time and not be tempted to imagine that you are failing or that you should have become a traffic warden instead of a teacher. The experience of most trainees is that there is a honeymoon few days when children weigh you up, followed by an anxious couple of weeks in which children test your resolve. This period of uncertainty is almost invariably followed by a state in which 'the tension of control and instruction is no longer a distraction' (Cullingford 1995, p. 123) and you can properly get on with the job of teaching.

Their independence in working

If the children concentrate on their work with little prompting, then your responsibility is to retain and, if possible, enhance the positive climate. Some children resent too much adult intervention and you have to tread a fine line between offering support and allowing children the opportunity to work things out for themselves. If they respond enthusiastically to your involvement, you are in for an exciting time as you introduce ideas and strategies for learning in the reasonable expectation that the children will not take advantage of the situation. If they are unresponsive, you need to adopt a more carefully managed approach, introducing creative methods gradually within a formal lesson framework.

Teaching principle

Children are as interested in you as you are in them.

Adjusting to the placement

Trainee teachers may find themselves at home in one school situation and not in another. This variation is frequently due to the quality of the relationship between trainee and class teacher. An open, supportive placement situation, where mistakes are tolerated by host teachers and used as a basis for discussion rather than a means of condemning the trainee, provide the best conditions for success. The vast majority of placement situations are of this kind. A small number are characterized by having a less sympathetic class teacher or mentor, who may be stressed or unhappy or have unreasonable expectations of the trainee, and it is difficult to be successful in such a barren climate. Similarly, large, unruly classes are bound to be more challenging than compliant, friendly ones. However, regardless of the situation, you will need to press on with determination and adapt your teaching to suit the conditions. Thankfully, the majority of placements provide a first rate learning experience for trainee teachers and the following are typical comments about their placement schools by satisfied customers:

> The school was very supportive during my time there. All the teachers were very helpful and friendly, which was a great relief.

> The welcome the school gave me was also very useful in helping me get settled in. It was such a warm welcome and it made me feel valued.

> The teachers made us feel very welcome and have been very supportive of our ideas.

> (Quoted in Hayes 2001, p. 15)

Sometimes a class of children can make life quite difficult for a new teacher. Mischievous children sense your vulnerability and they may try to bamboozle you or get away with behaviour that they would not even consider with their regular teacher. Timid children feel threatened by the presence of a different adult in the room and become defensive, even fearful. They will need gradual reassuring and gentle persuasion that may take a considerable time to have an effect. Learning to 'read' a class situation requires skill and experience. Nevertheless, there are signs that may give clues about children's disposition to learning and the effect of your presence, such as:

◆ Lack of eye contact, suggesting low self-confidence
◆ Arm used to conceal work, suggesting fear of criticism
◆ Surreptitious sniggering, suggesting a lack of engagement with the work
◆ Feigned yawns and sighs, suggesting insubordination
◆ Innocent questions designed to distract you, suggesting a perverse disposition

◆ Daydreaming, suggesting a short attention span or boredom
◆ Hurrying to complete tasks, suggesting keenness or superficiality
◆ Complaints about not understanding, suggesting a negative attitude or slow thinking.

You need to take account of such reactions, but do not allow them to distract you from the job. Thus, for each of the above:

◆ Low self-confidence can be counteracted by encouragement, a light touch and lots of gentle praise
◆ Fear of criticism can be counteracted by constructive guidance, clarifying intentions and focusing on positive aspects
◆ Lack of engagement can be counteracted by setting specific expectations within a given time limit
◆ Distraction techniques can be counteracted by refusing to be sidetracked
◆ Daydreaming can be counteracted by redirecting the child's attention on to the task
◆ Hurrying to complete work can be counteracted by raising expectations and attention to detail
◆ Complaints about lack of understanding can be counteracted by explaining carefully while refusing to accept them as excuses for poor work.

Of course, it is sometimes the case that apparently negative reactions are, in fact, the result of genuine confusion, uncertainty about the requirements or anxiety. Your ability to distinguish between real and feigned behaviour will influence your teaching effectiveness and reputation as a practitioner.

Other factors, such as the quality of your time management, communication skills and subject knowledge also contribute to the speed of your progress as a teacher. You may discover that your host teachers are very busy and cannot spend the time with you that would ideally be desirable. Sometimes poor health or family matters prevent you from making as much headway as you might have hoped for. Regardless of your commitment and perseverance, however, there are limitations on what you can achieve as a trainee teacher working in someone else's classroom, and it is not normally possible (and usually not desirable) to transform the situation or radically reform existing structures. In addition, it is important to recognize that class teachers are not free agents either, able to do what they like without reference to other factors. In fact, although teachers work actively to organize and manage their classrooms to reflect their educational ideals, they do so within various time and resource constraints and the expectations of the head teacher. Class teachers expect trainees to maintain the existing environment and enhance it where possible, and not to make clumsy attempts to alter things without consulting them.

What will be expected of me?

The college documentation that you are given before the placement commences will identify specific targets and expectations for the school experience. However, the requirements still need to be understood and interpreted for your particular circumstances. Teachers do not always have the time or inclination to read documents closely or may not absorb the details. It is your responsibility to agree with the mentor and class teacher a programme such that you have sufficient teaching responsibility to keep you alert, but not so much that it becomes overwhelming. It is generally better to begin slowly but to assume a *teaching* rather than an assistant role as soon as possible. It is preferable to start (say) by reading a few poems as part of a literacy lesson and gradually build your confidence and expertise, than to grandly volunteer to take over the class and struggle to cope. Again, the documentation should offer guidance about the staging of your teaching, though circumstances vary somewhat from one school to another. The following questions will help you to clarify key points with your mentor and class teacher.

How much will I be expected to plan during the different weeks of the placement?

Some schools have rigid sets of plans that give a lot of detail about individual lessons; others include only broad areas of the curriculum to be followed. Even if there are detailed plans available, linked to a published plan of work, you will still need to ensure that you have put your own 'fingerprints' on the lesson and plan it with the particular class in mind. Depending upon experience, it is normal for trainee teachers to begin by using existing plans produced by the class teacher for the first few days, then to take responsibility for planning lessons for a single group of children before assuming increasing responsibility for the whole class.

Am I always expected to be present in the room?

It is important to spend some time out to help you reflect upon your work, annotate records and reflect on your progress. Time spent in different classrooms, arranged in conjunction with your school mentor, form an integral part of your school experience. As a rule, time out of class should not normally be used for tasks such as marking that should be undertaken outside teaching hours, unless agreed with the mentor. If the college insists on trainees teaching for a specified percentage of the school week (75 per cent, say) you will need to clarify whether this time includes occasions when you are physically present in the classroom working with some children, though not directly responsible for the planning and teaching.

How much feedback can I expect about my teaching?

This varies considerably from situation to situation. It is important to establish and maintain a candid relationship with the class teacher so that s/he can comment on your teaching and suggest strategies. Mentors should give you regular written feedback and spend time discussing key points. However, in the midst of a busy schedule, snatched conversations may have to suffice. One way and another, it is vital that you receive and act upon the advice you are given.

Will I be expected to attend staff meetings?

It is normal for trainee teachers to attend regular team-planning meetings when they can discover how systems operate, ask questions and increasingly contribute their own ideas as they become familiar with the situation. Trainees' experiences are more varied in respect of attendance at full staff meetings, when the topic may not be relevant or a confidential matter is on the agenda. If you enquire about attendance and are told that you can come along if you want to but it is not very suitable, then it is usually better to wait for another opportunity when the topic is more appropriate. On the other hand, teachers are always impressed when trainees make an effort to attend meetings. Beware, however, that you don't spend lots of time at meetings and neglect more pressing matters such as lesson planning and marking.

Teaching principle

Attempting too much, too soon, will overwhelm you; avoiding responsibility will damage your reputation and your progress.

The placement cycle

It would be comforting to be able to say that your time on school experience will begin gradually and improve consistently until the end. Unfortunately, things are not always that simple. On a placement of about six weeks, the following cycle is fairly typical.

During the first few days you are feeling your way, finding out about procedures and getting to know the children. You tend to be more of an assistant than a teacher. The children are politely interested in you and, with one or two exceptions, generally co-operative. You feel quietly confident that you will be able to cope with the situation and begin to relax after your pre-placement anxieties. After the first week, and as you take more responsibility for lessons, the mischievous individuals start to make their presence felt more strongly, testing the boundaries and noting your reactions. However, you feel pleased about your teaching and relish the encouragement given to you by the class teacher and mentor. By the end of the second week, you have settled into the school routines and are more acutely aware of the children who will stretch your patience, question what and why they have to do things and, in a few cases, show signs of antisocial behaviour. Most of the children are responding well to your teaching and the class teacher seems pleased with the way things are going.

As the placement reaches the half way stage, there is sometimes a slight downturn in fortunes. You will be taking more of the teaching responsibility than you were earlier and begin to feel jaded. Your initial enthusiasm is being replaced by a realization that teaching needs qualities of gritty determination and staying power. You begin to understand better what teachers and tutors have said about the need to be consistently firm and not allow yourself the luxury of imagining that if you are kind to them, the children will be compliant. As you start to teach a broader range of subjects, you become more aware of the limitations of your subject knowledge. Taking lessons outside the classroom (such as PE, games, drama, using the ICT suite) obliges you to engage with a new set of organizational and class management issues. For example, organizing the children to move between the classroom and the hall requires you to exercise strong leadership and discipline. The class teacher may be absent from the classroom more often, leaving you to deal with the multitude of decisions that qualified teachers cope with every day. Although the teacher's absence relieves you of the pressure of being under constant scrutiny, it raises other challenges associated with taking full responsibility for the class, such as health and safety issues.

Towards the end of your school experience, fatigue claws at your mind and body. You struggle to get up in the morning and look forward to going to sleep at night. The teaching and non-teaching responsibilities are at their heaviest. You are also conscious of the directed tasks from college that remain to be completed and become nervously sensitive to comments from tutors or teachers that may indicate their dissatisfaction with your performance.

The final few days fly past. The class teacher begins to retrieve the lessons that have been allocated to you during your time in school. Depending on the way that the placement has gone, you will either reluctantly tear yourself away from the children or leave as quickly as decency will allow. Either way, there will inevitably be a mixture of emotions as you head back to college and the next phase of the course. If it is the final school placement, your thoughts will be firmly on next September and the prospect of having your own class.

As a trainee it is important for you to come to grips with the many diverse and challenging elements of the teacher's role. This takes a lot of perseverance and you will undoubtedly have ups and downs on the way to qualifying. However well you prepare and think through your teaching, it is only when you come to the moment of lesson delivery that you realize how difficult it is to translate ideas into classroom practice. The key principle is to learn from your mistakes, discuss issues and strategies with the host teachers or tutors, and be resolute in your determination to improve.

Teaching principle

You should not despair if, midway through the placement, it seems that you are actually getting worse at teaching. It is simply that expectations have grown, so hold your nerve and persevere.

Role diversity

There are many aspects of the teaching role that will occupy you during your school placement. Each element is further explored in Part 2, so for now it is enough to be reminded of the rudiments. First, those aspects that relate to classroom practice:

Planning single lessons

It is common for trainees at all stages of their course to begin by taking a small number of individual lessons rather than consecutive ones, often with a small number of children rather than the whole class. Solitary lessons must still be made to fit within the general pattern of the children's learning and, if you are inexperienced, it is a good opportunity to sharpen your teaching skills without undue damage. Some trainees plan too loosely so that they are not clear what they are doing and some plan too tightly so that they restrict opportunities for spontaneity. Those who are under-planned often do well initially, then run out of ideas. Those who are overplanned make solid but uninspiring progress. The middle way is best.

Planning sequences of lessons

After you gain more confidence and knowledge about the children, you will begin to teach consecutive lessons on the same subject. For instance, you may teach three literacy lessons on Monday, Tuesday and Wednesday. The advantage of lessons that are linked in this way is that you can refer back to the previous lesson at the start of the new one. In this way you provide a sense of continuity for the children and establish your authority as a teacher.

Classroom organization and management

Most organizing takes place before the lesson starts. Management happens during the lesson. The former is an essential prerequisite to the latter. Poor organization is not easily redeemed once the lesson begins, so thorough preparation is essential. See Chapter 9 for a more in-depth examination of classroom organization and management.

Dealing with paperwork

Most teachers hate doing paperwork. However, as it has to be done it is in your own interest to use the time effectively. If you view record keeping as an aid to teaching effectiveness rather than as a chore, it will give the process greater purpose and relevance. Remember, too, that your teaching files are likely to be different from, and more complex than, those of the class teachers, who have already proved their worth and do not need to keep the sorts of detail that are essential for you while you train.

Second, those aspects that relate to your professional life:

Conforming to the prevailing school ethos

Every school has its priorities and unwritten protocol. It is vital to find out as quickly as possible where the boundaries lie by watching and listening closely, and asking advice from the host teacher or a member of the support staff, avoiding any hint in your comments that you are challenging the status quo.

Relating to mentors

You will probably have a teacher from within the school who acts as your mentor. This person may or may not be your class teacher. If your class teacher is the mentor and you get on well together, it is a considerable advantage to you both. If the relationship is less positive, it is important to make effective use of other confidantes, such as your college tutor, a friendly teacher about your own age or a sympathetic, plain speaking friend.

Responsibilities towards children and colleagues

Even though you are a trainee, you share with other staff a responsibility for the welfare of every child. Less obviously, you also have responsibilities towards adults in the school. Despite your inexperience and novice status, your caring, helpful and understanding approach towards colleagues is part of belonging to the school community. It will be noted and appreciated.

Learning and contributing

As a trainee, you have a lot to learn but also a lot to offer. Do not underestimate the contribution you can make while you are on placement in respect of your enthusiasm, insights, fresh ideas and talents. Tired and jaded teachers are happy to feed off your zeal, providing you don't come across as supercilious. If you are in your final school experience, it is particularly important to establish a reputation as someone that is an active learner and will make a good staff member during the induction year.

Coping with comments about your teaching performance

Your tutor will normally offer comment and suggestions about improving your teaching. You may not agree with it all, but you must take it seriously, as tutors hate to think that their advice is being ignored. Sometimes your tutor's and host teacher's comments may be less commending than you hoped for. Some feedback may emphasize areas for development and take for granted, rather than highlight, the things you do well. Remember that a tutor who calls to see you once per week has not witnessed your other teaching and may catch you on a bad day. It is important to deal with issues about classroom practice calmly and ask for advice about developing strategies for improving weaker aspects of your teaching. Feedback is essentially to provide a basis for discussion that aids effective progress. It is not intended to depress you.

Dealing with setbacks constructively during your time in school

No school placement goes smoothly. Even the best of school experiences has its highs and lows, and yours will be no different. The secret is to persevere, refuse to be downhearted and keep things in proportion. The vast majority of trainee teachers eventually come out on top, and so will you.

Comment

Bubb (2000, p. 13) acknowledges that the road to successful teaching is a stony path with many hidden snags and unexpected setbacks. However, these are compensated for by some 'golden moments' that make the job worthwhile.

Like any skill or craft, learning to teach is a developmental process characterized by devastating disasters and spectacular successes.

Teaching principle

Role diversity characterizes the job of a teacher

Other professional requirements

We have noted that there are many responsibilities associated with the role of teacher, some of which are specific to the classroom, others that are non-teaching duties and contribute to the general life of the school (see Figure 2.1). It is important to build a good reputation as someone that listens closely to advice, responds positively to suggestions about improvement and gives every impression of being wholly committed to the job. It is also necessary to cultivate a pleasant and responsive manner as you move around the school, and to impress others by your cheerful and positive attitude. Whether you are going into school on placement for the very first time or as an old hand there is an expectation that you will make every effort to behave *professionally*. Professional is a difficult term to define but it presupposes that you will:

1   Communicate openly with colleagues, including associate staff, and not assume that they will always initiate the exchanges. This aspect of professionalism requires that you contribute to the maintenance of a regular dialogue.
2   Set a good example to the pupils you teach, through your manner and personal conduct. This aspect requires that you dress appropriately, speak courteously and act with decorum, even when they are being unreasonable.
3   Ensure that all children are given the opportunity to achieve their potential and meet the high expectations set for them. This aspect requires that you interpret achievement broadly, and include things that cannot easily be measured, such as the ability for the children to work as part of a team, take a leadership role and show concern for others.
4   Take responsibility for your own professional development and keep up to date with research and developments in teaching. This aspect requires that you give consideration to the implementation of new ideas and theories into your teaching.
5   Become familiar with school policies and practices, including pastoral, personal safety matters and bullying. This aspect requires that you see yourself as a responsible adult in the school acting in the best interests of all children.
6   Recognize that learning takes place inside and outside the school context, and liaise effectively with parents. This requires that you make the effort to involve parents and help them to feel that they have a significant part to play in their children's education.

These will include some of the following:

- Staff meetings
- Playground supervision
- Attendance registration
- Displays
- Photocopying
- Organizing furniture
- Basic computer repairs
- Extra-curricular activities
- Stock-taking
- Distributing letters
- Sports training
- Organizing and managing sports teams
- Advising on supply cover
- Administering charity collections
- Completing questionnaires
- Bus duty

Figure 2.1 *Non-teaching duties*

As an aspiring professional in school there are many frustrations and demands that can, if allowed to fester, hinder your development as a teacher, so it pays to adopt a positive but realistic view of the situation:

- Remind yourself that hard work and effort as a trainee teacher will pay off when you have your own class
- Think about how much you are achieving rather than how much there remains to learn
- Remind yourself that there are bound to be occasions when you experience self-doubt.

As a trainee teacher you therefore need to be able to:

- Work under pressure but not become overwhelmed
- View lessons as an exciting opportunity to help children learn
- Catch a vision of the end point of your teaching and the children's learning
- Deal with unexpected events calmly
- Accept that there will be times when you do not cope particularly well.

You can help yourself by:

◆ Knowing what you are talking about when you start teaching a lesson
◆ Spending a lot of time thinking about ways of organizing and managing the lesson efficiently
◆ Managing your own time carefully
◆ Co-operating fully with school staff, both teaching and non-teaching.

Consequently, during your school placement it pays to develop the following characteristics:

◆ A sincere interest *in* the children
◆ A sincere interest *for* the children
◆ A responsiveness to parents and staff
◆ A pleasant and engaging personality
◆ A willingness to contribute to all aspects of school life.

Some of these attributes may not come naturally. However, the best trainees view the challenges they present as part of their professional development and seek advice about how best to improve.

Teaching principle

Aim high but be patient with yourself and others.

In Chapter 2, many of the issues and practicalities associated with the start of school experience have been raised to help you to orientate and get off to a positive start. Chapter 3 now offers seven case studies that have been selected to illustrate the sorts of emotional and practical demands commonly experienced by trainee teachers in the period immediately prior to commencing the placement and during their first encounters with the new school situation.

Further reading

Gipps, C., McCallum, B. and Hargreaves, E. (2000) *What Makes a Good Primary Teacher*, London: RoutledgeFalmer.
Wyse, D. (2002) *Becoming a Primary School Teacher*, London: RoutledgeFalmer.

CHAPTER 3

The emotions of school experience

Dealing with your emotions

Teaching is a job that involves the emotions – in fact it is impossible to remain detached from the responsibilities and relationships that form a major part of the teaching role. As such, it is important to recognize that in addition to the mental and physical requirements of being a teacher, emotions also need to be managed. Hargreaves (1994) represents the emotional heart of teaching as 'desire', which is:

> Imbued with 'creative unpredictability' and 'flows of energy' . . . In desire is to be found the creativity and spontaneity that connects teachers emotionally . . . to their children, their colleagues and their work. Such desires among particularly creative teachers are for fulfilment, intense achievement, senses of breakthrough, closeness to fellow humans, even love for them . . . Without desire, teaching becomes arid and empty. It loses its meaning.
>
> (Hargreaves 1994, pp. 12–13)

The time prior to the start of your school experience is both a worrying and a thrilling time. Naturally, you are very interested to know the name and location of the school, the teacher and year group with which you will be working, and the expectations that will be made of you. Factors such as your own experiences as a pupil and student, your success on previous school placements, your attitude to life in general, and the extent to which you feel adequately prepared for teaching, combine to have a strong influence on your confidence level and attitude. One student teacher wrote about her feelings in this way:

> In the build up to the placement, my confidence was quite high as my previous school experience had been successful and I hoped to build on this, taking on more responsibility to prepare myself for having my own class next September. I was also a bit apprehensive because I did not know what the school was like, if the staff were supportive and what sort of backgrounds the children came from.

The weeks before the placement are like being in a 'phoney war' situation. You are gearing up for battle when all around you things are calm and peaceful. Most trainees are anxious to get stuck in and begin their time in school but also feel a little nervous about whether they will be adequately prepared and able to cope with the demands placed on them. As a trainee, your dominant emotion will, quite naturally, be one of *excitement* about the opportunity to go into a school and start teaching. After all, this was the main reason for starting a training course in the first place. However, some emotions will be born of anxiety and a fear of facing the unknown. This uncertainty takes a variety of forms:

◆ Doubts about your teaching competence
◆ Concerns about establishing a harmonious relationship with staff
◆ Worries about coping with college expectations
◆ Lack of confidence about your subject knowledge and ability to plan lessons
◆ Anxieties about adjusting to unfamiliar school and classroom norms.

In fact all teachers have to grapple with a variety of emotions associated with the job, including concerns about whether they can cope with the diverse demands made of them, so if you feel a degree of trepidation about teaching, you are not alone. Teaching carries with it a mysterious combination of factors impacting upon the emotions that can broadly be subdivided into those that tend to satisfy and those that do not. Every teacher needs the satisfaction that comes from a knowledge that children have been helped and their education advanced. The flash of understanding that lights children's faces when they grasp the meaning of something never loses its ability to thrill and encourage a teacher. Similarly, the enjoyment derived from moments of fun and intimacy with children based on the establishment of trust and mutual respect provides teachers with a huge incentive to persevere with the job. The emotions that do *not* satisfy are associated with the fact that no matter how hard you work and how sincerely you approach your responsibilities, you can never fulfil all your aspirations. It is also unsettling to face the rather bitter truth that some children fail to respond to your teaching or to you as a person, and others let you down. Thankfully, the satisfaction always outweighs the disappointment.

This chapter is based on the premise that the emotional dimension of teaching has a significant influence on classroom effectiveness and acts either as a springboard for success or a hindrance to progress, depending on how trainee teachers cope with it. You may feel at ease with children and be strongly motivated to teach, but still suffer from a nagging worry about whether you will, after all, be able to handle the demands of a school placement. It would be surprising if you did not feel a degree of anxiety prior to school experience but it is more difficult to distinguish between healthy concerns and damaging ones. Healthy concerns act as a spur to achievement, while damaging concerns affect confidence and lead to underperformance.

The ability to harness the emotions and employ them constructively is sometimes referred to as *emotional intelligence* and associated with the work of Daniel Goleman in the United States. Dimensions of emotional intelligence include the ability to speak and listen effectively, to think creatively about situations, to manage professional development, to work as part of a team and to influence others in order to make a positive difference. Bocchino (1999) prefers to use the term 'emotional *literacy*' as a 'key factor in determining and predicting future success in any aspect of life and in all types of success' (1999, p. 5). The terminology is not crucially important but the principles of being able to handle your feelings and marshal your emotions so as to retain self-esteem and empathize with others is very significant in negotiating the complexities of school life. This is particularly relevant as a newcomer in school with little idea about the vagaries that characterize the situation.

Pre-placement anxiety

The time between knowing where you have been placed and visiting the school for the first time is often one of especially high emotion. The following extract, typical of many, is taken from what a trainee teacher wrote about the days preceding the time spent in school:

> So here I am on the eve of the preliminary visit. For some inexplicable reason I am incredibly nervous. I don't know if it's just that it has been such a long break since the last time or because I had such a good time on my last placement in a different age group. This time it's an older age group, which I've had no experience of before. Whatever else, I'm sure that once I get there, get to know the teachers, pupils, other staff, parents and routines, I will be fine. I know I am capable. I know that I will give it my best shot and I know that support will be there. All I have to do is ask for it. So at the end of the day, what am I worried about? The fear of the unknown, that's what! Know the unknown, remove the fear.

Another trainee wrote of different, but equally powerful concerns that were at the forefront of his mind before commencing the placement:

> As the teaching experience approached, my feelings were that I simply could not be a teacher. In the build-up to the placement, many questions concerned me: Will I get on with the teacher? Will my planning be good enough? Can I motivate myself sufficiently? Am I good enough for the job? Will I fit in with the school?

In fact, once the school experience started, he soon found his feet and enjoyed his time immensely (see Wong's story, later and in Chapter 5). This did not mean, however, that he did not have to work hard and persevere to succeed. On the contrary, it was these very qualities that won over the school staff when they saw that he was willing to do his best and co-operate with them. Although you may similarly doubt your ability to cope, making a determined effort to do your best, remaining alert to the opportunities and keeping an open relationship with 'significant others' will impress key people such as the class teacher and mentor (Stephenson 1995). It is also important to recognize that the majority of your fellow trainees share the doubts and fears you entertain. It is possible to convince yourself that you are not cut out for teaching by paying too much attention to the inner voice of doubt, when this emotional turmoil is common among trainee teachers and even some qualified ones. Although you may have some feelings of insecurity about teaching, remember that you have lots to offer schools, too. Teachers prize your enthusiasm, bright personality and breadth of academic and other forms of knowledge. As Harrison (1995, p. 29) rightly claims: 'Student teachers . . . bring with them a myriad of experiences and skills, many very relevant to teaching.'

Another source of anxiety and concern for some trainees emerges when they are placed in a school at some distance from the college and therefore need to live in temporary accommodation. Whereas some people enjoy being detached from student life and its many distractions, others find living away from the campus in a strange area to be an unsettling experience. For instance, one trainee teacher wrote:

> I was worried about this school experience because, for the first time, I was living out in accommodation arranged by the college. I was worried about this because if I were unhappy there it could greatly affect my performance in school.

If you are living some way out from the main campus and do not have immediate access to your peers, or if you are the only trainee teacher in the school, it is essential that you maintain regular contact with other trainees. Establishing a regular network of connections with sympathetic friends can act as a conduit for your fears, help you to feel more settled and give you a fresh hope when things seem bleak. It also offers the opportunity to share ideas, discuss classroom issues and celebrate success. Whatever happens, don't try to fight your battles alone during school placement.

It is important to remind yourself that fragile emotions associated with *anticipation* invariably change following a successful initiation into school life, and that adopting an optimistic and confident approach to events plays a major role in allaying fears. If you allow a spirit of pessimism to dominate your thinking, it can lead to a sense of hopelessness and, in the worst cases, depression, so don't dwell on 'what if?' thoughts. Three facts may help you to adopt a more upbeat view of the coming placement:

◆ Failure on school experience is extremely rare
◆ Success on school experience is normal
◆ Struggles are part of learning to be a teacher, not a sign of incompetence.

Case studies

On the basis that the best means of combating anxiety is to confront it, the remainder of this chapter explores the experiences of seven trainee primary teachers on their final school experience. Extracts are taken from accounts written by the trainees, who describe their experiences and feelings at the start of placement and their initial reaction when facing new circumstances. Although anxiety is widespread amongst trainees before they commence time in school, the accounts show that with determination and management of the situation, it can be harnessed and used positively. Many of the extracts refer to the tension between excited anticipation and feelings of anxiety. This *emotional management* includes:

1   Self-awareness
2   Evaluating first impressions
3   Relating to others
4   Refocusing.

Each extract is accompanied by comment about the key issues that confronted the trainees and their implications for successfully negotiating the challenges that faced them.

Cindy

I looked forward to my final year teaching practice with a mixture of excited anticipation at the prospect of being able to have a 'proper go' and occasional, no, *frequent* bouts, of anxiety brought on by thoughts of 'What if I can't cope with staying up until all hours trying to plan, re-plan and re-plan again?' On my first day at the large city school (the school buildings were actually quite small for so many pupils) myself and another student teacher were greeted by a friendly but rushed and seemingly very busy school mentor. She laughed aloud when I told her my name, apologising at the same time, while explaining that I was working in class 1R. She gave me a knowing look as though even us wretched students should have heard of 1R. She cleared her throat and this time repeated her apology, only this time she said: 'I'm *really* sorry; they have a bit of a reputation for . . . wait for it . . . being a bit lively.' She continued: 'You will have to sit on them for a while to get them sorted.' By now I was starting to feel physically sick. Four years hard graft flashed before my eyes. Failure was beckoning me with a large crooked finger. I swallowed hard and said 'That's okay' in a feeble attempt to retain some confidence, all the while thinking that my bottom was not quite big enough to sit on thirty-one children!

We were shown to our respective classes after being given a brief tour of the school and I was introduced to the class teacher who turned out to have been trained at the same college as me and was in her second year of teaching. She was clearly as nervous as me and said that I was her first student so she felt a little unsure of her role. She went on to explain that the classroom had been converted from a cloakroom and originally used as an adjoining 'messy play room' for shared use by reception and other early years' classes. It was now, however, a classroom for thirty-one lively Year 1s.

'We are a little cramped', she apologized. She went on to explain that 1R was a very difficult class. 'I'm warning you now,' she said, 'they are very hard to manage. I've been at my wits end. They've improved a bit since September; well, they're not hitting each other so much. They also vary in ability, so you'll have to think about differentiation.'

The children were due back from assembly at any moment and hasty preparations occurred while we spoke. I offered to help her and was told that some pencils needed sharpening as the learning support assistants no longer did that job and she hadn't got around to it. I was happy to oblige and feel useful, so got on with trying to find the sharpener.

The children arrived, animated and bustling. Some of them were so tiny they were almost as small as my own four year old, but there was a large group of seemingly much more physically mature boys who jostled and giggled and pushed each other as they came through the door. Some of the girls clutched each other tightly, whispering comments while they stared at me shyly. For a moment I felt better. They weren't three-headed monsters and nobody appeared to have a gun. I smiled and tried to appear friendly but at the same time exude an air of 'I'm nice but don't try to mess with me.'

Issues for Cindy

The ability to cope with the new challenge

Doubt and uncertainty is a natural part of growth and development. Cindy was taking stock of her situation and preparing herself for the challenge that lay ahead. A strategy to reduce stress is, paradoxically, to consider the worst possible scenario and begin to shape strategies for coping (Carlyle and Woods 2002). It is a common phenomenon that once the worst is confronted, events become more manageable. An old saying declares that 'today is the tomorrow you worried about yesterday, and all is well'. It holds as true for teaching as any other situation in life. However, the rite of passage into a school (Van Gennep 1960) involves a variety of experiences which, if not understood for what they are, can lead to unnecessary stress. First, new situations need to be interpreted, understood and aligned to. This process takes time and invariably includes a degree of hit and miss. Second, it is important to remember that as other trainees have coped before, so will you. Third, schools invite trainee teachers to work with them by choice, not because they have to do so. This should help to reassure you that there is a reservoir of goodwill from which you can draw.

The initial encounters with host teachers

The school mentor did little to reassure Cindy when she first arrived by giving the impression that the class was a particularly difficult one to control. Although it is true that some classes are harder to manage than others, it is equally the case that a class that proves very challenging for one person is less so for someone else. It was significant that the class teacher was inexperienced and quite nervous about working with a trainee teacher. The more that you can reassure the class teacher that you are going to be an attribute, the more likely that you will establish a harmonious relationship with her or him. It helps to put yourself in the teacher's place. What would you want from your trainee?

The need to feel useful

It is sensible to get busy as soon as possible for three principal reasons. First, being busy allows you to complete a task, which is gratifying in itself. Second, it shows that you are willing to get stuck in. Third, it avoids the sense of being a 'spare part'. However, it is also important to spend time observing classroom events, so it may be better to volunteer for some relatively undemanding tasks early on that allow for more flexibility, rather than a complex one that demands your full attention and does not allow you to watch experienced practitioners at work. There is a balance to be struck between looking tentative and appearing overly assertive. Class teachers hope for a self-reliant trainee teacher who shows initiative and is not afraid to ask for clarification when uncertain.

First impressions of the children

Cindy was relieved when she saw the children but was also determined to remain a little aloof from the class rather than being too friendly. This strategy of remaining cool and slightly detached (while still being approachable) is an effective means of easing yourself into the class situation on the assumption that it is easier to loosen up after initially being stern than to retrieve a situation in which you have begun weakly. However, if the delay in establishing a rapport with the children is extended, it may be difficult to redeem, so don't take too long to thaw out! As you will not know the children when you first arrive in the school, you cannot depend on your relationship with them or knowledge of their backgrounds to guide your responses and decisions. You must therefore rely on being alert to what is happening, clear about what you are doing and exuding a quiet self-confidence that comes from feeling good about yourself and others.

Cindy's emotional management

1   *Self-awareness*: Cindy was sensitive to the fact that she had doubts about her ability to cope and appears to have entered school in a defensive mode. She would have been better advised to adopt a 'Yes I can!' attitude by refusing to countenance negative emotions.

2   *Evaluating first impressions*: Cindy made negative assumptions about the impossible task that lay ahead of her on the basis of the class teacher's initial comments. She would have been wise to avoid jumping to hasty conclusions and feeling gloomy about things as a result.

3   *Relating to others*: Cindy wisely made up her mind that she was not going to be a pushover and used body language (good eye contact, relaxed face, upright stance, smiles and frowns) to convey this impression to the children.

4   *Refocusing*: Cindy quickly became aware that the children, though lively, were not out of control. By concentrating on this positive element, she gained confidence and hope for the future.

Emily

My school experience was an immense learning curve for my professional development, classroom ability and, most importantly, my confidence. Before commencing the school placement there were the common emotional feelings of excitement and anxiety that are felt before embarking on any new venture. However, the most emotional issue for me was whether I was actually capable of teaching, as this had been questioned by some people previously.

I was placed with a Year 2 class and due to the SATs' pressure there was a slightly different arrangement. In the mornings there were three classes for literacy and numeracy, reducing the number of children per group to twenty-three. In the afternoon the three classes merged for their activities. I therefore found myself working closely with three teachers rather than my assigned class teacher for planning and organization, quickly contributing fully to planning meetings and general discussions, beginning to feel confident that my ideas would work. This was furthered when other teachers took on board my ideas and used them in their own teaching. This highlighted for me the importance of developing positive relationships with teaching and support staff, and although I achieved these almost effortlessly, I can contrast this with a more challenging experience. My second placement was one in which the class teacher did not make me feel welcome or part of the team. This negative relationship with the class teacher made it very difficult for me to progress during that time due to the feeling that I was an unwelcome intruder into her domain. Since that experience I have always worried about going into someone else's classroom for fear of never becoming an 'insider'. My final school experience was just the opposite from the start. When I entered the school I immediately felt welcomed and respected.

Issues for Emily

The impact of school experience on confidence

Emily had experienced a disappointing time during her second placement and this had the effect of making her more anxious about subsequent ones. She was unsure whether her previous experience in school was a true reflection of her ability or an aberration. She does not specify who the 'some people' were, but they had obviously sowed seeds of doubt in her mind and these had festered during the intervening time between placements. Most trainee teachers' fears quickly evaporate once they enter school and become involved in its life and work. Emily was no exception.

The different atmosphere in schools

Emily sensed that there was a different feel to the school in which she was placed and the previous one. She found the one school to be very welcoming but felt like an intruder in the other. The importance of feeling welcomed is something mentioned as important by most trainee teachers and is principally based on staff attitudes. However, the more that you can demonstrate your determination, sensitivity and competence, the greater will be the respect that you enjoy. It's as if the host teachers are saying, 'We are willing to extend a welcome to you, so now you must convince us that you deserve our respect.'

The impact of tests

End-of-key-stage tests (also known as SATs) are important in school as they are used as a measure of its success. Every year, test results are made available to parents and if a school is perceived by inspectors to be underachieving, it receives close and not particularly welcome scrutiny from the local education authority (LEA). Every school seeks to be above average to ensure that parents are satisfied, pupil numbers are maintained and the staff is left alone to get on with the job, rather than being constantly monitored. LEAs are also under pressure from central government for the schools in their area to raise standards annually. This process may yield better test scores but it is disadvantageous in respect of the way in which preparation for SATs squeezes out other important curriculum work. A culture of swotting for SATs has emerged, whereby teachers coach children (especially Year 6) before the tests to maximize scores. The time of year when SATs are being administered (usually in the month of May) involves additional strain for teachers, so the presence of a trainee can be extremely useful to share the load. It can also mean that the timetable is disrupted and you may find yourself asked to play a less prominent role until the tests are over.

Participation in decision-making

Involvement in collaborative discussions with host teachers forms an important element of school experience, when you can learn how the planning process operates. Although trainees are dependent upon teachers inviting them to participate, there is also a need for you to show an obvious interest in this important aspect of a teacher's work. It is helpful to contribute ideas where possible and learn about sources of curriculum materials, maintaining records and taking note of the different educational priorities and teaching approaches of staff responsible for the same age of children. Teachers will expect and hope that you make constructive suggestions about methods, ideas and resources, especially the use of ICT.

Emily's emotional management

1   *Self-awareness*: Emily grappled with the fear that she was not cut out for teaching but convinced herself that she should proceed. The past should inform but not constrain your attitude as each school experience offers a fresh chance to prosper and succeed. Emily's strategy of 'convincing herself' that she could do it was an effective one.
2   *Evaluating first impressions*: Emily was unsettled by the prospect of dealing with end of key stage tests but these fears proved groundless as the situation provided for a range of experiences that she would otherwise have missed. Emily could have avoided a lot of anxiety by viewing the unusual circumstances as an opportunity, not an obstacle.
3   *Relating to others*: Emily had three teachers to relate to, which might have been a disadvantage for her. Instead, by making the effort to contribute her ideas to group discussions, she found that she was soon accepted into the inner circle of decision-making and her confidence was boosted.
4   *Refocusing*: Thanks to establishing a positive relationship with the staff, Emily was quickly able to relax into her placement and enjoy the experience.

Nadia
I worked with a Year 1 class, next door to the early years' unit. My class teacher was very caring towards her children and had built up good relationships with them. At the same time, she seemed to have at the front of her mind that they were there to learn and so she used her relationships with the children to encourage the best work from them. One day I hope to achieve this. I think it would be fair to say that the whole school was very child-centred, with all

teachers expected to provide an extra-curricular activity and to encourage the pupils to be involved in these.

The school was very friendly and successful, with motivated teachers. As a result, one of the initial issues in my wider professional role was to try and become part of the ethos. I had to contend with many conflicting feelings, including establishing myself as a competent teacher and not just the student. I was worried about not meeting their expectations but knowing that I still had a lot to learn from the experience. Also, I wanted to fit in but needed to respect the fact that the other teachers were busy and to a certain extent only had time for professional relationships with me.

Fortunately, there was a recently qualified teacher in the school who helped me in my transition from outsider to insider. I was able to talk to her about how I was feeling and found that once I was friendly with her, the other teachers were friendlier with me. I believe that they were able to see that I was making relationships within the school and she could reassure me in what I was doing.

Issues for Nadia

The caring climate within the school

There is an ongoing debate about the extent to which teachers should be 'carers' or 'educators'; that is, how much responsibility teachers carry for the physical, moral and social dimensions of a child's development, and how much for the academic elements. Nias (1997) even argues that teachers may care too much, to the neglect of other important aspects of their role. Nevertheless, Nadia was struck and impressed by the evidence of care that pervaded the school and noted that the class teacher used this nurturing approach as a foundation for effective learning in the formal curriculum. It took time for her to establish a relationship with the children and gain their trust. After all, why should children have confidence in strangers, when they do not know them, what they stand for, how significant they are or their temperament? It is little wonder that early on in the placement children tend to go first to the class teacher or assistant rather than to the trainee. Over time, however, teaching becomes more fulfilling as you receive the children's seal of approval.

The place of extra-curricular activities

Nearly all schools run additional activities for the children. Sometimes a subject specialist is responsible (e.g. a computer club run by the leader of ICT). Sometimes it is a teacher who has a particular enthusiasm (e.g. netball, gardening). There are also booster classes for children who are deemed to require additional support in English and extension classes for children aspiring to high academic achievement. In all these cases, your help and support is greatly appreciated by the staff, and they will be pleased for any assistance that you can offer. Nevertheless, it pays to be cautious before committing yourself too eagerly. Your priority is to establish yourself in the regular curriculum before accepting further responsibilities.

The need to adjust to the prevailing ethos

The friendly and motivated staff made an immediate impression on Nadia. She, in turn, demonstrated her own willingness to reciprocate the teachers' goodwill. She was conscious, however, of the teachers' busy schedules and the need to be careful about making too many demands on them when they were preoccupied. In their enthusiasm to show that they are keen and able, some trainees overwhelm the host teachers with questions and requests. There is a fine balance to be struck between being keen to learn and sucking a teacher dry.

Nadia's emotional management

1   *Self-awareness*: Nadia was worried about not meeting the teachers' expectations and how to fit in to the school placement without being a burden to them. In fact, she was able to gain emotional support from an anchor person, who provided reassurance and friendship.

2   *Evaluating first impressions*: Nadia sensed that the school was friendly and teachers well motivated. While she was relieved, Nadia was also anxious about her ability to conform to the prevailing ethos.

3   *Relating to others*: Nadia found that the teachers were first waiting for her to demonstrate that she was friendly. She duly obliged.

4   *Refocusing*: Nadia was wily enough to discern that if she wanted to maintain a positive relationship with the class teacher, she must make the enhancement of children's learning her goal.

Wong
I believe that my biggest success when teaching children is when I am the concise and direct twenty-two year old guy from the big city and not when I try to be something I'm not. My aim is to probe deeply into my private, even personal, world of teaching and help ordinary people understand how difficult, antagonizing, daunting, rewarding and enjoyable teaching can be.

The feelings I had at the end of my third year school practice were very mixed. Initially I was pleased it was over. Emotionally the pressure was off, so I had time to readjust to normal life. Physically, I could catch up on those early mornings and I was nearer the distant goal of becoming a teacher. However, as the teaching practice approached, my feelings were that I simply could not be a teacher. In the build-up to the placement, many questions were in my mind:

◆ Will I get on with the teacher?
◆ Will my planning be good enough?
◆ Can I motivate myself?
◆ Will I fit in with the school?
◆ Am I good enough for the job?
◆ Is this what I want to do?

In addition, I knew that, once again, I would have to travel some distance to the school.

Whether I would fit in with the class teacher was something I spent many hours worrying about. The question I ask myself is 'Why should it matter so much?' I decided that it was the fact that for the first time on teaching practice I would be working with a lady class teacher. This is not due to the fact that I don't get on with women but that I did not know what to expect from her teaching. Would her approach be very different from that of a male? When I met the teacher for the first time I could observe the differences and similarities between male and female teaching styles and between her and me in particular. I watched her first lesson and observed her manner with the children. I would like to say that our styles were similar and I 'fitted' into her class with remarkable ease, but I can't. The following is what I noted of her:

◆ She was very calm.
◆ When dealing with discipline issues, she treated the children with a remarkable sense of control, without ever losing her temper.
◆ The children treated her as a mother.
◆ She taught from a three-page lesson plan.

These were immense differences from my approach that I felt I couldn't deal with. The resolution to the problem came from the teacher herself when, after the first day, she asked me if I had any problems. I had thousands but only admitted to one: 'I can't be like you in the classroom.' She looked at me with a look of misunderstanding and asked me what I meant. I responded by stating that we were so different that my teaching would be difficult. Her response to this was so comforting that it felt mightily profound. She simply said: 'I'm glad that we're so different, for the sake of the children. I have been having a bit of trouble with the boys in the class and I think that if they have a young male teacher around they might look to you in confidence.' Her reply answered two of my immediate worries. First, I could get on with this person. She was honest. She had the children's best interests at heart and we could converse. Second, I was made to feel the importance of my own personal style and, though teachers are so very different, children still respond to them.

Issues for Wong

The need to be natural in school

Teachers are those who do not feel the need to project their character synthetically to create a relaxed and purposeful classroom climate because they are spontaneous, warm and at ease with their role. Trainees who strain to 'be like a teacher' fail to understand that children quickly spot a fake. Although there will be times when you have to feign anger, amusement and interest, these occasions should be kept to a minimum. While it is important to use appropriate vocabulary and terminology when talking to children, this should not be confused with affected speech.

The range of questions intruding upon self-confidence prior to the placement

The questions that Wong asked himself at the beginning of the placement will be familiar to most trainees. They varied from pragmatic ones (such as the adequacy of his planning) to more profound ones (such as whether teaching was the right job for him). As we have noted on several occasions elsewhere, it is natural for trainee teachers to entertain doubts, not only at the start of their placement, but during the time in school. The prospect of a lengthy journey added to Wong's worries about the whole experience but particular concerns focused on fitting in with the female class teacher. Wong's open approach to the issue facilitated its relatively easy resolution. In other circumstances, the class teacher might have felt threatened or upset by his remarks but in this case she responded constructively and this facilitated the establishment of a strong working relationship.

The difficulty of reconciling contrasting styles

There are occasions when trainees are placed with a class teacher whose style is so different from their own that they face a stark choice about whether to conform, adopt a different approach or compromise. For example, the teacher may use a loud voice to gain the children's attention when the trainee prefers to use a more subtle approach, such as raising a hand and waiting for children to follow suit. The teacher may tolerate queues of children when the trainee prefers to circulate throughout the room and attend to children as they request help. The teacher may ignore the actions of certain children when the trainee's instincts warn that swift intervention is needed. In all these matters it is important to spend time observing the teacher, asking careful questions and honing your classroom technique as a result. It pays to avoid making premature value judgements and to keep an open mind. Teachers usually have very good reason for acting the way they do, so it pays to find out.

Wong's emotional management

1   *Self-awareness*: Wong was a highly reflective person and cared passionately about his work. However, he allowed the fact that he was male and working with an older female class teacher to influence his expectations. He came to realize that stereotyping is unhelpful and creates unnecessary psychological barriers to progress.

2   *Evaluating first impressions*: Wong was unsettled by the class teacher's teaching style. He would have been well advised to adopt a more professional attitude and view diversity as a positive chance to consider alternatives.

3   *Relating to others*: Wong discovered that talking through the issues in an unthreatening way with the teacher resulted in peace of mind instead of emotional turmoil.

4   *Refocusing*: Wong began to take a more productive view of the situation and acknowledge that there are many successful teaching approaches. His scepticism turned to admiration.

Tracey

During the ten-week experience I was working within one of the two reception classes. The class teacher was in her fifth year of teaching at the school. She had completed her NQT year at the school and had remained there ever since. A formal teaching style that allowed very few child-initiated tasks had been developed by this teacher. This surprised me greatly, particularly with the introduction of the Early Learning Goals. However, I felt that her philosophy had been greatly influenced by her training. Having qualified after the introduction of the National Curriculum, there would have been heavy emphasis during her training on subject teaching.

Before I entered the school I felt very confident about the forthcoming practice. This confidence had manifested itself out of the success of my previous school experience, so I was hoping to continue to develop from where I had finished on my last placement. On reflection, I realize that this was unrealistic. First, because it is the norm to take a few steps back before you can move forward, and second because the ethos and philosophy that govern each class can differ enormously.

As each preliminary day went by, I realized that I was growing increasingly uncomfortable and anxious about certain elements of the practice in my class. The teacher's didactic, controlling approach differed considerably from my child-centred approach. To add to this problem, the teacher expressed her initial reluctance to hand control over to me. She explained that the decision was not related to my professional competence but was because she wanted me to observe, fully understand and then implement the existing classroom practices and procedures throughout my teaching experience. This caused me concern as I had had visions of developing my own pedagogical style on my final school placement. I did not want to mirror someone else, becoming her carbon copy.

This situation presented me with a huge dilemma. Should I mirror the teacher's 'top-down' method or develop my own 'bottom-up' approach? I realized that my decision to either ignore or implement the teacher's request would make the difference between a happy, supportive experience and an unhappy, disappointing one. I decided to conform and make every effort to fit in. However, as I was gradually allowed to take on more responsibility, it soon became apparent that I was finding some of my principles difficult to suppress.

Issues for Tracey

Continuity between school experiences

It is very difficult to carry on where you left off in a previous school. The circumstances are different, and whereas at the end of the previous placement you have established a relationship with the children and adjusted to the school's expectations, the process has to begin afresh in a new situation. Qualified teachers often experience something similar when they change schools. It is essential for trainee teachers to evaluate their progress at the end of the placement and set sensible targets for the next. In this way, the idiosyncrasies associated with a particular circumstance can be viewed as opportunities rather than problems. For instance, it is common for trainees to find difficulty in differentiating work to accommodate the range of learning abilities in the class. At the end of the school experience, this issue would become one of the key targets for the trainee during the next placement or the induction year.

The formal teaching style of the teacher

Like Wong (earlier), Tracey was faced with a dilemma about the extent to which she should conform to the class teacher's style or promote her own child-centred preference. It is interesting to note that she elected to 'fit in' and gradually introduce changes, rather than take the more forthright approach adopted by Wong. On the whole, Tracey's tactfulness was successful, though she discovered that her own educational principles impelled her to teach in a more informal way than the class teacher. The issue with which all trainee teachers have to contend is that in contrast to experienced teachers, who have already determined their approach and are unlikely to deviate very much from it, trainees are still developing their preferred style. This does not mean, however, that teachers are unwilling to tolerate a different style from trainees, as most are happy to discuss alternative strategies if they are convinced that the children will benefit from them. If you view differences as a rich source of issues for consideration rather than a stumbling block, your outlook will soon be more optimistic.

Limitations on modelling

Trainees have a lot to learn from experienced teachers but there is no way in which they can, or should, try to replicate their approach unthinkingly. In particular, it is essential to discover their *reasons* for teaching and prioritizing in the way they do. One teacher will put a lot of passion into interactive teaching, question and answer, and eliciting responses from the children. Another teacher will use her skills in storytelling to get across important concepts. A third teacher will spend time preparing a variety of interesting activity sheets, providing resources or utilizing ICT. Some teachers are extremely systematic in lesson planning, while others rely more on spontaneity. Some teachers foster collaboration, while others favour individual work, and so on. Additionally, the class teacher has already established a rapport with the class that you have yet to gain and you cannot proceed on the assumption that the children will react towards you in the same way. Tracey was faced with a serious ethical dilemma. On the one hand she wanted to demonstrate to the class teacher that she was ready to fit in and provide continuity of experience for the children. On the other hand she wanted to be true to her convictions. To a large extent, Tracey's sensitive handling of this dilemma influenced the success of her school placement.

Tracey's emotional management

1   *Self-awareness*: Tracey gained considerable comfort from dwelling on her past success in school.
2   *Evaluating first impressions*: Tracey made rapid judgements about the teacher's style and expectations that unsettled her. She needed to spend a little more time weighing up the position before jumping to negative conclusions.
3   *Relating to others*: Tracey judged that in order to maintain a working relationship with the class teacher it was better to 'go with the flow' and conform.
4   *Refocusing*: It soon became evident that conformity had its limitations and that replicating the teacher's actions was no substitute for passionate teaching, based on conviction.

Kate

I spent my final school experience with a Year 4 class in a large primary school in which there were separate buildings on the same site for children in KS1 and KS2.

My emotional condition before the placement was shaky for several reasons. First, I did not have an enjoyable third year school experience and although I passed the practice I was worried that I would be in a school that I hated for ten weeks. The reason for not liking my previous school placement was largely down to a tyrannical class teacher who was not approachable and made it perfectly clear that I was not wanted in her classroom. I was petrified that I would be in a similar situation again, but this time for ten weeks. So although I was wary about being in such a large school after spending previous placements in much smaller ones, I made a conscious decision to do the best I could with staff relationships and to try very hard to have a communicative and happy relationship with my class teacher.

The second reason for being nervous about this practice was that for the first time during a school experience I was living out in accommodation arranged by the University. I was worried about this because if I was unhappy there it could greatly affect my performance in school. If, for example, I did not like the family, the food or the bed was uncomfortable, then my unhappiness would seek an escape. This would probably result in me venting my feelings at school. Although I risk sounding fussy when I write about these worries, I believe the idea of the 'whole person' comes into focus here. Teachers are now expected to educate and care for the whole child and it is a commonly accepted idea that children who are unhappy at home for whatever reason do not perform their best in school. I believe that this is true of teachers and of myself in this case, because teachers are human beings, too, and outside factors affect their performance.

During the Christmas holidays I held a full-time job for three weeks and I believe that this helped me to get used to the routine of getting up early and going to work every day. With the money I earned, I bought some smart new clothes and had my hair cut so that I could go into school feeling self-assured and professional. Although this may not be of importance to some people, it is very important to me as I think that how you feel about yourself reflects how you come across to others. I did not want to give the impression of being sloppy, either to the children or other members of staff. It also gave me the idea of making a new start in this school.

Apart from the above factors I was worried about the workload which I had to undertake during my time in school. As I had never been in school for such a period of time, I was worried about losing the momentum and being able to keep up with the paperwork. I am not the sort of person who can stay up into the small hours working. I didn't want the factors of tiredness and a treadmill of paperwork to affect my performance when teaching.

Because of the above concerns, my emotional state was therefore apprehensive but not without some positive thoughts, too. I was looking forward to being in school and working with children because I had not had much contact with children for about a year. I find that if I do not have this contact for a while I miss the company of young people. I was determined to do my best in this placement and to overcome pessimism resulting from my last experience in school. This may have been a subconscious effort to 'show the previous teacher' that I was capable of doing well in a classroom. I also knew that this was to be one of the most important ten weeks of my life, as my future rested on my time in school. I was not aiming for perfection but to do my personal best so that if my future took a different direction, I could look back with pride, not regret.

From the start I made a huge effort to be polite, helpful, interested and enthusiastic, but luckily I soon realized that I did not have to force these qualities. I shared some common ground with the teacher, as she was the same age as my sister and also a newly qualified teacher. She was, therefore, not much older than me, so I used this fact as a starting point on which to build our relationship.

Issues for Kate

Size of school

Kate was right to note the individual circumstances of her placement, and avoided the trap of making assumptions about being in a large school. In fact, the main differences between large and small schools are often as follows:

◆ Teachers in large schools usually have a responsibility for a single curriculum subject or area, teachers in small schools often have to be responsible for several
◆ Larger schools tend to have a lot of sophisticated equipment and resources, smaller schools more often have to 'make do'
◆ The staff of small schools, especially in rural areas, are often involved in additional tasks, such as bus duty
◆ Classes in smaller schools are frequently composed of two or more year groups (such as reception and Year 1)
◆ Teachers in large schools meet together to plan as year teams, whereas the teachers in smaller schools often meet in key stage groups.

However, despite the size differences in schools, they share a large number of common factors. The school day tends to be designed along the same lines, teachers and pupils interact in similar ways, parents bring their children to school each morning and pick them up at night, lunch boxes and coats abound, displays cover walls. In fact, whether you are placed in Rosebud Petal Primary or Cactus Prickle Primary, the job is basically the same. Children need to be taught and teachers are there to help them learn. It's as simple and complicated as that!

Concerns about personal well-being

Kate was keenly aware of her emotional and psychological disposition, and was conscious of the fact that her self-esteem and happiness would influence her effectiveness in school. She recognized that if she felt good about herself she could approach the placement with greater confidence. The situation was not helped by the fact that her previous experience had left her feeling bruised and disillusioned with teaching. Kate was worried about finding herself in a similar position and was nervous about being in unfamiliar circumstances in a strange town. However, Kate's determined attitude ensured that when she went into school, she had given herself the greatest chance of making a good impression and looking the part as a teacher. The strategy worked!

Concerns about workload

Studies show that qualified teachers work long hours every week, including administrative tasks such as record keeping, planning meetings to plan work, liaising with and advising colleagues, and so forth. Trainee teachers also spend a lot of time preparing lessons, making resources, marking work and completing paperwork. As a result, weariness and fatigue can creep up on them and badly affect the quality of their teaching. Tiredness can also result in depression and self-doubt, and minor incidents assume a meaning that is wholly out of proportion to their actual significance. Kate was determined to establish a work pattern that took account of her metabolism and give herself the best chance of reaching optimum performance. There is a mythology among trainee teachers that unless they are pushing themselves as hard as possible and living on the brink of exhaustion, they are being negligent. Such a martyrdom philosophy invites disaster, as the trainee becomes increasingly unable to cope with the strain. You will need to be wise and disciplined in such matters.

Looking forward to being with children in school

The majority of primary teachers choose to teach because they enjoy being with children and helping them to learn. Kate was eager to re-establish her contact with children and relished the satisfaction that comes from engaging with young minds. Regardless of how challenging school life becomes, remind yourself that you achieve something that few others have the opportunity to do as you make a direct impact on children's education and welfare.

Kate's emotional management

1   *Self-awareness*: Kate focused on the unhappy time she had experienced in a previous school placement and allowed this to dominate her thinking instead of being cheered by the thought that it was highly unlikely she would have such ill fortune again.

2   *Evaluating first impressions*: Kate made up her mind to adopt a positive approach to the situation, regardless of the outcome. Her attitude provided the momentum that was needed for success.

3   *Relating to others*: Kate knew that relationships held the key to success and rightly decided to enjoy the time in school. Sensibly, she drew on her original motivation for teaching as a spur, rooted largely in the pleasure and fulfilment she gained from working with children.

4   *Refocusing*: Once Kate had met the class teacher she was able to relate to her through the medium of her sister and positively realign her own expectations. The foreboding evaporated thanks to her effort to be polite, helpful, interested and enthusiastic about her work.

Sarah

For my final school experience I was placed in an inner city school in a deprived area, working with a Year 5 class taught by the deputy head teacher. On finding out my placement I experienced a range of emotions ranging across fear, disappointment and excitement.

◆ Fear about 'can I do this?'
◆ Fear of failure and the consequences that accompany failure
◆ Disappointment that my placement wasn't in a leafy suburban school with excellently behaved children (if there is such a thing)
◆ Excitement that this was going to be the final chance for me to prove my worth as a teacher.

Prior to this school experience I would have described myself as a confident teacher who was aware of my limitations. However, as I walked into the school on that first day I felt as if I was an inexperienced first year. I didn't feel confident. As soon as I walked into the classroom, however, I felt reassured. I could do this. I was determined to be a success and be enthusiastic, something I maintained throughout the practice.

Settling into school life and understanding the unspoken school rules was, perhaps, the most challenging aspect of the beginning of the practice. This was the first time I had been the only trainee teacher in the school. I realized how much I missed the friendly competition and reassuring advice from fellow travellers. Adjusting to school life wasn't helped by the fact that on the first day

I wasn't introduced to the staff or given a list of the staff names and their responsibilities. Sitting in the staff room was a lonely experience. I couldn't distinguish between teaching staff and learning support assistants. The staff room was a bustling hive of activity where everyone seemed to have a hundred and one things to do. There was the temptation to run back to my classroom and spend the rest of the lunch break in there. However, I reasoned that if I was going to spend the next three months in the school, I didn't want to spend every lunchtime in the classroom. So I took the plunge and introduced myself to all of the staff and sounded enthusiastic about the practice. This was definitely a turning point. I began to feel like one of the staff and one of the team. This experience helped me to identify that staff membership is a crucial part of school life, and how important it is to establish good working relationships with all of the staff, both the teaching and the non-teaching.

Issues for Sarah

The deprived nature of the local area

Many trainee teachers dream of an idyllic placement in a quiet, orderly school on the outskirts of a small town, with a cheerful, welcoming staff and enthusiastic, well-behaved children. Sarah was realistic enough to accept that such situations do not necessarily provide the challenges and demands that give trainees the best preparation for the time when they take their own classes. Some teachers elect to work in tough situations because of the camaraderie and sense of winning through against the odds. You may not have the placement of your dreams but if the children were impossible to teach, the school would have closed down before you got there. It is important not to make children's backgrounds an excuse for classroom management problems, though they may be a contributing factor. As we shall see in Part 3, children will be sensible if the work is appropriate and interesting, the boundaries for behaviour are clear, explanations are given about the nature of the work and teacher expectations are specified.

Discovering who was who on a large staff

The larger the staff, the more difficult to distinguish the personnel. It is not uncommon for trainees to discover after some weeks in the school that the person they thought was a supply teacher is, in fact, a parent, and the caretaker turns out to be the Chair of the Governing Body! If the school has a board containing pictures of the staff, it is worth taking a photograph of it during your preliminary visit and making sure that you are not only familiar with the names of people and their positions in the school but something about their different roles. It goes without saying that a positive and respectful attitude to everyone is a prerequisite for getting on well with adults in the school.

Balancing time spent in classroom and staff room

It is not easy to decide how much time it is appropriate to spend in the classroom and staff room. On the one hand you will want to ensure that you do not seem to be avoiding the opportunity to mingle with other teachers during breaks. On the other hand, you will want to ensure that you have prepared the classroom for the next lesson, tidied the room, checked resources, attended to displays, and so on. In terms of priorities, it is more important to be adequately prepared for the lessons than to socialize. However, it is worth examining the structure of your day from time to time to see if you can find more opportunities to interact with colleagues. Many decisions are made informally by teachers as they talk together during breaks. It pays to be present to hear what is said. Your continued absence may be interpreted as unprofessional conduct. Chapter 9 contains further advice about time management.

Taking the initiative

Although it is natural to expect the host staff to initiate conversations and make hospitable overtures towards visitors, rather than the other way around, Sarah found that there were ways in which she could be proactive and foster relationships. It took a lot of courage to introduce herself and chat to people she did not know, but the rewards were considerable, as it facilitated a more relaxed atmosphere and endeared her to the staff, who quickly accepted her as one of the team. More importantly, their responses encouraged Sarah and liberated her to do her best in the confident knowledge that she was accepted and affirmed by her colleagues.

Sarah's emotional management

1   *Self-awareness*: Sarah fell into the trap of imagining that working in leafy suburbia would provide for success, whereas the inner city school would be a nightmare. She might have taken a more positive view if she had realized that (a) tough challenges can bring out the best in teachers and (b) there is more to learn from difficult situations than tame ones.
2   *Evaluating first impressions*: Whereas Sarah was anxious that the placement would prove beyond her capability, she discovered, like so many other trainees, that meeting the children has an uplifting effect on attitudes.
3   *Relating to others*: Sarah grappled with ways to facilitate her rite of passage into the staff body. She rediscovered that schools function effectively on the basis of caring and consideration for one another as much as systems and procedures.

4   *Refocusing*: Once over the first difficult hurdle of engaging with other adults in the school, Sarah immediately felt more at ease. The initial effort and perseverance had been worthwhile.

Combating emotional insecurity

Some of the trainees in the case studies were confident people by nature and others were less secure about their ability to cope. They all spent time reflecting on their ability to prosper on the placement and several were affected by previous experiences in school. However, whereas negative thoughts and expectations beset some trainees, others were able to draw on their successes and use them to foster a spirit of determination. They were all aware of the importance of establishing fruitful working relationships. Some trainees felt it necessary to acquiesce and conform to the class teacher's present working pattern, others decided to address the situation directly and talk through the issues that were troubling them. The emotional upheaval that accompanied the initial adjustments resulted in a realignment of priorities and opinions that created an agenda for progress as the trainees eased into the new situation.

You may be assertive in manner or timid. You may have had encouraging school experiences in the past or disappointing ones. You may find it easy to make friends or not. You may be quick or slow to settle. Regardless of your experiences and temperament, however, the need to feel good about yourself and take a positive view of your ability must precede all else. The following principles will help you to do so.

Six ways to reinforce a positive view of yourself

1   *Don't think or say negative things about yourself or apologize for who you are.* Turn negative thoughts into positive ones and remind yourself that no-one is perfect.
2   *Don't be afraid to adjust your approach in the light of mistakes or assume that everything that goes wrong is your fault.* In fact, don't look to apportion blame at all; instead, look for solutions. Avoid saying damaging things like 'Trust me to mess things up again' and sink into despondency as a result.
3   *Don't spend all your time moping over what you cannot do or have not done.* Instead, be thankful for all that you have achieved and use it as a spur for taking positive action and advice about what you perceive to be areas for development. Anything that is worth achieving takes time and perseverance.
4   *Don't allow yourself to get physically exhausted.* Maintain a sensible life style, eat regularly and incorporate rest times into your schedule. A healthy body and mind often go together. Burning the midnight oil is a sign of poor time management rather than a high level of commitment. It has been said that a school's greatest resource is a fresh teacher. The maxim is equally true for trainees.

5   *Don't stop learning but retain an appropriate sense of humility about your progress.* Celebrate your previous accomplishments and view them as a platform for further advancement rather than an end point. All effective teachers are keen to learn. Humility comes through accepting yourself for who you are and not trying to meet other people's aspirations for you.

6   *Don't take your gifts and abilities for granted.* Acknowledge them, be thankful for them and determine that you will continue to refine and hone them. If you neglect them or assume them they will quickly fall into decay.

Six ways to promote a positive approach to others

Bolton (1979, p. 7) comments that 'eighty per cent of people who fail at work do so for one reason: they do not relate well to other people'. It is a paradox that if you want to improve your own self-confidence, you need to pay attention to the emotional needs of others. By adopting a positive approach towards colleagues, you will not only enhance your relationship with them but also discover that your outlook on life is brighter and more optimistic. The following six principles parallel those listed earlier under 'Six ways to combat emotional insecurity'. Thus:

1   *Don't say or think negative things about other people.* Be generous in your opinion of them and give them the benefit of the doubt.

2   *Don't look for things to blame people for or hold against them.* Concentrate on strategies to improve situations in the future.

3   *Don't resent people's weaknesses.* Affirm their strengths and support them when they are struggling.

4   *Don't burden people with your own concerns and fears to such an extent that they become physically and emotionally exhausted.* It is important to be open and honest about your worries but don't be like the trainee who used to wait in the car park each morning to pour out her woes to the mentor before she had even got out of her car!

5   *Don't keep knowledge to yourself.* Freely share your insights with others. Teachers are always grateful for fresh ideas, insights and expertise.

6   *Don't take people's gifts and abilities for granted.* Show and express your appreciation. Tell teachers that you admire what they do. Ask them how they do it and if they can help you to emulate their high standards.

Strategies to settle your fears at the start of a placement

Excited anticipation is healthy; darkening fears are not. If you allow anxiety to overwhelm you it will not only undermine your confidence but also erect a wall of doubt instead of laying a path of certainty. It is not merely a case of convincing yourself against your better judgement that things will work out, but making a decision that you will adopt a resolute approach to school placement and not allow your feelings to grieve you. The following strategies will assist you in settling your fears:

1   *Talk yourself into a positive frame of mind.* Do not allow pessimism to linger in your head; banish it as soon as it appears. Don't permit past failures to become a yardstick for future success.

2   *Make a list of your anxious thoughts.* For each thought, write an antidote alongside it. For instance:
    Anxious thought: I may not get on with the class teacher
    Antidote: I am a friendly person with a big smile and a listening ear. If I show a willingness to learn and co-operate, there is every reason to believe that the teacher and I will work well together.

3   *Avoid jumping to conclusions.* Schools are complex places and it is difficult to move from being an outsider to an insider. Persevere to find out about the inner workings of the school. After the first school visit, write down a list of all the opportunities that the placement offers.

4   *Seek a friend in the school.* This person may be a teacher but could equally well be an assistant or member of the support staff. You will quickly discover who is a potential ally by establishing good eye contact with adults in the school. Your ally will quickly reveal her/himself. If you find such a person, be careful not to overwhelm her/him with your troubles before you have established a trusting rapport.

5   *See yourself as someone with rights.* You have a right to be treated with respect and dignity and in the vast majority of schools this will be the case. Remind yourself that you are not at the mercy of circumstances. You may be a junior but you are still a contributor to the life and work of the school.

6   *Dwell on the contribution you can make.* Give yourself credit for having abilities and talents that will be of use to the school. Think of yourself as a novice teacher rather than a student.

7   *Accept that a bumpy rite of passage is normal.* Regard the settling in period as an interesting element of your school experience rather than a barrier to be overcome. See it as a preparation for when you start your first teaching post!

8   *View teaching as a vocation, not a life-sentence.* You have an identity outside school. You may be a parent or a sister or a musician or a neighbour or a friend. You can make people laugh, read books, write letters, show kindness, be passionate. Membership of the human race does not reside solely in your achievements as a teacher. Remember that!

In this chapter the significance of the emotions and how trainee teachers coped with their feelings have been exposed through using case study material. In Chapter 4 we examine a range of strategies and attitudes by which trainees can fit in to their school placement, create a good impression on the staff and settle quickly to the task in hand.

Further reading

Atkinson, T. and Claxton, G. (eds) (2000) *The Intuitive Practitioner*, Buckingham: Open University Press.

Gilroy, P. and Smith, M. (1993) 'Introduction to teacher education: rout or route?' *Journal of Education for Teaching*, 19, 4–5.

Prospering on school placement

Being a guest in school

Being a trainee teacher on school placement is the most exciting and useful element of your training but it can sometimes be the most frustrating, too. First, as you are in someone else's classroom, it is difficult to establish yourself as the teacher because the children understandably look to their regular teacher. Second, it takes time to discover the way that things work in a new situation. This can lead to moments of embarrassment, as you may be unable to answer children's queries, you are unfamiliar with the procedures and might unintentionally do or say something inappropriate. Third, the host teachers are busy people and may not have a lot of time to spend with you. Fourth, there is always an interval of settling and getting to know significant adults, during which time you have to make a special effort to be personable. Fifth, the host teachers may underestimate or overestimate your ability to cope with the class.

Being a guest means that there will be a certain protocol that has to be observed. Schools are distinctive in both obvious and subtle ways. Obvious ways include the structure of the timetable, the extent of specialist teaching, the design of the playground and the types of extra-curricular activities. Subtle ways include the nature of the relationship between teaching and support staff, the tone and content of staff room conversations, the social divisions within the staff and the emphasis on creativity or conformity in teaching. As a guest in the school, you will always have to tread a fine line between demonstrating your confidence and aptitude for teaching, and inadvertently coming across as supercilious or overbearing. Some trainees tend to err too much on the side of caution and may, therefore, give the impression that they are *too* tentative, thereby alarming the host teachers, who may be convinced that they have landed a poor student. One way and another, it pays to be sensitive about the impression that you create to the staff and parents, and avoid the following:

◆ Looking or sounding as if the world owes you a living
◆ Giving the impression that the school is there solely to service your needs as a trainee teacher

- ◆ Expecting to be given priority treatment
- ◆ Expressing doubt about your vocation
- ◆ Taking for granted the effort that the host teachers make on your behalf
- ◆ Making yourself 'invisible' by avoiding contact with staff.

There are also a number of practical, common sense issues to watch out for, such as:

- ◆ Dressing or acting in a slovenly way when you ought to be setting a good example
- ◆ Arriving late or leaving early without explanation
- ◆ Being static in the classroom when you should be lively and bright
- ◆ Taking care of your own needs at the expense of others
- ◆ Making inappropriate comments to colleagues about their professional or personal conduct.

Maynard (2001) underlines the point that as part of the process of fitting in to a situation, trainee teachers have to adopt the class teacher's practices and priorities, and that it takes time before a trainee is properly aware of the reasons underpinning the teacher's actions.

> It was through acting like a teacher, initially through becoming someone else, that students began to develop an identity as a teacher. In addition, student teachers appropriated their teachers' discourse, even though they did not appear to be aware of doing so, nor initially share the same conceptual understandings as their teachers. The use of this discourse enabled student teachers to gain acceptance into the community of practice, the approval of their class teacher, the means by which they could negotiate richer and more appropriate understandings.
>
> (Maynard 2001, p. 49)

Although trainees may initially imitate their host teachers' actions and words, they need to progress towards understanding why things are done and said, and formulate their own principles for action.

Creating the right impression

In your first few days it is not worth committing yourself to a lot of teaching responsibilities until you have begun to find your feet and your head stops spinning. Orientation to a new situation can be quite nerve-racking for some trainees, who feel daunted about being left in charge of a little known group of children for any length of time. Although you will need to be courageous and determined, it is sensible to gradually increase the range of your contributions to class life rather than be magnanimous and offer to do too much, too soon. Don't attempt to be a super-teacher in your first week on the job! The pace of school life is so rapid that you will have enough trouble just keeping up with the basic duties, let alone demonstrating your dazzling expertise to a mesmerized audience of children! Ideally, you should incorporate the pattern of teaching that you used successfully towards the end of your last teaching experience but also recognize that just as it took some weeks to induct the children into your methods then, so it will now. It may also be the case that you are teaching an entirely different age group from previously. Be patient. If you are very inexperienced, it will normally be sufficient to work alongside the class teacher in the first week or two, rather than taking any major responsibility for planning and teaching. All of this has to be negotiated with the teachers and mentor.

Teachers are realistic enough to recognize that trainee teachers have their fair share of trials and tribulations during a school placement. It pays to maintain an open and constructive relationship with the class teacher, whereby you can celebrate successes, share concerns, express uncertainty and generally engage with the issues that form the heart of the job. There is a big difference, however, between analysing your teaching to highlight areas for improvement with a teacher or tutor, and deconstructing aspects of a lesson into isolated fragments. Constructive talk examines issues, evaluates their relevance and advances solutions. Deconstructive talk examines issues, evaluates their relevance and admits to hopelessness about ever bringing about useful change. Mentors and teachers in school who work regularly with those in training often comment on what they consider to characterize the ideal trainee teacher. The following are a compilation of the expectations they have for trainees based on a study carried out by Hayes (1999a). Trainee teachers are expected to:

Adopt a forthright attitude

Make sure that you get stuck in from the very start. Do not hold back due to anxiety. Learn to occupy the classroom space by telling yourself that you have a right to be present and an important job to do. Don't find excuses for keeping your head down. Show a genuine interest in what the children are doing. Stay calm, poised and vigilant. Volunteer for jobs where appropriate, including the messy ones. Do not, however, give the impression to the children that you are another classroom assistant or parent helper. Let the teacher see that you mean business but don't get frantic.

Stay focused

Offer your help and expertise to the children. Make every effort to concentrate their attention on the work in hand. If they start to show off or behave in a silly fashion while you are attempting to help them, simply walk away and help another child. Do not allow the children to tease you or treat you like a favourite cousin. It is unwise to court popularity; although showing that you are a lovely person and one of them may result in temporary benefits, it will be a major disadvantage when you need to exert discipline.

Be concerned about the children

Show that you like the children by establishing eye contact and taking an interest in their activities, but avoid being sucked in to child-orientated conversations. When children approach to speak to you, smile invitingly. Offer your help willingly but watch that you don't end up doing the work for them. Some children are so keen to please the teacher that they will feign confusion about the work to get attention. Concern is not the same as wrapping in cotton wool! In fact, your ultimate aim is to encourage pupil independence, so the sooner you begin, the better.

Enjoy the work

Make it clear to the teacher that you are enjoying your time in school and appreciating the opportunities it presents. Accept that some school situations are more attractive and pleasant than others, and be determined to make the best of it. If you speak and act to show that you are keen to be in the school, staff will immediately adopt a more sympathetic attitude towards you. Despite the many challenges that trainee teachers face, teaching is still a fulfilling job. Remind yourself of this fact often.

Have a determined attitude to their own learning

Ask the teacher how you can improve your teaching. Don't be fobbed off by general comments to the effect that you are 'doing fine'. Ask for specific advice. Carefully monitor your professional progress, but don't be too hard on yourself. When you evaluate your lessons first write down five or six things that went well and then two or three areas for improvement.

Express appreciation

Thank the teacher regularly for her or his help and support, and show that you appreciate the effort that has gone into making you welcome and giving you opportunities to gain experience of teaching. Give the firm impression that you value and appreciate what the teacher does, but don't be patronizing. Whenever possible, volunteer for tasks that will help and encourage the teacher. For example, you might offer to mark some work, look after the class for five minutes while the teacher sorts herself out after being on playground duty or set up the computers.

Generally, if you are willing to learn, respond to advice and determine to be a positive influence in the school, you will create the right sort of impression and be well received by both the staff and the children.

Comment

Nias (1989) carried out a major study about the way that primary teachers approached their work and their experiences of doing the job. Amongst many other interesting findings from her extensive research, Nias documents the demands and rewards of the job:

> Primary teaching has a bottomless appetite for the investment of scarce personal resources, such as time, interest and energy. The more of these resources that individuals choose to commit to their work, the better for pupils, parents and fellow staff, and the more rewards the individual teacher is likely to reap in terms of appreciation, recognition, self-esteem and, perhaps, self-extension.
>
> (Nias 1989, p. 208)

Principles to prosper by

School placement is often exciting and enjoyable, sometimes unsettling and always challenging. There is so much to do and think about that you could be working every minute of the day and still have things left to complete, so having some strategies to guide your actions is well worthwhile. The following points will act as a checklist to help you to get the best from your time in school:

Be friendly but not chummy

Children want to like their teachers and be liked by them, but in your desire to be accepted by them, be careful not to compromise your adult status. The children do not expect or want the adults in their lives to act like big brothers and sisters. It is, however, important to learn children's names quickly. The effort to do so gives you a considerable advantage, as when you use a child's name it signals two things. First, children cannot hide behind their anonymity. Second, you are interested in the child as an individual and not merely as a number on a register. However, never allow a child to share an intimate secret with you. Make it clear that you cannot guarantee confidentiality but would like to help if possible, though with the help of the class teacher.

Be conscientious but don't drive yourself too hard

Many teachers claim that teaching is not a job but a vocation and their own motivation resides in a desire to work with children and help them to learn. These aspirations are commendable but need to be kept in perspective, as many issues that affect children's well-being and attitude to school lie outside your control. As a trainee you will, of course, want to demonstrate a thorough commitment to your chosen career and work hard to be the best teacher that it is possible to be. However, fatigue and ill-health are constant threats and there is little point in driving yourself to a point where teaching effectiveness suffers as a result. Enthusiasm is highly desirable for effective teaching but a gushing manner and artificial tone can be off-putting for children and irritating to the class teacher. It is better to look and sound interested in all that is happening and come across as an interesting person yourself.

Sound enthusiastic about the lessons

Unless you are enthusiastic about the lessons, it is difficult to inspire the children to feel that way. The use of a rich and varied tone, a sense of anticipation, a bright countenance and alert eyes, combine to give children the feeling that the lesson is going to be worthwhile. Incorporating moments of public celebration enlivens the proceedings and revives flagging spirits, but your enthusiasm should not detract from the serious purpose of learning.

Take time to pause and reflect

In addition to completing the many different tasks required of you, it is essential to spend time thinking about their implications, how they influence your development and the impact upon your educational philosophy. Trainee teachers who make thinking and reflecting an integral part of their school experience are more likely to make good progress than those who do not. You will be expected to keep a log of 'significant events' as part of your evaluation. In doing so you should ask yourself how the things that you have seen and learned assist you in being more effective in future. This process is best served by (a) describing the event, (b) identifying key points that stand out for you, (c) discussing the implications for teaching and/or being a staff member.

Take careful note of the strategies that teachers employ

Effective teachers have honed their skills over many years and you will not be able to emulate their achievements overnight. It is desirable, however, to take note of the strategies they use to maintain order, keep the class on task, help the children learn and operate routines and procedures. As you make these observations, consider the principle that underpins the action, as well as the action itself.

Be cordial with colleagues and parents

Reputations are hard won and easily lost. A hasty word or ill-considered remark can damage weeks of careful relation-building work. It pays to be cautious when speaking to parents, as a casual comment may be taken very seriously by them in a way that you never intended. Nevertheless, if you are pleasant and responsive in your dealings with other adults they will soon warm to you.

Think of yourself as an inexperienced teacher

The process of becoming a teacher has two distinctive, but inseparable, parts. One part involves being a student of your subject and gaining appropriate teaching skills. The other involves putting the knowledge that you have gained into practical use in the classroom. While it is true that you are a student of teaching, you are also a teacher of children every time you have contact with them. To be inexperienced is not a crime. However, to be inexperienced and make this condition a regular excuse for continuing lack of progress is irksome. Throughout the process, it is important to remind yourself that the person who has never made a mistake has never made anything!

Employ both talent and perseverance

Outstanding teachers are invariably the most modest about their achievements and realistic about their successes. Some trainee teachers seem to possess a natural ability for the job and appear to be comfortable in the classroom from day one. Most trainees have to battle their way through countless challenges and over numerous hurdles to achieve the same result. Talent can become a hindrance if success relies wholly on it. Those who consider themselves devoid of natural talent may be inclined to use this as an excuse for underperforming or avoiding challenges. Those who believe themselves to have a surfeit of talent may become demoralized when they are outperformed by those they initially considered less capable. The ideal situation occurs when talent is combined with determination and carefully designed and articulated learning targets.

Distinguish between advice and criticism

Teachers and mentors often recommend ways in which your teaching can be improved and strengthened. You may occasionally feel that the comments are unjustified or wrong; you may also feel incensed that your actions and motives are being misinterpreted or impugned. Such sentiments are understandable but not helpful. First, experienced teachers have a view of teaching and learning that you simply cannot possess. They notice things that you, buried in your teaching, are unlikely to be aware of in the same way, so comments that you perceive as criticism are invariably meant to be helpful. Second, protests about things being unfair rarely cut much ice with hard-working teachers. While it is perfectly right and proper to give an explanation to clarify misunderstandings, it is equally necessary to affirm the advice received and press on with renewed determination.

Take an interest in the child as a whole

When children arrive in school, they carry with them a wealth of previous experiences, interests and hobbies, friends and acquaintances, talents and aptitudes. The more that you know about children, the easier it becomes to interpret their behaviour, understand their motives and respond appropriately. Discovering about a child's interests and experiences outside school is worthwhile in its own right as it provides a basis for informal conversation and demonstrating to pupils that you are interested in more than academic results.

Allow children to share with you

In a busy classroom, it is difficult to give every child the opportunity to speak to you at length. A certain pace and purposefulness needs to be maintained during lessons, and break times are usually filled with minor preparation tasks, liaising with teachers and gaining a well earned breathing space. It is far from easy to find time for a gaggle of excited seven-year olds eager to tell you about the birthday party or bright-eyed eleven-year olds desperate to share their news about the school sports team. Nevertheless, wise teachers make certain that they leave some room for spontaneous conversations such as these that cement relationships and enrich the social climate.

Give children the benefit of the doubt

Most children behave well most of the time, respond to the teacher's directives and are eager to please adults. It is unusual for children to tell lies, attempt to deceive or wriggle out of responsibility. While you will not wish to be naive or overlook obvious transgressions, your work will become more pleasurable if you learn to trust children, take them at their word and develop a spirit of appreciation rather than condemnation. It is easy to jump to conclusions about a child's behaviour. It is more professional to ascertain the facts first and, wherever possible, make a considered judgement about their consequences. Of course, if children are found to be lying, it is vital to make them face up to the fact and not allow them to wriggle out of their responsibility in the matter. When caught out, some children will protest or cry or shout or walk away or offer a big-eyed 'sorry' in the hope of avoiding blame. It requires great presence of mind, coolness of thinking and firm insistence to move beyond this point and resolve the matter.

Keep a sense of humour

Humour must not be confused with comedy, jesting or tomfoolery. However, laughter eases tension and helps the body and mind to relax. Pleasant remarks and gentle witticisms in the classroom help to soften the atmosphere without detracting from the main purpose of the lesson, though younger children may not understand drollery and may even find it threatening or upsetting. Early in a school placement it is better to spend a few days weighing up the situation before injecting your particular brand of humour. Take account, too, of the class teacher's approach.

Accept that learning is an unpredictable process

Life for teachers would be straightforward if they merely had to plan lessons, teach the class, assess the extent of children's progress and move along in the certain hope that the intended learning goals had all been met. In practice, learning is a much less clinical process, involving sudden bursts of understanding, long periods of uncertainty, perseverance to consolidate knowledge, opportunities to implement ideas and time to ask questions, clarify details and explore implications. The complexity involved in the learning process inevitably means that there is going to be a mixture of encouragement and disappointment. Sometimes, the occasions when children seem least able to grasp what is happening or required of them are important processing times when their brains are organizing information and the establishment of long-term memory. The ability to recall facts and explain concepts are useful strategies for identifying areas of uncertainty in learning (see Chapter 6 for further details).

Value effort as much as achievement

Success is a difficult term to define. On the one hand there are obvious goals for every child, such as high standards in reading and writing. On the other hand, success can be measured with regard to the ability to co-operate, show leadership, promote innovative and creative ideas, accommodate the aspirations and whims of other people, encourage and help others, and so forth. Some children try hard but achieve little. Others seem to make minimum effort and achieve a lot. The bright, articulate and capable child may achieve more than the less able child but be capable of doing much better. Less able children may achieve less than the clever ones but have made more progress (relatively) than their academic classmates. Success lies as much in the heart as it does in scholastic effort.

Get children to talk about their work

One of the best ways to discern children's progress and understanding is to ask them to explain to you what they are doing. Children may be completing the tasks and activities with apparent ease, yet failing to learn a lot from doing so. This process requires that you are trusted by the child and are sufficiently clear about your expectations for the work. By asking the children to explain what they are doing, you not only gain insights into their grasp of the subject but allow them to reinforce their understanding. Children should be encouraged to set targets for their own learning and this is most effectively achieved through dialogue between teacher and child. To assess the quality of their own work with any exactness, the children must understand what constitutes satisfactory or good, and be encouraged to make honest comments about the standard that they have reached. Some under-confident children will respond by saying that they have underachieved because they are bored or confused. This gives you a vital opportunity to intervene, give fresh direction and encourage them to greater things. It goes without saying that children should be judged on the basis of their potential and the less able should not be unfairly compared with their more illustrious classmates.

Advise them specifically about areas of improvement

Teachers think a lot about standards of work and, particularly in an educational climate where formal academic achievement is highly prized, they are anxious about improved test results. Children, on the other hand, only become anxious about high scores if teachers and parents make them feel that way. When advising children about their work it is essential to point out areas of success before indicating weaknesses. Where aspects of the work need improvement, it is your job to give the children unambiguous direction and not merely tell them to do better. Avoid rewarding good work with yet more work of the same kind.

Be systematic but not rigid

Planning and preparation for the school day requires a systematic approach, with time and attention being paid to the nuts and bolts of the job. The development of good working habits pays dividends as they act as a scaffold within which innovation and creativity can flourish. A small number of trainees believe that they can live on their wits, putting in minimum effort on the basic preparation, and relying instead on their personality and ability to think on their feet. In fact, both the thorough preparation and spontaneity are important in teaching. If you are an inexperienced trainee or in a new situation, you will probably want to stick rigidly to your lesson plan and deviate only slightly from the text. As you grow in confidence, you will realize that it is possible to prepare in such detail that you become wholly dependent upon the script and suppress your teaching instincts as a result.

Get paperwork under control

Trainee teachers spend a lot of time on paperwork and sometimes question the wisdom of doing so. There are three main areas that absorb time and effort. The first, and most important, is in lesson planning (see Chapter 7). The second is in recording pupil progress (see Chapter 11). The third is in writing evaluative comments about your own performance and targets for improvement. The amount of detail and emphasis will depend upon the college's demands and the expectations of the tutor involved. It is important to recognize that paperwork is a means to an end and of little value in itself. You may spend hours recording, writing, evaluating and so forth, but unless it helps you and the children you teach, it is wasted time. Trainee teachers will always have to spend more time writing than the average class teacher because of the need for them to engage with the many key issues and refine the associated skills that qualified teachers already possess.

Establish and maintain wider professional contacts

Being a teacher involves a range of professional tasks and responsibilities that involve almost as much expenditure of energy as teaching a class of children. These include the duties such as break-time supervision and attending meetings, but also a range of less apparent ones, such as liaising with colleagues, sharing subject expertise and offering support to those around you who are feeling discouraged. It is common to think of trainee teachers as the people who need all the sympathy and support as they undertake their training, but serving teachers and assistants also benefit from a kindly and supportive word.

Get to know parents as soon as possible

As you settle down it is worth making a deliberate effort to associate with parents informally and interact with the children as they arrive and go home. It is important to bear in mind that unbeknown to you, many of the children will have mentioned to their parents that there is a new teacher in the classroom (you!). Parents will naturally be interested to know who the new teacher is and reassured when they see that you are an open, responsible and communicative individual, who clearly enjoys being with the children. A study by Harrop and Williams (1992) indicated that the reward that children prize above all others is to be commended by a teacher to their

Teaching principle

You are a teacher from the moment you enter the school.

Comment

Teaching, of course, is charged with emotion, positively and negatively. It is a passionate vocation. Good teachers are not just well oiled machines. Computers can never replace them. They are emotional, passionate beings who fill their work and their classes with pleasure, creativity, challenge and joy . . . Being passionate does not mean blindly loving all pupils; some are hard to love on given days. But passionate and caring teachers are more likely to set the right course, to stay with it when the going gets rough, and to avoid a permanent fog of fatigue, ritual, routine or resignation.

(Hargreaves and Fullan 1998, pp. 56–7)

---

parents. They also found that the punishment that most of them feared most was being reported to their parents. For the latter group, it is significant to note that some parents may have heard little other than bad news since their children began school. Others hold a poor opinion of their children's ability and potential. It is not uncommon to hear a mother (in particular) express the view that, as she was 'useless at maths', her daughter will be equally poor because it runs in the family. Your affirming comment to a parent about a child's progress, character and latent ability can help to transform attitudes and strengthen hope. Remind yourself that their children are the most important people in the world to parents.

Relating to host teachers

If there are problems on placement, they are most likely to be the result of misunderstandings between you and the mentor or class teacher. Campbell and Kane (1998, p. 93) make a salient point in this respect: 'The importance of hitting it off with one's mentor is crucial to a good experience and there is often a high correlation between doing well and getting on with the mentor.' Indeed, the possibility that they will not get along with the host teachers, especially the class teacher, is one of the prevailing fears for many trainees, one of whom wrote:

> Specific worries included how I would manage to build good relationships with the other staff in the school and whether my contributions as a staff member would be valued.

Another openly admitted:

It was not only the classroom responsibilities that gave rise to my anxieties but also other areas of school life; for example, life in the staff room. I was distinctly worried that I would find the staff room to be a 'closed shop' to me as I had before. It was, perhaps, this aspect that plagued my mind more than any other concern, as I understood the importance of forging good working relationships with other members of staff.

In one respect, these trainees were right to be concerned about their relationships with the host teacher, as this is certainly one of the most crucial factors influencing the extent of trainee teachers' success in school. On the other hand, it pays to remind yourself that host teachers are just as keen to enjoy a good working relationship as you are.

The adults and children who are in the school when you arrive consider it to be *their* school and are proud of where they work and study. When you enter a school, you are, to some extent, entering a social microcosm, with its own traditions, expectations and priorities. It will always take a while before you adjust to the school norms and feel at home. In the meantime you have to be patient and remain resolute. As Calderhead and Lambert (1992, p. 26) point out: 'newcomers have to adjust quickly to a new community, getting to know people, routines and facts, appreciating the ethos of the school and understanding protocol'. Many trainees find that they struggle to relate to children and teach effectively during the first few days of being in a new placement. It is only after acclimatizing to the unfamiliar school and classroom context that they are able to build securely on previous experiences.

Host teachers are usually very pleased to see you but they still have to put the welfare of the children first. This may mean that teachers are not always able to give you the time or attention that you would ideally like to receive or they would like to give. If other teachers in the school appear somewhat aloof on occasions, they are not being supercilious. They are simply too preoccupied with their own work to get involved or may not wish to be seen as interfering with another teacher's student.

The one quality that host teachers value above all else is when trainees show a willingness to contribute and be helpful. If the teacher is convinced that you are such a person (and some teachers take more convincing than others) it is up to you to do your utmost to repay their faith in you. If you go into school with a generous heart and a resolute spirit, you won't go far wrong. Try to think well of the staff and children. Show as much enthusiasm as you can muster but don't get physically drained. Staying up into the early hours to finish some preparation or marking is counterproductive if you are tired out the next day and cannot teach properly or become irritable with the children.

Responding to advice from teachers and tutors poses a number of issues for trainees, not least the extent to which they incorporate the suggestions into their teaching. In most situations the advice is appropriate and reasonable, in which case it should be followed as closely as possible (option 1). However, there are occasions when the advice, though useful, is inappropriate for you at that stage, in which case you may choose to delay implementing it (option 2). A third possibility is that you disagree with the advice and, after careful thought, you decide to adopt a different approach (option 3). Although from your perspective, the three options offer a menu from which to select your response, the teacher will assume that you will follow the advice unless you give powerful reasons for not doing so. Your failure to respond wholeheartedly will be perceived as negligence or arrogance and not as the exercising of your professional judgement as you intended. If you decide that option 2 or 3 would be more appropriate, it is essential that you talk at length to the teacher or tutor concerned about the reasons for your decision and secure their agreement and support. Figure 4.1 lists the attributes of an ideal trainee teacher.

The final area of willingness that host teachers like to see concerns trainees' attitude to their *extended professional role*. Trainee teachers are not only expected to teach their classes well but become involved in wider aspects of school life, such as:

◆ Helping to carry out supervisory duties (e.g. assisting in the playground)
◆ Tackling regular administrative duties (such as registration)
◆ Talking to colleagues in an open and respectful manner (particularly in the staff room)
◆ Availability for additional, unforeseen duties (such as assisting another class teacher where there is an urgent staff shortage).

An ideal trainee teacher is:

◆ Mature but not supercilious
◆ Confident but not cocky
◆ Assertive but not arrogant
◆ Thoughtful but not too idealistic
◆ Willing but not fawning
◆ Chatty but not verbose
◆ Interested but not intrusive
◆ Helpful but not interfering
◆ Well-prepared but not inflexible
◆ Sensitive but not soft
◆ Careful but not hesitant
◆ Cheerful but not frivolous
◆ Enthusiastic but not hyperactive

Figure 4.1 *Trainee teacher attributes*

Comment

School life is normally exciting and enjoyable. However, it is important to recognize that even the best school has its moments of crisis and tension. People get tired, misunderstandings occur and hasty words are exchanged. As a trainee teacher you may feel that such matters are beyond your control, but it is surprising how your calm and pleasant response can pour oil on troubled waters. Thody *et al.* (2000, p. 84) reminds us of the variations that all teachers experience:

> At bad times the teacher's job can seem to be a constant round of aggravation with awkward colleagues, demanding parents, detached senior management and pupils from hell. To deal with conflicts with these, we need to keep a sense of balance. Remember that our schools are also full of warmth, with friendly, helpful colleagues, co-operative pupils and supportive parents.

If you experience misunderstandings with a host teacher, console yourself with the thought that despite your very best efforts there is always more to learn and experience about interpersonal relationships. Hansen (2001) refers to the need for all teachers to develop a sense of 'moral sensibility', whereby 'thoughtful emotion' and 'sympathetic reason' are brought together (p. 32). Hansen stresses the need for teachers to be 'neither blind nor sentimental'. He argues that a moral sensibility 'includes a reflective capacity: the ability to stand back from the scene at certain moments in order to discern the issues at stake, to appreciate differences in point of view that may be involved, and more' (2001, pp. 32–3). The ability to stand back and reflect is not, however, to be confused with being aloof. It is, rather, a process for coming to terms with a situation by taking account of the opinions and feelings of others without becoming emotionally overwhelmed.

Teaching principle

Your arrival has an impact that is positive or negative, but never neutral.

Hindrances to progress

Despite careful, consistent planning, sensitivity to the class teacher's priorities and the potential to engage meaningfully with the children, there are four issues that may hinder your endeavour to make optimum progress as a teacher:

1   *Hesitancy.* As a guest in the classroom you may be reluctant to act decisively for fear of being seen as too bossy. However, the children may interpret your hesitancy as indecision and it will unsettle them or encourage them to be mischievous in the belief that they can get away with it. The class teacher or tutor may think that your hesitation signals a lack of preparation.
2   *Poor decisions.* As an inexperienced teacher you will not always know the best way to react to situations and will inevitably make mistakes. However, inappropriate decisions annoy the children concerned and can make them feel victimized if viewed as unfair. They also sap your own morale as you become increasingly desperate about your ability to make wise judgements.
3   *Tentativeness.* As someone who may still be grappling with subject knowledge and classroom management, it is unlikely that you will have the confidence to teach as imaginatively as will be the case when you are more experienced. This tentativeness can sometimes lead to rather drab lessons.
4   *Erroneous expectations.* When you first meet the class, you will not know the children or their capabilities. It takes time to discern whether children are unable to do work or unwilling to try, and to understand whether children are uncertain about what is expected of them or tentative for fear of making a mistake. This can result in making unreasonable expectations of the children, sometimes referred to as a 'lack of match' between task and child. As a consequence, some children struggle with work that is too difficult, others get bored with work that is too simple and lose motivation for learning.

During the early days of a school experience, your hesitancy, wrong decisions, tentativeness and unfamiliarity with children's capabilities may cause some children to get restless and for you to feel frustrated with yourself. You can make a more certain start to your teaching and improve your effectiveness by addressing the four issues above as follows:

Hesitancy

If in doubt about the appropriateness of a strategy, gain the class teacher's approval for it. For instance:

◆   Whether to move Andrew away from George when they continue to chat
◆   Whether to spell words for the lowest ability group if they get stuck

◆ Whether to ask the assistant to prepare the resources in advance of the lesson or do it yourself.

By establishing and maintaining good communication with the class teacher and assistants, it is much easier to raise such issues. If something is troubling you, it is better to ask advice than to stumble on uncertainly.

Poor decisions

Unfamiliarity with the classroom situation and anxiety about your ability as a teacher combine to create the conditions for making poor decisions. Bear in mind the following principles:

◆ *Do not* make a decision before the facts are clear. Instead, spend time clarifying the position.
◆ *Do not* jump to conclusions about a child's intent. Instead, check that you know what is going on first.
◆ *Do not* pretend to believe a child, when inwardly you do not. Instead, ask directly for the truth.
◆ *Do not* assume that children know your reasons for taking a decision. Instead, make a habit of telling them.

There are also a number of positive rules:

◆ *Do* keep an open mind about children's motives
◆ *Do* be firm and insistent when the facts are clear
◆ *Do* be consistent in your responses
◆ *Do* explain your decisions (but do *not* seek to justify them).

It has been estimated that teachers make hundreds of decisions every day of their working lives, so little wonder if you get some of them wrong. A little humility is useful here: if you make an obvious blunder, apologize briefly and move on smartly. There is no point in agonizing over your mistake.

Tentativeness

Many children seem to have the ability to smell fear in a teacher. There is something in the tone of voice, body language and action that immediately alerts them to the adult's prevailing insecurity. Combating the message that you are nervous and tentative about what you are doing requires a lot of determination and courage on your part. Thorough lesson preparation and mental rehearsal of key lesson points will help you to be positive in your approach and exude more confidence (regardless of how you feel). In the same way that actors on stage can disguise the fact that they have forgotten their lines by speaking out boldly, you must learn the art of coming across as a competent performer. Of course, the best time to practise your lines is before, not during, the session. You can also improve the confidence with which you teach by making certain that you have sufficient subject knowledge and by anticipating potential difficulties. It pays to write down some key questions that you can use to open up the issues relating to the topic and a list of key vocabulary that may require explanation. Assertiveness springs from self-confidence and well-refined people skills (Bolton 1979). Actively banish self-doubt from your mind.

Erroneous expectations

Find out as much as you can about the children's capabilities during your preliminary visits and in the early days of the placement. An hour spent after school looking at samples of the children's work will give strong clues about their ability, attention to detail and application to work. Of course, discussions with the class teacher will enlighten you, but it is still important to make your own evaluations of children's capability, as a child may respond to you in a way that is substantially different from the way he or she does with the class teacher. As a stranger to the situation, you may also spot things that the teacher hardly notices or fail to see what is blatantly obvious to her. The secret of improvement is to keep thinking about the issues and seeking advice about improvement. As you do so, accept that progress is often more of a marathon than a sprint!

Adopting a positive perspective

We have noted that a small number of trainees are so unnerved by the prospect of spending time in another teacher's class on school placement that they begin to doubt that they want to teach at all. It may be reassuring for you to know that even experienced teachers can suffer from a loss of confidence before the start of each new term. The belief that 'I cannot possibly cope' seems to be a common feeling that afflicts many practitioners, from novice to seasoned professional. The following extracts from three trainee teachers give a flavour of these concerns:

> The build-up to the final school experience was not without its problems, as even after three successful teaching practices I was still unsure as to whether I really wanted to become a teacher. To me this was an important issue as I had encountered a number of teachers who had a severe lack of motivation for the profession and I vowed never to continue teaching if this state of mind ever affected me.

> I started this week not knowing whether I have what it takes to be a teacher. I feel that if I can't make it in this school then I won't be able to make it anywhere.

I had always known that my final school experience would be the hardest and most tiring, yet I believed that I would be ready for the challenge when it arrived. However, as the time approached I started to doubt my ability and willingness to teach and, as such, my commitment to the teaching profession.

Despite the fact that all three of the above trainee teachers went on to make a success of their time in school, the extracts demonstrate that emotional anxiety can undermine confidence and create irrational tension. As we noted in Chapter 3, however, the good news is that your zeal for the job is quickly restored once you have begun the placement and adjusted to the fulfilling task of working with children again. If your confidence slips to a low level and you begin to entertain genuine and serious doubts about your sense of vocation, you need to discover whether your feelings are born of anxiety or reflect a more deeply held conviction that teaching is not for you. Three questions are particularly helpful in situations where you are struggling with this type of uncertainty:

1   *Did you feel this way before you heard about the school placement?* If not, it is likely that the prospect of facing time in school is clouding your judgement.
2   *Are your doubts due to an aversion to teaching or to being a trainee teacher in school?* This is a significant issue as many committed qualified teachers disliked being a trainee but felt differently about things once they were in charge of their own classes.
3   *Would you feel the same way if you were placed in a familiar (as opposed to a new) school setting?* Sometimes the prospect of being in a strange school can stir doubts and fears about teaching that would not otherwise be present. Once the unfamiliar becomes familiar, you can relax and enjoy your placement.

It is in everyone's best interest that you do well in your teaching and make a positive contribution to school life, and this is considerably enhanced if you feel confident and well supported in your efforts to become an effective teacher. You may need convincing that even though you have struggled on previous placements, this does not mean that you will have similar problems in your new school, providing you have learned from your mistakes and made a genuine effort to respond to advice. Although you should do everything you can to demonstrate that you are enthusiastic and committed, it is unhelpful for you to arrive in school feeling that you have to perform extraordinary feats to compensate for your previous shortcomings. On the other hand, a positive experience in school A does not mean that in school B you can pick up from where you left off and carry on without a care in the world. Occasionally, a trainee teacher fits in well with one situation and struggles to feel comfortable in the next. Every new situation requires time for you to find your feet, get to know the children and staff, and generally to adjust to the new circumstances. It is also worth remembering that the vast majority of student teachers enjoy a successful school

Teaching principle

Do not confuse confidence level, which varies with circumstances, and vocation, which does not.

placement. Despite the ups and downs, it is only a small number of trainees who drop out or fail to achieve the necessary standard. Make up your mind that you will not be one of them!

Measuring success

Success as a teacher on school placement can be measured across a range of skills, including the ability to plan and teach effectively, co-operate with other adults, evaluate children's progress and resource lessons. All teachers are conscious of the requirement to raise standards in literacy and mathematics in accordance with government targets. Parents partly assess teachers on the basis of their concern for children's welfare, openness and friendly personality. Children consider teachers to be successful when they teach interesting lessons in a relaxed but purposeful environment. There are no guarantees that your teaching experience will be a success but your effectiveness will be considerably enhanced as you listen carefully to advice from more experienced teachers and tutors and constantly reflect upon your classroom practice. It is worth remembering that success in teaching over the long period is dependent on three basic qualities:

◆ Knowing what you are doing
◆ Persevering to do it to the best of your ability
◆ Being determined to do it even better next time.

One of the stumbling blocks for trainees is a fear of failure in front of the children, as this can have a depressing effect and suppresses creativity. Although a little nervous tension is often needed to stimulate maximum effort and attention to task, constant unease does nothing to inspire effective teaching and can lead to depression. Maintaining an open dialogue with teachers and tutors is an important factor in airing issues and reducing anxiety, so it should be carefully nurtured. It is useful to list some of the challenges that you face while teaching in your school experience journal or diary. However, as well as listing the challenges, it is essential to consider the *strategies* that you will employ to address them. For instance, imagine that there were four key points of concern for you during a lesson:

1   Children became restless during the introduction
2   Two silly boys distracted one another when working as a pair
3   The more able group finished the activity sooner than expected
4   Children made a lot of noise leaving the room.

These sorts of concern are familiar to most novice practitioners. A second set of statements outlining strategies to improve each area might include:

1   Make the introduction more forceful and less protracted, and use a few visual stimuli to interest and raise more speculative questions.
2   Separate the two boys and place them in a part of the room where they have minimum chance of eye contact.
3   Include a related problem-solving element to follow the main activities so that the faster workers can get their teeth into something interesting.
4   Stand next to the door as children leave the room and supervise their exit more closely.

It is also important to refer in your journal entries to the *triumphs* of the lesson as well as the areas for further development. For instance:

◆ You made sure that learning aids were available during the lesson (successful resourcing)
◆ Children completed the tasks in the allotted time (successful management)
◆ Less able children showed a high level of interest in their work (successful differentiation/inclusion)
◆ The creative methods you used helped the children to improve their understanding (successful teaching method)
◆ The room was left tidy and in good order after the conclusion of the lesson (successful organization).

The examples given above act as a reminder that despite the tensions and struggles that are often experienced by trainee teachers, there are usually a number of encouraging aspects too. A lot of trainees refer simplistically to their lessons as 'good' or 'dreadful', as if the situation were clear cut. As indicated throughout this last chapter, however, all teaching tends to be a mixture of triumph and tribulation.

Teaching principle

'If at first you don't succeed, try, try, try again'
(William Hickson 1803–70).

Chapter 4 has explored how being sensitive to school norms and using carefully considered approaches will help you to make better use of your time on placement. In Chapter 5 trainee teachers describe in detail the issues they faced during school experience and the strategies they used to cope.

Further reading

Cole, M. (ed.) (2002) *Professional Values and Practice for Teachers and Student Teachers*, London: David Fulton. In particular, see the section about the school community.

Johnston, J., Chater, M. and Bell, D. (2002) *Teaching the Primary Curriculum*, Buckingham: Open University. See Chapter 1 of the book.

CHAPTER 5

Key issues during school placement

One of the challenges facing trainee teachers in a new placement is that they have little idea about the school's prevailing ethos and 'the way it is done here', so they have to expend time and effort in interpreting the situation. As you enter a new placement situation, there is always a period of adjustment and the need to accommodate new knowledge, both situational and non-situational. During this time, you are bound to make some mistakes, misjudge the significance of factors and fail to 'read the runes' on occasions. This is all part of the rite of passage referred to in earlier chapters, and can be emotionally demanding, particularly if you inadvertently misconstrue priorities or quite simply put your foot in it. Elliott (1993) argues that the attitude that teachers adopt to pupils' learning is partly based on their experience of non-situational factors as well as situational factors that relate to the immediate place and time. An example of a non-situational factor is a boy who experiences pressure from his parents to do as well in school as his older sister. An example of a situational factor is the child who behaves well for her regular teacher and misbehaves when there is a supply (substitute) teacher. It is essential to keep matters in proportion and acknowledge that the process of moving from outsider to insider relies on an initiation into the community of practice based on:

1 Explanations from staff about what is done and what is not done.
2 Your own observations and questions to discern what is acceptable.
3 Your ability to adjust your approach on the basis of children's responses.

The following passages from trainees' logbook entries expose the issues that were significant for them in school. As the trainees negotiated their school experiences and eventually brought them to a successful conclusion, they had confronted and weathered a variety of challenges and enjoyed many enriching experiences. It is interesting to note that although each trainee faced dilemmas and periods of uncertainty, the tantalizing fears that existed at the commencement of the experience were largely dispelled once the placement got properly underway.

As you read the accounts, try to place yourself in the shoes of the trainee and consider how you would have responded and whether there were alternative strategies that they might have employed. A summary and list of key points are given after each extract to provide you with issues to consider and discuss.

Cindy

During the first few days in school it was evident that the class of Year 1 children were quite a handful. Registration was interrupted by a lot of chatter and restless behaviour. I was not sure whether or not the teacher noticed what was going on or chose to ignore it, so I did not intervene. However, the poor behaviour continued throughout the day and the teacher kept raising her voice to be audible. Children shouted across the table to each other when they were doing group activities and the noise level was very high. I was asked to work with the shared reading group during literacy sessions but found that the volume of noise made it impossible to hear properly.

I was very concerned about the children's behaviour. The class had obviously been having the run of things for a considerable length of time and it was now the spring term. How on earth was I going to manage if more experienced teachers had difficulty controlling them? The class teacher was a bit embarrassed and apologetic about the standard of behaviour, explaining that the children had been the same since they were in reception and had never settled down. I went home feeling depressed and anxious about how I was going to handle the situation. I was sure that the class teacher was similarly worried. I couldn't help wondering why the least experienced teacher on the staff had been given the toughest class in the smallest classroom.

In my favour was the fact that I had come across a similar class on a previous teaching practice. On that occasion I had received some excellent support and gentle advice from my tutor, and managed to gather some effective strategies for dealing with the situation. I shared my concerns and ideas with the mentor and college tutor. The mentor advised me to be very firm and establish control as quickly as possible in order to continue to make good progress in my teaching. The college tutor's advice was that I should be careful not to use an approach that was too different from the class teacher's for fear of confusing the children. This contradictory advice left me in something of a dilemma, however I decided that the mentor was probably more familiar with the situation and I determined to adopt her suggestions.

The next time I met the class was when I read them a story. I decided to use the occasion as an opportunity to lay down the rules and my expectations of them. I explained how I wanted them to concentrate on what I was saying and to sit still. I warned them about my quiet voice and the need for them to listen carefully. I told them about my very good eyes that could see everything that was going on in the room. After making sure that they understood what I was saying, I continued with the story and was aware that a number of the children were watching me intently to see if I meant what I said. I finished the story without interruption. Even the children seemed surprised at how well they had behaved, though, to my disappointment, the class teacher made no comment.

Over the following few days I tactfully suggested to the class teacher my ideas for improving class behaviour, and with her approval and support initiated some changes. We identified three key areas that were causing significant disruption: noise levels, the transition between activities and the children's inability to stop and listen on request. Over the next few weeks, and not without frustration, effort, tears, joy, praise, anger, exhaustion, lots of talking and, most of all, patience, the children and I began to understand one another better. By week four, we reached a level of understanding by which a 'little glance' and the 'wait a moment' was usually, though by no means always, sufficient to nip the action in the bud. It was only after this point had been reached that I was able to focus more on learning objectives, assessment of children's progress and related issues. Classroom control and management remained a challenge, but much less so than hitherto.

The benefits of spending time establishing control and cementing a positive relationship with the children only became fully evident during the last couple of weeks in school. I was so thrilled when one little girl, who had previously been shy and reluctant to come to school, came up to me as she was leaving to go home and said that she had enjoyed the day and liked coming to school now.

The experience taught me that a more relaxed, generally quieter and purposeful atmosphere, in which there is both a desire for success and support for those children who struggle, contributes in a significant way to children having a more positive attitude to learning.

Summary

Cindy was faced with a restless class of children whose teacher was struggling to establish acceptable boundaries of behaviour. She made the decision to concentrate on building a stable learning environment, sometimes at the expense of teaching in the way that she would have ideally liked to do. Fortunately the class teacher adopted a realistic view of the situation and was thankful to have Cindy working alongside her. Although the school experience was challenging, it proved to be eminently worthwhile.

What Cindy learned

1   Some classes establish a bad reputation for themselves that they may not deserve.
2   Class teachers do not have all the answers and are continually learning, too.
3   The most effective learning takes place in a settled and orderly environment.

Emily

When you begin to get to know a class of children, there are always those who make themselves known because they are mischievous, those who stand out because of ability, and the remainder who are just quiet and pleasant. I made up my mind that I would try to get to know all of the Year 2 class, regardless of personality or aptitude. Nevertheless, despite my good intentions, the lower ability children proved to be a challenge, both in respect of their academic progress and maintaining their self-esteem. The lower ability children were generally less well motivated and more easily distracted. I found that I had to strike a balance between giving them straightforward tasks to raise their confidence, and more challenging ones to stretch their thinking.

The quality of learning was not, in my opinion, assisted by the physical arrangement of the classroom. Although there was a lot of space, resources were inaccessible and the board was inconveniently positioned. The computer facilities were good, but they were separated from the main classroom in an adjoining room. A computer suite was available for use, but it was too small to accommodate the whole class at one time, creating organizational complications. I hope that when I have my own classroom I will create a working environment that is clearly defined, versatile and accessible.

I discovered during my placement that the nature of school life is not quite as straightforward as the National Curriculum and educational theorists make it out to be. In fact, school life was very unpredictable and sometimes chaotic. Although routines were established, with timetables for teaching and break times, there were numerous unscheduled incidents that were beyond my control. For example, the photographer visited the school, children arrived late or left to go to the dentist, some children had to be sent home with head lice, vital pieces of clothing seemed to disappear into thin air! All these unexpected events and circumstances had to be managed and dealt with. I gradually realized that the class teacher's role includes a significant pastoral dimension, as well as planning and teaching lessons.

One of the best moments during my school experience took place about halfway through, when the class teacher asked me if I could take the class at short notice, adding that I could choose what I wanted to do with the children. Despite having only 'head knowledge' of the lesson, and no written plan, the session went really well and the children produced some excellent work. It made me aware of the fact that flexibility, spontaneity and the ability to think on your feet are important dimensions of effective teaching.

Summary

Emily's school placement was valuable for many reasons, not least because she recognized the complexity of the teacher's role and the importance of combining thorough planning *and* being alert to spontaneous opportunities. Emily was disappointed that the physical layout of the classroom did not facilitate effective learning and determined that she would take special care over organizing the room when she had charge of her own class.

What Emily learned

1   Classroom layout influences teaching approach and the quality of learning
2   Teachers have to be ready to respond to unpredictable events
3   Spontaneity is facilitated by thorough planning.

Nadia

As a trainee teacher, I attended the regular staff meetings, which were focusing on the school's development plans. I was invited to contribute to the discussion if I wished to do so. To begin with I felt a bit uncomfortable about this because as the student I did not want to say anything that might have offended the teachers there. On the other hand, I was aware that they had expectations about my role in their school, even though I was not going to be there very long. Eventually, I realized it was not the staff who viewed me as a student, only myself, so I made up my mind to be more confident and act as if I was a newly appointed teacher at the school. If I wanted to be seen by the host teachers as an insider, I needed to have the confidence to think and act like one.

Another element of the staff training in which I was involved related to the school's marking policy. The head and deputy had been on a course about marking as a part of assessment, and had brought back an exercise to do with the staff. There was a mixture of good and poor examples for us to examine and consider. We discussed the purpose of marking and what we considered to be good practice, reflecting upon the worth of our own approaches. We agreed that comments on a piece of work were for the child to get feedback and to set future targets for development. In the light of this decision, we decided that the written comment should reflect the learning objective for that lesson, as it was unfair to ask the children to concentrate on one thing and then to mark the work based on different criteria. In addition, they agreed that a tick on a page or a comment such as 'Well done' was insufficient because it would not tell the children what they had achieved or how they might improve. These decisions presented a problem to me because while I could see their point of view and agreed that it was desirable, I felt that it was going to be very time-consuming and a little unrealistic for a teacher to write a formative comment and target on every piece of work. Not only this but the younger children or those with limited reading skills would not benefit from the comments unless the teacher or assistant could find time to go through each item of work with them.

Nevertheless, I did my best to respond to the expectations, even though I did not find the process to be altogether satisfactory.

The other major issue for me during school experience concerned classroom management and developing strategies for dealing with one particular child, Ben, who found it difficult to work with some of the class rules. Ben did not seem able to sit still, he would always talk over others, call out, crawl under tables when he should have been with the rest of the class, and fiddle with items from his and other people's trays. He also regularly irritated other children by playing with their hair and clothes, and argued when asked to do something. I believe that most of his actions were for the purpose of seeking attention and gaining approval from the rest of the class. At times, I was aware that Ben's actions resulted, in part, from my own inexperience as a teacher. For instance, I sometimes kept the children too long on the carpet during literacy or, having insisted that he put his hand up like the other children if he wanted to speak, then allowed him to get away with calling out.

To cope with his behaviour, the class teacher said that I must follow the school's system of consequences very firmly with him, as with other children. The system involved the following steps:

- ◆ A child acting unsuitably is told to stop
- ◆ If the behaviour continues the child is separated from the group and sat on a chair
- ◆ If there is no improvement, the child is sent to be dealt with by a senior member of staff.

Although I knew that I had to follow these procedures because I had been told that I must do so, I had concerns about them. Most importantly, I was unhappy about sending Ben out of the room to be told off by another teacher because I knew that he would be brought back into the classroom to be told off and made to apologize in front of everyone and humiliated. I hoped to avoid this situation occurring because he was already viewed by the other children as being different, and this action would worsen the situation. However, I knew I had to do something decisive as he was preventing the other children from learning properly. I tried different approaches, such as ignoring his behaviour as best I could, pretending that I thought that he had a different motive from his real (mischievous) one and sharing the motive I made up with the class. In this way he would not receive the response he was hoping for. I also used sensible children as models, publicly commending their good behaviour and hoping that Ben would imitate them. I also used a firm voice with him, but did not shout, kept him in at break time if he failed to complete the work because of his silliness, and warned him about the possibility of being sent to another member of staff.

My experience with Ben showed me that although school behaviour policies are normally useful, there are occasions when I will need to persevere to find other solutions to difficult behaviour. I want to find out the reason for the behaviour and use strategies that I, as the teacher, feel comfortable with. As a trainee teacher I was, to a large extent, a prisoner of the existing system.

Summary

Nadia discovered that becoming an insider required that she conform to the collaborative staff decisions. In her account, it is interesting to note that when she feels happy about the decision she refers to 'we' but when she is unhappy about a decision she uses 'they'. Nadia was sufficiently perceptive to recognize that as a guest in the school she had to tread a careful path between conformity and autonomy. While she somewhat reluctantly followed the agreed marking policy, her unease about dealing with Ben led her to exploring other strategies without directly contravening the regular procedure.

What Nadia learned

1   If you think like an outsider, you will remain an outsider
2   Teachers sometimes have to conform to policies to which they may not be totally committed
3   The behaviour of one child can have a major influence on teaching and learning strategies.

Wong
During my first day I watched the class teacher's lessons and observed her manner with the children. I would like to say that our teaching styles were similar and that I fitted into her class with ease, but this was not the case. I noted the following characteristics:

◆ She was very calm at all times
◆ She never lost her temper when addressing issues to do with the children's behaviour
◆ The children seemed to treat her like a mother
◆ She taught from a three-page lesson plan.

Her overall approach differed significantly from my own and I was worried about how I would cope. Fortunately, she asked me early on if I had any problems and I admitted to her that I was concerned that I would not be able to teach like her. At first she could not grasp what I was saying, but I explained that I thought that our styles would be very different and that this might be confusing for the children. I was relieved when she responded positively by saying that she would welcome the differences and that the children would benefit from experiencing another approach. She also confided that she had been having trouble with some of the boys in the class, who did not seem to be able to make friends, and might benefit from having a young male teacher to relate to.

After we had finished the conversation, I knew that I could get on with the teacher. She was honest and had the children's best interests at heart. I also knew that we would be able to converse openly. I was made to feel confident about my own style of teaching, in the belief that the children would benefit from it and not suffer from it.

Summary

Wong was anxious that he would not fit in to the classroom ethos owing to the differences he perceived to exist between the class teacher's approach and his own. He courageously raised the issue at the first opportunity, rather than allowing it to fester, damage the relationship between himself and the teacher, and ultimately jeopardize the school experience.

What Wong learned

1   There is no single correct model of teaching
2   There is no single correct model of relating to children
3   It is essential to establish and maintain an open and courteous dialogue between class teacher and trainee.

Tracey
Despite the wide-ranging support for discussion as a tool for enriching learning, it was not widely encouraged by the class teacher. It was made clear to me that she did not approve of my efforts to use discussion as a learning tool and I was chided because I had not conformed to her way of working. For instance, during my lessons in week two, the teacher frequently told me that I spent too much time talking with the children and not enough time dealing with the noise level. Her reaction surprised me greatly, particularly as my lesson plan had identified collaboration as its principal objective and all the children were richly engaged in task-related discussion. The teacher seemed to ignore the distinction between productive noise and misbehaviour. She seemed unaware that the collaborative

tasks that I had planned were not only facilitating the completion of the task but had the potential to promote and extend learning.

Regardless of my concerns, I wanted to conform to the teacher's expectations of me with the intention of fitting in, so I altered my approach and modified my planning to eliminate collaborative learning. I became very sensitive to the occasions when the children talked to one another, as the teacher and I had a different definition of noisy that made it difficult for me to judge when the volume was reaching the limits of her tolerance. This uncertainty caused me further anxiety and an almost obsessive preoccupation with noise. I hate to admit that I even resorted to the ubiquitous 'sshh' technique. I felt that I was shifting from a child-centred philosophy because of the need to conform to the class teacher's wishes.

This uncharacteristic behaviour made me feel very frustrated, particularly as I was consciously denying the children opportunities to scaffold their learning through peer interaction. I was also telling the children to be quiet when I knew that they were talking about things relating to the task, which was something that I had previously been encouraging. As I think back it makes me shudder. Because of my concerns over the class teacher's opinions of me, I feel that I was squandering valuable learning experiences for the children. I felt great relief when I began to share my anxieties with other trainee teachers. They empathized with my desire to conform and one of them compared being a trainee teacher working in another teacher's classroom with wearing someone else's shoes: they just don't fit!

At the end of the placement my practice was deemed by the tutor to be very good. Comments in my final report indicated that I had built a good working relationship with the class teacher. Of course, I was not going to tell anyone the truth but inwardly I did not get much personal satisfaction from the experience. In terms of my development as a teacher I would deem it unsatisfactory. I will always be left to wonder what would have happened if I had been strong enough to justify and successfully demonstrate my educational principles. Notwithstanding this disappointing time in school, the knowledge that I shall have my own class next September gives me great strength. I will be the one responsible for governing what teaching strategies are most appropriate, valid and in the best interests of the children in my charge.

Summary

Tracey had clear views about the way in which children learned most effectively but was frustrated by the class teacher's contrasting philosophy. Maintaining a balance between conformity and innovative teaching proved to be a considerable challenge for her. Dialogue with the teacher did not resolve the problem and, sensibly, Tracey decided that self-preservation as a trainee teacher outweighed her ideology. Only when she had her own class would Tracey be able to reconcile her preferred theory with classroom practice.

What Tracey learned

1   Teachers are concerned with what works for them
2   Working in another teacher's classroom involves compromises
3   Satisfaction in teaching has its roots in professional autonomy.

Kate

I was surprised about being placed with an NQT and thought that it was a controversial situation to be in, as she should not have been expected to deal with the pressure of having a student, especially someone on their final placement. Also, an NQT does not have the experience to be able to advise and help a trainee teacher. I was worried that she would find me a nuisance and a burden during her first, important year in teaching. However, I found that there were benefits in being placed with a new teacher. She had been in my position just a year earlier and was knowledgeable about what I had to do and how to go about it. She was also sympathetic towards any problems or queries I had. Sometimes we would sit down and work these out together. Learning together in this way helped to cement our relationship and made me realize that I did not need to be worried about her thinking I was stupid, as she did not have all the answers either. It was only towards the end of my time in the school that she admitted that initially she had not been keen on having a student but had not been given a choice in the matter. She was relieved that things had worked out so well for both of us.

Apart from getting on with the class teacher, I wanted to develop solid relationships with other members of staff. They were most welcoming and, on my first day, I paid £10 to cover my tea and coffee consumption for the term. The atmosphere in the staff room was relaxed and informal, and conversations were generally open for anyone to join in with. Occasionally, a couple of teachers would whisper in the corner or go to another place to continue talking privately. There was a light air of cynicism about teaching threaded through the conversations, and sometimes gossip or tittle-tattle, but I thought it best to remain silent during these times. I wanted to learn how to get on well with everyone so that I could work as a member of the team and contribute my ideas. If the class teacher was unable to help me with a problem, I learnt the art of asking other teachers, rather than keeping it bottled up. This process of approaching staff other than the class teacher or mentor was a significant step for me as a professional, and came from a growing confidence in myself that I should have a voice in the school.

One of the main challenges for me was coping with the workload of planning, marking, evaluating, keeping records and writing reports. To cope with everything that had to be done, I developed the habit of keeping about two days ahead of myself, especially organizing resources for lessons. A large proportion of my resourcing required access to a photocopier, which frequently broke down and, in one case, took a week to be mended. After being caught out a few times, I learnt to do my photocopying in large chunks, rather than relying on it to work every morning before school began. I gradually weaned myself away from a reliance on photocopied materials and would, for instance, sometimes write out what I needed on a large sheet, using a bold felt pen. This made me feel more secure and in control of my own destiny!

Apart from resources for lessons, I had to keep up to date with paperwork, especially lesson plans and marking. I developed my own ways of dealing with the amount that I had to do. For instance, I found that it was better to do the marking little and often, rather than to spend ages in a single go. Wherever possible, I marked literacy straight after the lesson when the class was in assembly, as staff only had to attend it on Fridays. I marked the numeracy during lunchtimes and the afternoon work immediately after school. This system worked reasonably well and I did not end up with over ninety books to mark each evening, during which time I got up to date with records, evaluations of my own teaching and mounting displays.

The other main challenge for me as a teacher was keeping control over my class of eight and nine-year olds. I was worried that they would run riot as they could see that I was young and inexperienced. I therefore went in with a strict attitude, believing that this was the best way to cope. I used a range of strategies for gaining the children's attention, ranging from clapping my hands to shouting for them to be quiet. I soon found my voice going croaky and I began to feel quite stressed because the learning environment was not the positive one that I wanted it to be. I did not want my class to be disciplined through fear. After a few weeks I realized that I needed to rethink how I was coming across to the children and my expectations of them. I made a mental note to step back and assess the situation. To my surprise I found that much of the noise was productive and work-related, and only a small percentage was unnecessary. After I began to relax, the children seemed to be less nervous of me and I started to feel more comfortable as the teacher.

I faced many challenges during my time in school, ranging from coping with temporary accommodation, pressure of work, relationships with staff and how I controlled and communicated with the children. I look back at this time in school as a period of great learning and useful experience to reflect on and use as an inspiration when I have my own class.

Summary

Despite the initially unpromising prospect of working with a newly qualified teacher, Kate discovered that the situation offered some distinct advantages. Her willingness to persevere in developing effective relationships with all staff was worthwhile, both in the knowledge that she gained and her professional status. Kate constantly evaluated her progress and adjusted her practice accordingly. Unlike Tracey (see pp. 107–8), Kate was allowed by the class teacher to develop her own preferred strategies for the organization of learning, especially dealing with the sensitive issue of noise level.

What Kate learned

1   Even unpromising situations can be turned to advantage with perseverance
2   Time management is a central issue for teachers
3   Sustained use of stern control strategies can damage adult–pupil relationships.

Sarah
Success in teaching did not happen immediately or easily. The first week of the practice really felt like trial and error, as I was getting to grips with the school's planning and knowing the children, and which classroom strategies worked and which ones did not. After the first week, my confidence was at an all-time low because I didn't feel that I was progressing at all. After working with lower key stage 2 children in my previous school experiences, I found that working with this Year 5 class was so different from anything I had done before. The children's behaviour was very challenging, with a high number of them having special educational needs and behaviour problems.

The class teacher was extremely helpful and supportive. During the first fortnight he observed me frequently and focused on the positive rather than the negative points. He would say to me: 'Okay, so that didn't work, so what are you going to do next?' We discussed techniques and strategies, but he was keen to emphasize that I should not imitate him but develop my own approach. This issue was at the heart of the difficulty I was experiencing, as I was trying to use the same control and teaching methods that worked for him. In part, my actions were subconscious, as I wanted the children to have consistency. However, I soon realized that this was not going to work and that I was going to have to find my own strategies, which proved to be a challenge. At first I tried strategies that I had previously used with other classes, but most of these were unsuccessful. I needed to develop an approach that specifically suited these children. It took a lot of courage for me to discuss the problem with the class teacher. After all, I was just a trainee and he had been teaching for twenty years.

Fortunately, he was very understanding and supportive, and allowed me to develop my own teaching methods and groupings. This freedom led me to experience more success in my teaching and also to enjoy it, which I had not been doing before despite the fact that as deputy head the class teacher was often absent from the classroom for lengthy periods of time.

The ability to handle this difficult class did not happen overnight. For the first few weeks of the practice I really felt that I could not control them or influence their behaviour. It felt like a constant battle, with me the loser! The problems I encountered were principally due to a small group of children whose bad behaviour dominated the whole of the class. I found that as the practice progressed, my class control improved. First, the children were getting to know me, and I was getting to know them, and they knew what standards of behaviour I was expecting. I used opportunities to discuss with the children the importance of good behaviour and explain what it 'looked like'. The school already had a reward system in place using merit marks. However I was convinced that the children needed something extra, so I set up a system of behaviour cards, which set targets for the behaviour of individuals and groups, and gave a choice of rewards. The rewards included spending time on the computer during break time, spending time drawing instead of writing, sitting with a friend, and bringing a special item to school for a day to show to everyone in the class. This strategy was fairly successful, particularly with the naughty ones, as the children had a reason to stay on the straight and narrow. Looking back, the introduction of this reward system was a turning point. I cannot claim that the children's behaviour was impeccable for the rest of the time I was teaching them but at least it improved gradually.

The placement helped me to identify the main issues and priorities for a teacher. At the end of the placement, my dominant emotion was gratitude at not only having survived the time in school but prospered. By the end of my time at the school, they really felt like 'my' class, a point commented upon by the tutor. It was particularly nice when parents started to address notes to me and not to the regular teacher. The placement proved to be daunting and challenging but one in which I felt that I was successful as a 'nearly qualified teacher'. The experience of being in charge of the class showed me just how complex the job of the teacher is, and also confirmed for me that teaching was the right profession for me!

Summary

Sarah found that the contrast between her previous school experiences and this placement was stark. The situation was complicated by the absence of the class teacher and the heavy teaching responsibility that Sarah had to cope with from an early stage.

Sarah struggled for a time with discipline and began to wonder if she would survive, but by taking advice, being imaginative in her use of a reward system and employing a variety of teaching strategies, she made steady progress, grew in confidence and made it to the end. She was also more convinced than ever that teaching was the right career for her.

What Sarah learned

1   All teachers have to develop their own style of teaching
2   Establishing and maintaining discipline requires skill and determination
3   Teaching is demanding but immensely satisfying.

Reports on trainee teachers

At the end of a school experience, mentors and tutors summarize a trainee teacher's achievements in a final report. The following examples have been selected to show the characteristics of successful teaching that tend to be noted by staff in school and invite you to gain a clearer picture of the aspects of your work that teachers and tutors expect to see, and for which you should strive. The selection of trainee teachers are different from those who provided the extracts above.

Camilla (teaching nursery)
Camilla understood how important effective relationships are within a school and demonstrated a natural ability to liaise amicably with staff. She was keen to learn and to improve her skills. She was extremely easy to work with and always cheerful. Camilla adapted well to teaching nursery class children and demonstrated a consideration for their individual needs.

Key points
◆ Camilla was keen to learn and improve
◆ She was cheerful and personable.

Esther (teaching the foundation class)
Esther worked well with children in a variety of situations. She took the opportunity to visit and work in a key stage 1 class. She also took the chance to take responsibility for the registration group when the teacher was ill. This gave her the chance to manage the class and the ancillary staff. Esther was always well prepared. She spent time making her own resources and producing interactive starting points for children's activities. Esther is an adaptable, resilient young teacher, who has made a positive contribution to the group she has worked

with. She coped well with the challenges and variation of this large early childhood centre.

Key points
◆ Esther made the most of every opportunity
◆ She impressed the staff by her willingness and positive approach.

Saliah (teaching reception)
Saliah set a very good example to pupils through presentation, personal and professional conduct. She was committed to ensuring that every pupil was given the opportunity to achieve his/her potential and meet the high expectations set for them. Saliah proved to be a natural teacher of young children. All her lessons were supported by visual aids, pictures and books. The children responded enthusiastically to her teaching and progressed under her care. Saliah created a very colourful and attractive learning environment. She regularly changed or added to her displays. Saliah also established very good relationships with the parents of the children in her care. Parents respected her and felt confident in her teaching.

Key points
◆ Saliah used visual material effectively in her lessons
◆ She gained the trust and support of parents.

Jess (teaching reception and Year 1)
Jess is a warm and caring person who obviously enjoys working with children. Her confidence has grown and her expertise developed throughout her time in school. She is very willing to accept and act on advice, and eager to learn as much as possible. Jess has high expectations of herself and values children's opinions and efforts. She interacts well with adults and children alike and will become a valued and competent teacher.

Key points
◆ Jess's personal qualities shone through
◆ She demonstrated a positive attitude towards the children.

Rhonwen (teaching Years 1 and 2)
Rhonwen established professional relationships with all staff. She demonstrated commitment through attendance at staff meetings and whole school in-service training. She communicated effectively with parents and produced three highly effective classroom displays. Rhonwen will develop into an excellent teacher. She is prepared to listen and act on advice, and this has led to greater confidence in the classroom and in her own abilities. Her classroom management skills are

very good and, through concentrating on effective planning and challenging tasks, the class has produced work of some quality.

Key points
- ◆ Rhonwen was wholehearted in all her work
- ◆ She planned thoroughly and imaginatively.

Millie (teaching Year 3)

Millie has a very lively approach and the children responded to this well, finding work with her great fun. She developed a good relationship with the children. In her planning, Millie was very thoughtful and enthusiastic. She had good ideas and was able to adjust her planning, using her own ideas, the class teacher's feedback and the children's responses. When Millie slowed down a little and explained clearly and calmly, she had a good-humoured authority with the children, and they worked well as a result.

Key points
- ◆ Millie was dynamic and interacted well with the children
- ◆ She improved her delivery with practice.

Brenda (teaching Years 3 and 4)

Brenda has worked very successfully with a number of teachers and assistants throughout the school. Her ability to undertake tasks at short notice reflects her very positive and professional attitude. She has attended many staff meetings and in-service days, and liaised with parents in a friendly but professional manner. Brenda has made herself familiar with school policies and practices, and incorporated these into her teaching.

Key points
- ◆ Brenda had a school-wide influence
- ◆ She took time to read school documentation.

Leroy (teaching Year 4)

Leroy has taken on a lot of responsibility and become very much a part of school life. He worked with two class teachers and made changes to the teaching programme in consultation with them. Leroy has had contact with parents to discuss their children's learning difficulties, celebrated pupils' writing in a class assembly, carried out playground duties, created displays and taken extra-curricular hockey and gymnastics. He has shown himself to be highly professional and hard working.

Key points

◆ Leroy was involved in many aspects of school life
◆ He maintained a consistently high work rate.

Gurwal (teaching Years 5 and 6)

Gurwal developed good working relationships with teaching and associate staff. He demonstrated excellent professional commitment and had an excellent rapport with the children through high expectations of their behaviour. He was a great asset to us during our recent Ofsted inspection, showing a very professional attitude.

Key points

◆ Gurwal exuded professionalism in his work and attitude
◆ He was highly supportive during a critical period of time for the school.

Nelson (teaching Years 5 and 6)

Nelson has a calm manner within the classroom that provided a good role model for pupils. He established a purposeful working atmosphere, gained the respect of the pupils and consistently valued positive behaviour. Nelson monitored and intervened when teaching to maintain discipline and dealt with negative behaviour in a low-key, understated way. Nelson participated in extra-curricular activities with enthusiasm and was involved with swimming and cricket.

Key points

◆ Nelson was a good role model for the children
◆ He used his skills and knowledge outside the classroom

Sam (teaching Year 6)

Sam has been keen to benefit from the opportunities to observe lessons, both in his own class and assisting in other classes. He has always been willing to broaden his experiences by taking on new activities. He has worked very closely with the class teacher, who has fed back regularly on aspects of his teaching as well as providing guidance for further action.

Key points

◆ Sam benefited from observing other teachers at work
◆ He worked closely with the class teacher throughout the placement.

The extracts quoted above are, in the main, about positive aspects of the trainee teachers' time on school placement. It is important to remember, however, that none of them were attained during the first week! All the trainees had to persevere, make mistakes, address issues and agonize about seemingly intractable problems. All the trainees were commended for aspects of their work and attitude, but each report also contains suggestions about further improvements and parts of their teaching and staff membership that were less than ideal. For example:

◆ Jess took time to settle and adjust to the pace of school life. It wasn't until the second half of the placement that she began to blossom as a teacher.
◆ For a long time, Millie spoke too quickly due to her anxiety, and 'lost' some of the less able children when she was giving instructions. Even by the end of the school experience she occasionally lapsed into the habit.
◆ Nelson was almost overwhelmed at first by a very tough class but was determined to persevere with a calm, firm approach rather than succumb to the temptation to shout and become fierce. Eventually, he had them eating out of his hand.
◆ Sam worked closely with the class teacher because he was having difficulty with a group of poorly behaved children. It took several weeks before he learned to deal effectively with a number of hardened boys and gain their confidence and respect. Sam's strongly developed educational values gave him a sense of purpose and direction in his teaching.

It takes time to develop, refine and improve the many and various skills and attributes required for successful teaching. However, as the extracts show, a positive attitude, a determination to learn and progress, and a willingness to work wholeheartedly are considerable assets. These personal and professional attributes need to be reflected in high quality lesson presentation and teaching skills. Schools need people with your drive, commitment and enthusiasm. Teachers are happy to work alongside you and help you to achieve your goals. They ask only that you do your best to ensure that your priorities coincide with theirs.

Part 2 has dealt with the emotional and practical challenges and opportunities in school that are faced by trainee primary teachers. Part 3 addresses the knowledge and abilities that form the heart of your professional learning. Chapter 6 opens this section with a consideration of the ways that children learn and how this can be enhanced through insightful teaching.

Further reading

Acker, S. (1999) *The Realities of Teachers' Work*, London: Cassell.

O'Hara, M. (2001) *Meeting the Standards for Initial Teacher Training and Induction*, London: Continuum.

PART 3

Practice

Children learning

The teacher, Mr Singh, asks his Year 4 class if they have learned their multiplication tables. 'Yes', they chorus. The following day he gives them a test and only eight children get full marks. 'I thought you told me that you had learned your tables!' he grumbles. 'We had sir, but we forgot them.' In the room next door, Miss Clark is shaking her head with disbelief as her eleven-year olds struggle to subtract fractions despite a series of lessons and supporting activities in which they seemed to have grasped the concept. In reply to her expression of surprise about their problems, one of the bolder children comments: 'We sort of know how to do it but we don't quite know what it all means.' Out in the playground Mrs Richards admonishes a boy who had been saying some nasty things to another boy about his appearance. 'After all we have been doing in citizenship classes about caring for one another and being responsible people', she fumes, 'have you learned nothing?' The boy looks away and shrugs his shoulders.

Although we refer to children learning, the above examples illustrate that it is easier to say it than to understand it! Learning comes in all shapes and forms, sometimes involving the intellect, sometimes the emotions, and sometimes both. It is rarely smooth and continuous but invariably benefits from knowledgeable and capable teaching.

Learning that resides at the level of memory without understanding has limited value. For example, children might learn to sing a song in an unfamiliar tribal language, yet have little idea about its meaning or significance. The singing might be angelic, but devoid of interpretation it would have limited value beyond the pleasure of performance. Again, children might chant a religious creed, but if it seems purposeless or confusing to them it is unlikely to impinge upon their behaviour and thereby fail to achieve its primary purpose.

Learning can be functional, such as knowing how to cross the road safely. Learning can involve securing knowledge, such as memorizing historical dates. It can be experiential, such as the sights, scents and sounds of walking through a wood in the autumn. So when we ask the question 'Have they learned anything?' it is important to be clear about the range of possibilities that exist:

◆ Acquiring knowledge that informs action and clarifies understanding
◆ A process that transforms current understanding
◆ Using previous experiences to respond to, and make sense of, new ones
◆ Creating something new and familiar from something unfamiliar
◆ Refining skills to increase competence.

The position is further complicated when we consider the various *purposes* that learning serves. Thus:

◆ *Transient* learning does not have to be retained after the event; for example, remembering directions for a one-off visit
◆ *Superficial* learning is required for a period of time only but needs to be retrievable when needed; for example, following a recipe
◆ *Deep learning* is permanently engraved into the mind; for example, riding a bicycle
◆ *Transferable* learning is employed in a variety of contexts; for example, knowing how to use sentences correctly
◆ *Social* learning promotes empathy, sympathy and conviction; for example, working collaboratively.

Teaching is purposeless until you take careful account of its impact on children's learning and what you are hoping they will achieve. However, children may learn many unintended things too, so a lesson plan must make some allowance for the unexpected.

The complex nature of learning

Potter (2000, p. 63) muses that 'human learning is highly complex and, even as we enter the new millennium, far from fully understood. Indeed, it is probable that this entire book could be filled with what we don't know about learning.' The range of children's needs and aptitude for learning in an average class is considerable:

> All young people have different capacities, aptitudes and biographies. They have different pasts and different futures. One of the roles of education is to help them find their future and understand their pasts. This begins by helping them to discover their own strengths, passions and sensibilities. Young people spend most of their formative and impressionable years at school. Their needs are not only academic. They are social, spiritual and emotional. All young people need an education that helps them to find meaning and make sense of themselves and their lives.
>
> (DfEE/NACCCE 1999, p. 23)

Some children learn best when given the chance to use tactile senses, others through visual stimuli, others via careful listening, others by means of enquiry-based activities, others through conversation and yet others by paper and pencil exercises. Most children benefit from a variety of learning opportunities, facilitated by teacher explanation and reinforced through activities, the use of visual aids, collaboration and written work. Part of your job as teacher is to take note of the individual differences that children exhibit and respond appropriately. In practice this necessitates wise use of teaching strategies so that a range of methods allows all children to benefit from some time engaging with their preferred learning style.

Some forms of learning relate to the acquisition of practical skills (such as the correct use of equipment), necessitating careful guidance about their application. Some forms of learning relate to understanding procedures and require practice in following a sequence, as well as understanding why things happen (e.g. use of computer software). Some forms of learning relate to the ability to solve problems and require plenty of time for ideas to be explored and investigated (e.g. in design and technology). Most forms of learning relate to absorbing facts, understanding principles and putting them into operation in a practical context.

When children enter the classroom they bring with them a multitude of experiences, ideas, interests, dispositions and questions. Some children come with a hunger to learn whatever is on offer; others turn up because it is part of the daily routine. Most children want to please their teachers, but some of them arrive at school with a less compliant attitude. Every class contains such a mixture of types. Fisher (1996) argues that one way to foster learning in all of them is through being 'active'. Thus:

> Being active means that young children engage with experiences actively . . . bringing their existing knowledge and understanding to bear on what is currently under investigation. Being active is what causes children to both physically and cognitively construct their own view of the world, to personalize the experience and to apply it in ways which make sense to them as individuals.
>
> (Fisher 1996, p. 9)

Howe (1999, p. 23) makes the point that however clearly presented and interesting the lesson material may be 'no learning will take place unless the learner attends to it and engages in the *mental activities* being undertaken by the individual learner' (my emphasis). Howe underlines the seminal principle for effective learning that children make sense of things for themselves. Merely providing children with tasks to occupy the space of a lesson does not, in itself, ensure thorough learning. You have a crucial role to play in this process in helping children to evaluate the position and apply their knowledge and skills to a variety of situations and challenges (see Costello 2000; Wallace and Bentley 2002).

Social factors

By the time you arrive at the placement school, most of the children will have established a strong bond with the class teacher and assistants, and some of the children may initially resist your attempts to play a significant role in their learning. This reaction is quite common and you should not take it personally if it happens. It is also natural for trainee teachers to feel a surge of sympathy when they first encounter children who seem to be disadvantaged but it is wise to bide your time before jumping to conclusions. Every classroom has networks of relationships, dependencies and unspoken agreements, and these complexities take time for a newcomer to unravel and understand. The process of making sense of the classroom networks may require days or weeks of close association with the situation before your contribution to the learning process becomes fully functional. In the meantime, take your cues from the class teacher's actions and priorities, glean information from the assistants, and gradually demonstrate your capability by becoming closely involved with children and their activities.

Do not underestimate or overestimate the impact of your presence in the classroom. Until your arrival, the children had been used to following well-established procedures, conforming to expectations and working in ways that satisfied the class teacher. Now you have arrived and need to be accommodated and absorbed into the vagaries of classroom life. The children know nothing about you and, for the most part, will be curious to discover what they can about your status, personality and approach. The majority of children will not know much about why you are there, how significant you are, what your preferences are, and whether you might disturb their settled world. Some children will be pleased that you have come because it offers the prospect of new and exciting experiences. A small number will be pleased because they think (probably correctly) that they can get away with things more easily with you than with the regular teachers. One way and another, your presence has an effect on the classroom's social order and the children's learning.

Theories of learning

A theory is a way of explaining phenomena, accounting for circumstances or establishing rules and principles. To assist in the quest to understand better the process of teaching and learning, there are three well-attested theories that offer teachers insights into the process (see Pollard 1997): behaviourism, constructivism and social constructivism.

Behaviourist theory

This theory is posited on a belief that an external stimulus produces an inner reaction in individuals that is manifested in an outward response. The implications for teaching reside in the fact that the teacher normally exercises control over the nature and purpose of the stimuli, while pupils respond to them. For instance, the teacher's tone of voice and questioning elicit observable responses from the children, as witnessed by their facial expressions, comments, observations and so on. Behaviourist theory is reflected in teaching approaches where there is an emphasis on teacher instruction and close control over children's learning. Learners are in a relatively passive role, leaving the teacher to determine the content, pace and evaluation of the lesson. The teacher transmits information to pupils in an orderly way on the basis of a predetermined curriculum, using rituals, rewards and sanctions as deemed necessary. There is an emphasis on repetition, rehearsal, revision and regular practice until mastery is achieved.

A number of recent initiatives, such as the literacy hour, have been established, in part, on the principle that the direction of children's learning should be firmly determined by teachers and delivered in lessons of a given length and type, with specified learning objectives and assessment criteria. It is also recognized, however, that children need to have some ownership over their learning and should be encouraged to participate and offer their own ideas and suggestions. The importance of viewing children as individuals with specific learning needs and capabilities is increasingly acknowledged and has highlighted the need to differentiate work levels for children of differing abilities. This issue is especially relevant with the recent emphasis on developing an *inclusive* education in which all children have opportunity to reach their full potential (see Chapter 7).

Coaching children for the narrow range of learning outcomes included in their end of year tests that may or may not connect with their everyday experiences is a further example of how behaviourist theory has influenced education practice. This emphasis means, however, that there is a danger that children may lose opportunities to explore and enjoy wider educational opportunities, especially in arts subjects. Direct and interactive teaching methods are important but need to be used in conjunction with hands-on experiences, collaborative activities and enquiry-based investigations if learning is to be enriching and relevant.

Constructivist theory

This theory suggests that people learn when thought and experience interact, resulting in the sequential development of more complex understanding (cognitive structures). The most influential constructivist was Piaget, who argued that children accommodate their existing thinking into new experiences and gradually assimilate aspects of the new experience to construct a more detailed and accurate understanding. He suggested that the construction of these stages follows a distinctive sequence, characterized by the type of cognitive operations the child uses at each stage. The impact of constructivist theory in classrooms has been to emphasize the need for children to play, discover things for themselves and carry out practical investigations. This links to the notion of child-centred learning, the integrated day (where subject boundaries and individual lessons are more flexible) and stimulating classroom environments. Constructivism casts children in the role of *active participants* in learning, where they exercise some choice about the work they do and how they carry it out.

Sometimes constructivist theory has had the unfortunate effect of restricting the advancement of more able children because they were not considered ready to progress. In fact, although conceptual development is sequential, children move through the stages at different rates. All children should be encouraged to reach their full potential by being given opportunity to progress as far and fast as possible, providing their learning is deep and they know how to transfer it to new situations. Speed for speed's sake is counterproductive. It is also important to recognize that, whenever possible, children prosper when they are dealing with *meaningful* situations rather than contrived ones. For example, writing and sending letters to real people and receiving replies from them is preferable to letter-writing for its own sake, though the skills have to be taught before the letters are finalized and sent.

Constructivist theory is associated with a form of teaching in which the teacher takes on the role of facilitator, by meeting the children's resource needs, advising them about alternatives and directing them into new areas of learning. Critics point to its relatively unstructured approach, the level of responsibility entrusted to the children and the difficulty in monitoring curriculum coverage. One casualty of this widespread criticism has been a reduction in the amount that children have been allowed to play and learn through discovery. However, if children are given opportunity to construct their understanding through practical and experiential means it stimulates their curiosity, enhances their motivation and can lead to innovative thinking. Time spent on self-directed problem-solving can, therefore, foster 'a creative approach and creative activities which involve practical and first-hand experiences' (Beetlestone 1998, p. 13).

Dean (1992) also quotes Harlen (1985) in suggesting that the learning needs of different age phases are characterized in specific ways. Younger children tend to learn through concrete experiences, be less aware of other people's perspectives and the consequences of actions, and more egotistic. Older children tend to be more flexible, accommodating of other people's opinions, sensitive to the way things relate to one another and able to extract principles. A modified form of Dean's abbreviated version of Harlen's statements follows (Dean 1992, pp. 17–18):

5–7 year olds . . .
◆ They cannot think through actions but have to carry them out in practice
◆ They can only see things from their own point of view

- They focus on only one aspect of an object or situation at a time
- They tend not to relate one event to another when they encounter an unfamiliar sequence of events
- They are not able to anticipate the results of actions not yet carried out.

7–9 year olds . . .

- They begin to see a simple process as a whole, relating the individual parts to each other so that a process of change can be grasped and events put in sequence
- They can think through a simple process in reverse
- They may realize that two effects have to be taken into account in deciding the result of an action
- There is some progress towards being able to see things from someone else's point of view
- They can relate a physical cause to its effect.

9–11 year olds . . .

- They can handle problems with more than one variable
- They can use a wider range of logical relations and so mentally manipulate more things
- They show fewer tendencies to jump to conclusions and a greater appreciation that ideas should be checked against evidence
- They can use measurement and recording as part of a more systematic and accurate approach to problems
- They can go through the possible steps in an investigation and produce a reasonable plan of action.

Of course, the above model is, in common with all models, an idealized view of a complex situation. In practice, there are always exceptions to the broad principles outlined, but the overview provides a helpful starting point when you are planning for learning. It is worth noting that Dean also adds a timely warning that 'such skills will be present only if there has been good teaching at each stage' (Dean 1992, p. 18). The teacher's role is therefore crucial in helping children to achieve their potential in learning.

Social constructivist theory

Vygotsky and Bruner are the people most often associated with propounding this theory, which suggests that the social context and interaction with other children are important factors in learning. Bruner was concerned with how we make sense of the world and the ways in which meaning is ascribed to thought and language. Vygotsky was also intrigued by the way that learning is influenced by language. Social constructivism has two practical implications for teaching:

Comment

McCallum *et al.* (2000) interviewed children to find out their views about teaching and learning. Among their many findings, they discovered that there were marked differences between the perceived needs of younger and older primary children. Thus:

> The Year 2 children did not talk about classroom ethos in the way that the Year 6 children did. The Year 2 children emphasized that for learning, they needed constant access to help, preferably through one-to-one interaction with the teacher, which sometimes meant the teacher simply giving them an answer. This implied that when the teacher was teaching from the front of the class, it was harder for them to learn.
>
> (McCallum *et al.*, p. 281)

---

1   If a more knowledgeable person working alongside children offers appropriate support, they will make more rapid progress than would otherwise be the case.
2   Children learn better in social groups than they would if working alone.

The hiatus between a child's present and potential level of understanding is sometimes referred to by the odd-sounding phrase Zone of Proximal Development (ZPD). The active intervention and support of others is likened to a scaffold placed around a house as it is constructed; consequently, the help and guidance offered to children as they try to narrow the ZPD is therefore referred to as *scaffolding*. Once children have grasped the concept or gained the necessary understanding and are in a position to progress independently, the scaffolding of teacher or peer support can be reduced.

The use of scaffolding has many implications for teaching. For instance, teachers need to be aware of a child's *present* and *potential* understanding to identify the extent of the shortfall in knowledge. There is little point in trying to establish more advanced learning targets for children without having a reasonably precise grasp of what they currently know and what they are capable of achieving. This level of insight is far from easily acquired. However, by drawing alongside children, talking to them and allowing them to respond, offering feedback, advice and explanation, and discussing the next step in the learning process, it is possible to discern the extent of the shortfall and decide the best course of action. It is also important to remember that scaffolding strategies such as advising about options, demonstrating skills, pairing less and more able children and promoting group discussion require careful monitoring and employment if they are to be effective. You should always be on the lookout for children who are underachieving and offer a modest amount of support initially, gradually increasing the level if it becomes clear that a breakthrough in learning is not being achieved.

Pupils should be given a chance to share ideas, engage in a critical dialogue and talk about the work with one another, as opportunities for discussion cause children to examine their thinking and to develop a better informed view of events. Teachers need to use their experience to influence and shape the direction of children's learning by allowing them space and opportunity to ponder, evaluate, express opinions and ask questions. Teachers can channel children's enthusiasm for speaking into creating opportunities for exchanging ideas informally, debates, problem-solving activities and other united ventures, but must be ready to teach the skills and strategies needed if such interactions are to be of maximum benefit – for example, stressing the importance of turn-taking during discussions and establishing a simple rule framework to enforce it.

Comment

Selley (1999) emphasizes that learning rarely takes place unaided and requires an appropriate context and guidance from a well-informed adult to help children make optimum progress. Thus:

> If pupils are to develop generic intellectual skills . . . they must be given the opportunity to do so in contexts which they already understand well. We must beware of the discovery learning fallacy that a pupil can, unaided, discover or appraise new ideas at a higher level of cognitive demand.
>
> (Selley 1999, p. 35)

Theories inform classroom practice and vice versa. Your beliefs about education also influence the way that you view learning and your role as a teacher. If you are convinced that school is purely for academic purposes, then you will only see other dimensions of the role as peripheral to the main part of the job. If, on the other hand, you see school as a nurturing environment, where children should be helped to grow and develop as well adjusted people in society, your teaching, relationships with children and the way you allocate your time will reflect this principle. Hutchinson (1994, p. 311) argues that although reflecting upon your teaching is important to avoid a purely mechanistic approach to assessing its effectiveness, it needs to involve the 'flexible definition and redefinition of the complex situations in which class teachers work'.

One of the fundamental challenges for you as a trainee is to re-evaluate your educational beliefs in the light of classroom experience. As we saw in previous chapters, trainee teachers have to take account of the class teacher's priorities and make some adjustment to their approach accordingly, despite any reservations they may hold. For instance, you may believe that young children should be given time and opportunity to play, agreeing with Griffiths (1998) who, in common with many other writers, argues that exploring themes through play is an essential part of learning. Thus:

> Such play is crucial to the child, as it provides many of the experiences and interaction necessary for the child's healthy, intellectual, physical, emotional and social development. It allows the child freedom to explore and make sense of his or her ever-changing world, to solve problems, to set new challenges and to follow his or her natural curiosity.
>
> (Griffiths 1998, p. 3)

However, if the teacher adopts a more teacher-led approach and does not favour informal play, you may have to compromise your views by (say) negotiating to introduce *structured* play instead of the free play that you would ideally prefer. Again, the class teacher may overlook the quality of work that a troublesome Year 6 child in the class achieves in his work, providing he keeps out of mischief, while you want to spend more time on a one-to-one basis with him. In all such cases, you will need to negotiate with the teacher about ways forward without giving the impression that you are criticizing present practice. It may be that in discussion with the teacher you discover that they have already tried the approach that you favour and found that it had little influence on the child's learning.

Teaching principle

Theories have to be interpreted with regard to the classroom situation.

Influences on learning

Every teacher must take account of three fundamental factors that have a direct bearing on children's learning: context, attitude and teaching approach.

Context

Learning experiences are influenced by the physical and social context. For instance, it would be difficult to learn to play the violin in a games hall or share intimate feelings with total strangers! Learning is also hindered when there is a prevailing mood of antagonism or a sense of despair. The quality of the interaction between a child and an adult, and between a child and a child, has a significant effect on learning. If you promote or allow an intolerant or intimidating atmosphere, where mistakes are lampooned and unusual suggestions dismissed unthinkingly, then learning suffers as a result. While anxiety can hinder learning, enthusiasm produces a surge of energy due to the fact that more oxygen is pumped around the body and chemicals are released in the brain, stimulating its operation as a result. Teachers can help to make learning pleasurable by promoting a 'can do' mentality and ensure that the children enjoy the work and find it satisfying. It goes without saying that while there needs to be a sense of urgency about completing work, it should be done in such a way that it avoids unduly raising tension, thereby inhibiting children's ability to think clearly. If teachers sponsor a supportive climate where mistakes are seen as a normal part of life and mutual support is promoted, then learning will happen more spontaneously.

Attitude

Teachers' attitudes affect learning because they are transmitted to the children and influence the classroom climate. Pupils' attitudes towards themselves are also significant. Some children are very positive about learning and will always try hard despite their academic limitations. Other children are negative about their prospects despite having the advantage of natural ability. It is not difficult to see that the child with a positive outlook will make optimum progress, whereas the child with low self-esteem will probably underachieve. A lot of children have a strong achievement orientation; that is, they think solely in terms of what they have to accomplish and are too busy getting to the end to enjoy the journey. Such children may be characterized as follows (see Fisher 1995):

- ◆ They only feel satisfied if they succeed completely
- ◆ They make excuses if they perceive that they might not achieve all that they intended
- ◆ They see their ability to learn as fixed, rather than dynamic and capable of developing
- ◆ They see the difficulties rather than the possibilities
- ◆ They become upset by failure or partial achievement
- ◆ They give up rather than face the prospect of losing.

The best teachers encourage children to adopt a positive attitude to learning so that they are:

◆ Determined to make an effort to succeed even if failure is likely
◆ Curious about problems and eager to discover solutions
◆ Able to get failure in perspective and use it to inform progress
◆ Persistent and determined
◆ Willing to seek help and advice from others in pursuit of success
◆ Unwilling to allow their natural limitations to deter them from making progress.

Children with a positive attitude may not possess as much talent as their more illustrious peers, but they compensate by their energy and commitment to the task. They do not allow their weaknesses to become an excuse for not making an effort. They relish achievements but also find pleasure through engaging with the task.

Teaching approach

Effective teachers allow children the space to think, reflect and develop their ideas. They give them opportunity to express doubts, uncertainties and reservations. Through skilful questioning they help children explore issues and make sense of them at their own conceptual level. By offering constructive feedback, such teachers provide a secure basis for children to extend and enhance their learning. They promote a 'one for all and all for one' ethos where mistakes are used constructively, children support one another and a strong sense of purpose is dominant. Good teachers make sure that they share with the children the lesson's intentions and encourage them to feel a sense of ownership in the educational endeavour. One way and another, teachers who succeed in making children spend time thinking about the work they do rather than merely getting them to comply with the requirements are more likely to produce a vibrant learning environment (Gipps *et al.* 2000).

Teaching principle

Children learn because they want to learn.

Framework for action

On the assumption that your main task as a teacher is to help children learn effectively and enjoy the adventure of finding out new things, gain fresh understanding and master new skills, Dean (1992, pp. 59–60) provides a useful framework for action. The following section reflects her analysis.

Learning is related to motivation

This statement prompts us to consider what forms of motivation should be employed in teaching. Interesting and challenging work is obviously preferable to the monotonous variety, but developing a classroom climate that promotes a thirst for learning does not happen by chance. Positive motivation stresses the personal rewards to be gained from the enterprise; negative motivation stresses the consequences of failing to respond. The best teachers emphasize the positive. Littledyke (1998, p. 17) suggests that constructive teaching should anticipate learning that is 'meaningful, lasting and transferable to other contexts' and take account of children's experiences and views. However, he is at pains to point out that the teacher's role is to facilitate learning of identified curricular objectives and not to allow a free-for-all in which children discover things without guidance or direction. Consequently, motivation cannot be relied upon solely to achieve the stated goals, though other outcomes may unexpectedly be achieved if children are given freedom to follow their instincts (see also Gilbert 2002).

Children are motivated by problems that stretch them but lie within their capability

The requirement for teachers is to gauge the appropriate level of challenge for every child that will stimulate their interest but not overwhelm them. As a newcomer to the classroom, a trainee teacher cannot be expected to match questions and tasks perfectly to the children's ability straight away. However, the sooner this can be achieved, the quicker the children will settle and make progress. There will always be some children who, owing to anxiety or low self-esteem, will be tentative about their work and a few who will have the confidence to try anything. The teacher's task is to help them through their uncertainties by providing ongoing support and encouragement to persevere. Your affirming comments, careful directing and willingness to understand their problems will provide children with a positive spur to learning.

Reward and praise are more effective than blame and punishment

Although this is an excellent principle, there are occasions when praise has not been earned and should not, therefore, be offered too freely. On the other hand, teachers must not fall prey to the temptation of blaming children and using extreme sanctions for minor misdemeanours, rather than addressing the underlying issues and creating a more affirming learning environment. Gootman (1997) warns teachers against offering too many tangible rewards because they 'end up robbing children of the desire to do something because they know inside that it is the right thing to do' (1997, p. 56). Even the use of innocent rewards needs to be evaluated, such as listing on the board the names of children who have worked hard or giving a sticker to those who have been especially good without acknowledging other children who have tried. If not handled sensitively, these well intended rewards can lead to divisiveness, especially between 'average' children who always try hard and are invariably good but hardly get noticed by the teacher, and those who are normally indolent but happen to work hard on one particular occasion. The most effective rewards are ones that benefit the whole class. For example, a teacher might tell the class that because they have cleared up so carefully, everyone can have an extra five minutes playtime. However, even this approach has its pitfalls, as after a time the children may expect the reward as a right, rather than as a privilege to be earned. Providing they respect you, your encouragement and applause for their efforts will enhance children's self-belief and confidence, and be reward enough.

Children need time to talk about a piece of learning

The challenge is to provide opportunities for constructive talking to take place, either directed by the teacher or independent of the teacher, involving small groups of children working towards a common purpose. However, the teacher needs to ensure that the children have the necessary skills and experience to talk with intent, as children will happily chatter if left unsupervised and lacking guidance about the intended outcome of the collaborative venture. Even in ideal circumstances, teachers have to accept that not all of the talk will be positively directed. Just as adults stray from the subject, some parts of the children's talk will be inappropriate, but the main thrust of their discussion should focus on the designated task or issue. It requires fine judgement by the teacher to know how much off-task conversation to permit. This is made more difficult by the fact that the children usually cease such diversionary talk when the teacher approaches. However, don't be too hard on the children if they sometimes err. They are children, after all!

Language means only as much as the experience it represents

The connection between experience, language and understanding is not fully comprehended. However, it is clear that children need the opportunity to be immersed in a rich variety of activities if they are to grasp principles and be able to employ them in different circumstances. All children benefit from knowing what it feels like to touch, handle, play with, manipulate, organize and puzzle over ideas. Language flows from these first-hand experiences as children grapple to explore themes, explain processes and express uncertainties. The more children have a concrete reference point that is rooted in familiar situations, the more they will be able to talk meaningfully. In practice, this means that teachers should start any explanation by referring to something that the children know and understand or have experienced. Teachers also have to be careful that they use vocabulary with which children are familiar and not use unfamiliar expressions without explanation. Children, too, can contribute their own forms of spoken language, metaphor and figurative language, which though not strictly accurate, facilitates discussion and explanation and should therefore be encouraged. One way and another, it should be your goal to make the classroom a rich tapestry of constructive talk and careful listening.

Out of school influences on learning

The importance of home–school links to promote effective learning has become increasingly recognized (e.g. Wolfendale and Bastiani 2000). Children come to school with a wealth of knowledge, language and understanding that has, in the main, been gained from their parents. The teacher's task is to provide a structured learning environment within which children can increase their grasp of these areas, investigate the unknown and reorganize their thinking as a result. The increase in parental rights, closer ties between the school and community, and emphasis on extending learning beyond the school gate, mean that parents have assumed an increasingly significant place in their children's education. If you are an inexperienced trainee teacher it is unlikely that you will to be expected to attend to parents directly other than at the level of being polite and helpful, though parents of very young children often have more immediate dealings with the adults in the classroom. In all circumstances, but especially when you are new to the classroom, bide your time and don't jump to conclusions about the quality of parenting or the appropriateness of their attitudes. Bryans (1989, p. 36) comments that for some parents, their contact with school is 'based around a series of negative events when their child has behaved badly or shown signs of a learning difficulty'. He goes on to say that in such circumstances 'it is hardly surprising that so many parents lose contact with the school or see head teachers in particular as social workers or therapists' (1989, p. 36). You may discover that you are also viewed in this way.

Alexander (1997) warns that merely being with children constantly over a long period of time does not necessarily generate a deep understanding of them. For instance, his research indicated that teachers found it difficult to provide a suitable curriculum for children who were socially and materially disadvantaged. Alexander also found that some capable children from less wealthy backgrounds were under-achieving because teachers believed that gifted children must be from materially secure homes. He concluded that 'the full range of human potential is, of course, to be found in every social context' (Alexander 1997, p. 21). Although teachers must not prejudge children's propensity for achievement, it is clear that a supportive home environment and children who feel at ease about life generally provide the ideal conditions for them to achieve their potential. If children are unhappy, teachers face a considerable challenge in capturing their trust, interest and desire to learn. However, your enthusiasm and positive attitude to achievement may be the means by which that needy child finds fulfilment.

It is unwise to assume that every child has a father as well as a mother in the family home. It is also important to avoid any jesting about prison, death or hooliganism, as one parent of a child in the group may be behind bars, another may have died and a brother or sister may be on probation for anti-social behaviour. It is also wise to give careful thought before making firm statements about moral issues relating to matters such as judgement and wickedness, heaven and hell. You would not be the first teacher to make a well-intended remark, only to find a child in tears or an angry parent on the doorstep demanding to know why Lucy had lain awake half the night worrying what might happen to her if she died.

Children need opportunities to come to terms with difficult concepts and realities, though they may not grasp their full implications. For example, you may tell the class that poor people in Africa will starve without food. Sheena (aged seven and a half) is not listening to your stirring pleas about equal distribution of resources in the world; she is thinking about when her mother told her that morning that they were too poor to afford a holiday abroad. Sheena hears the word 'poor' and associates her own plight with those of the starving people. She does not differentiate between poverty as defined by Third World standards and those in the West. Clarity, careful use of vocabulary and giving children opportunities to ask questions is essential in such situations. Teachers need not only to state facts and make suggestions, but also to allay children's fears and sense of helplessness by proposing positive action (such as a small fund-raising project). Even a child from a home with limited income is wealthier than most people who live in the developing world.

As a trainee teacher, you need to face up to difficult questions about the way in which children's backgrounds influence your attitude towards them and your expectations of them. As a rule, teachers who assume that children cannot do well have their beliefs confirmed. However, teachers who have high expectations of children and offer them appropriate support and encouragement, discover that the children are capable of achieving far better results than initially seemed possible. Small successes in learning can have considerable additional benefits, as the under-achieving children gain self-confidence that positively affects their behaviour.

All parents want the very best for their children and the majority will do everything in their power to ensure that they make progress in their learning. On occasions, this desire encourages parents to make unreasonable demands upon the teacher or to have excessive expectations for their children. Nevertheless, it is better to see parents as part of the solution to children's learning needs rather than part of the problem.

Confidence in learning

Knowing about children's backgrounds and previous experiences is not being inquisitive, but serves a vital purpose in helping a teacher to respond to their learning needs more appropriately than would otherwise be possible. In addition to their basic intelligence, children's confidence and determination in the classroom depends on a combination of three factors:

◆ The level of their self-esteem
◆ The support and encouragement they receive from adults and their peers
◆ The way that adults respond to their efforts.

Children are not born with a particular view of themselves or their level of self-worth. It is something that they develop over the years, shaped through their relationships with others and their social experiences. Although some children are naturally tentative and anxious, those who develop high self-esteem are more willing to take risks and be enterprising than those who do not possess much confidence. Esteem is closely linked with inner contentment, influenced by factors such as security at home, strong friendships and academic progress. If self-esteem is high and fear of failure is low, children will normally approach work with optimism and cheerfulness. If the opposite conditions apply, children will be hesitant and fearful, often accompanied by restless behaviour. Merry (1998) even suggests that children's responses to fear of failure may take the form of regressing to more infantile and helpless forms of behaviour or venting their frustration on a weaker child. Although you cannot alter the way that children in your class have been or are treated by adults outside school, you can make a significant contribution to their well-being by concentrating your efforts in six areas:

1   Find out what the children already know and understand. This process requires that you talk to the children, listen to what they say, check previous school records, observe the way that they tackle tasks and use systematic elicitation techniques to expose their existing knowledge and understanding.
2   Model a positive attitude towards learning by celebrating achievement, commis-erating with failure, being enthusiastic about discovering new facts, thinking aloud about alternatives, and offering help and guidance whenever possible.
3   Give close personal attention to children who are struggling, restless or claim to be bored. It is worth remembering that most disaffection is caused by a lack of motivation or fear of failure.
4   Involve children in their learning by talking to them about lesson purpose, establishing manageable learning targets and asking them to comment on the quality of their work and effort.
5   Make it clear to children that you sympathize with their point of view and feelings.
6   Emphasize, especially among the boys, that success is 'cool'.

Dealing appropriately with individuals is not always straightforward when you encounter the realities of classroom life. One trainee teacher was honest enough to admit that her initial criticisms of the way that the class teacher handled teaching situations was tempered after she tried to implement her own ideals:

> I decided that I was going to try and spend more time with the children on an individual basis to review their work, discuss what they had done well and what could be improved next time. When I actually gained sole charge of the class, I realized that it was easy to criticize but not so easy to practise what I preached!

For instance, it is difficult to match children's self-confidence and view of themselves with their potential to achieve. As a trainee teacher and new to the class, it is easy to confuse the natural ebullience of a child with her or his capability. The bright-eyed, responsive child may or may not possess a good brain. The lacklustre child may have considerable potential to learn. There will also be some children that need your regular approval and are delighted and relieved when you commend their efforts. With your guidance and support they can surprise themselves with how much they can achieve. This is one of the great privileges of being a teacher.

Case studies: children's learning needs

In the following case studies, we see that the quality of learning is related to the children's personalities and their attitudes towards aspects of school life. The cases show that individual learning needs do not fall neatly into predetermined categories but require careful attention to circumstances and a range of extraneous factors. The cases also demonstrate that there are often no easy or immediate solutions to the challenges of helping some children to learn.

Paul

Paul, aged eleven, enjoys doing practical activities and has a keen interest in mechanical toys but hates doing formal English, especially writing. Conse-quently, he always rushes this element of the work. His teacher has tried to persuade him to adopt a more careful approach by insisting that he fills in a 'writing frame' proforma in advance and incorporates specific vocabulary and phrases into his work. She has even paired him to work co-operatively with a slower child. All these strategies have little visible impact on him. The teacher cannot fault Paul for his keen application to the task and enthusiasm to get the work completed, but sometimes despairs of ever making him work more prudently. By encouraging Paul to talk about his ideas and helping him to see where they might be expanded, the teacher gradually notes an improvement in Paul's quality of work. However, she is also aware that Paul's father has high expectations of his middle-ability son and senses that this fact partly explains the prevailing sense of urgency in everything he does.

Mishka

Mishka, aged seven, listens for short spells of time but allows his attention to wander. The teacher has lost count of the number of times she has gently spoken his name to draw him back from his silent world. Over the months, she has tried many different strategies with Mishka, including saying his name sharply without looking at him, asking him a direct question, making him sit right in front of her, putting him next to a lively child and using a small tinkling bell to signal his need to concentrate. Mishka reacts positively to these stimuli but quickly resumes his dreamlike pose. His mother speaks limited English but has indicated that Mishka is a solitary boy who prefers his own company. The teacher is anxious that he may become isolated and has already noticed that Mishka is beginning to show signs of restlessness during whole class sessions. In consultation with his mother, the teacher has started to encourage Mishka to bring in things from home that will motivate him and cause other children to talk to him. The situation with Mishka continues to be a delicate balance between gentle encouragement and firm insistence.

Jannine

Jannine, a rising five, steadfastly refuses to participate in messy activities. The assistant has tried to encourage her by bringing in a 'special' apron with pictures of animals for her to wear, letting Jannine watch other children engage with activities and working closely with her on straightforward, undemanding tasks. However, despite Jannine's obvious pleasure at watching others at work, she resists all attempts to persuade her to try for herself. The teacher has had several conversations with Jannine's mother, who comments that 'she is like this at home, too'. The teacher is concerned that Jannine is missing out on an important dimension of experiential learning but feels that for the time being it is better not to be too insistent. Fortunately, Jannine will happily draw and colour pictures using crayons and felt pens while her classmates paint.

Wanda

Wanda, aged six, is a capable child, but lacks the confidence to work on her own without a lot of adult support. She sits quietly on the carpet and will occasionally answer a question, but seems to freeze when she is given tasks to complete and waits to be told specifically what to do and how to do it. She often looks at other children's work in the hope of copying from them and is then told to 'stop cheating' by her classmates. Wanda frequently puts up her hand to ask the assistant for help but is more reluctant to ask the teacher and will not respond to strangers. The teacher encourages Wanda to work with a more confident child, praises anything that she attempts on her own and directly intervenes to help her whenever possible. However, the teacher and assistant agree that if Wanda receives too much support she will become over-dependent on adult intervention, so they hesitate to be unduly sympathetic and hope that she will improve with maturity.

Adriana

Adriana, aged four, refuses to share the toys with other children and resorts to pinching and pushing to get her own way. She is well behaved when left alone but becomes aggressive if another child invades her territory. Requests from the teacher and assistant for tolerance fall on deaf ears and several children have been injured in their attempts to share the play equipment. Adriana is the youngest of five children and because her mother gets angry with her daughter if the teacher mentions her poor behaviour, dialogue between them is limited. The teacher has tried a variety of strategies, including giving Adriana her own set of resources, removing her from the situation as soon as she becomes possessive, and maintaining a 'good girl' star chart with small rewards when she behaves for a given period. The staff of the nursery is anxious that Adriana will become isolated from class activities and have problems when she begins more formal schooling. The issue is made more complicated by the fact that Adriana is also capable of being extremely considerate and helpful when the mood takes her. The staff make a point of commending her kind deeds at every opportunity.

Kristan

Kristan, aged nine, is extremely unco-operative when working as a member of a group and insists on working alone. The teacher acknowledges that Kristan generally concentrates well on his own and makes good progress, but she is concerned about his unwillingness or inability to contribute to a team effort. Problems arise when the activity necessitates collaboration. The teacher has compromised by putting Kristan with a compliant boy who does not seem to take exception to Kristan's impulsive and single-minded approach. However, she is uncertain about whether she is allowing Kristan to have his way too much for the sake of having a settled classroom. The teacher consoles herself that there is little to be gained by forcing Kristan to work in a way that he so clearly dislikes, so the detachment continues. The teacher sometimes compromises by allowing Kristan to select the group he works with, though his arrival is usually greeted with complaints or sour comments from other members.

Enoch

Enoch, aged ten, loves to look at books but is very slow at reading and tends to fall behind in his work as a result. Other children are reluctant to work with Enoch because he slows them down and, in a co-operative effort, contributes little to the enterprise. The teacher has set Enoch short-term, manageable targets to encourage him to achieve more, and chosen texts for him to use that look suitable for his age but contain a limited vocabulary. The teacher has also kept in close touch with Enoch's mother, whose cheerful, relaxed attitude to life offers a clue about her son's lack of engagement with work. Even with additional support in reading from a volunteer parent, Enoch is not expected to do very well in his end of key stage tests, owing to his ponderous application to task. The teacher struggles to find other ways in which Enoch might find success, so she is pleased that he generally seems at ease with himself and quietly contented with life in general.

Jasper

Jasper, aged eleven, knows far more about the computer than anyone else in the class and, though extremely helpful, tends to vaunt his knowledge and irritate other children. The teacher is not an ICT specialist and secretly worries about her own lack of expertise in the subject. Whole class sessions using the computer suite are particularly galling for her, as Jasper looks and sounds bored for most of the lesson. After consulting with the ICT co-ordinator, the teacher allows Jasper to spend longer using a computer than other children to accommodate his insatiable desire for information. However, she is anxious that Jasper's fascination with technology is affecting his attitude in other areas of his work and has noted a gradual deterioration in his willingness to persevere with writing tasks. She has decided that she will use the computer as an incentive, contingent on Jasper completing his other work satisfactorily.

Gina

Gina, aged nine, gets stressed during mental mathematics, and blurts out the first thing that comes into her head. Her answers are often considerably at variance with the correct one and, when challenged, Gina seems at a loss to explain how she arrived at them. The teacher has sometimes found opportunity to speak personally to Gina afterwards and discovered that she is usually able to answer correctly when allowed time and given encouragement. Gina has begun to lose confidence and, where once her hand shot into the air regularly, she now prefers to claim that she doesn't know the answer. The teacher is worried because he has noticed that this passive attitude is spreading to other elements of her work. As a result, he is reluctant to ask Gina a direct question in public for fear of further alienating her from learning. She is far from being the weakest in mathematics in the class, so he cannot justify a request for additional support. The teacher has decided that for the present he will try to include Gina in co-operative responses (asking everyone to respond simultaneously) and give her effusive praise for her small achievements elsewhere. However, he is fearful that in a few years time she will conform to the stereotype of a female who 'never could do maths'.

Ahmed

Ahmed, aged eleven and a slow learner, is inclined to be curt and dismissive when offered help by the learning support assistant assigned to him. He is bright and articulate, but the combination of English as an additional language and minor brain damage at birth mean that Ahmed does not grasp basic principles easily and soon forgets what he has learned. He is able to repeat facts but struggles to transfer his knowledge to other situations. For instance, he can learn spellings for a test but has difficulty using them in free writing. Ahmed wants to be like everyone else and resents the presence of the learning support assistant (LSA) which he interprets as a slight on his character. The teacher has regular conversations with Ahmed to explain the importance of keeping up with his work and liaises with the father, who is extremely supportive. However, Ahmed is becoming increasingly restless with the LSA arrangement, so after discussions with the Special Education Needs Co-ordinator (SENCO), the teacher and the assistant have agreed to loosen the close adult–child ties. As a result, the LSA will spend time with other less able children, while maintaining a watching brief over Ahmed.

The case studies demonstrate that the idea that learning can be neatly packaged and offered to eager children in orderly chunks is a fabrication. Effective learning relies not only on basic intelligence but the classroom context, personality of the child and social factors such as friendship patterns, peer pressure and the desire to conform. Shrewd teachers take careful note of these special factors and try to use them as prompts to increase motivation for learning. For instance, children with a pleasant personality can usually be cajoled along if they lapse. Children who enjoy being part of a group effort can be reminded about the progress that the other members are making in the hope that they will not want to fall behind and make more effort to keep pace. A desire to conform can be used as a basis for classroom practices and procedures that apply to the whole group or class and helps to create a mutually supportive environment in which all children can flourish and fulfil their potential.

Teaching principle

Deal with each child as a unique and special individual.

Case studies: teachers' impact on learning

School can be a great place when the teachers are knowledgeable, confident and committed to the children in their care. Every survey shows that the majority of primary-aged children love going to school and like their teachers. Three trainees, reflecting on their own school days, each recalled what one of their teachers was like.

The contrast between them could hardly be greater. The teacher in the first example transformed the attitude of the fearful child. The teacher in the second example nearly destroyed the self-confidence of the timid child. The teacher in the third example was imprinted on the memory as someone who valued children and showed it through his words and actions. The accounts remind us that every teacher exerts a significant influence on children's attitudes to learning, one way or another.

Miss Thompson

I was six years old at the time. I had just moved to a new primary school and so I was very unsettled to start with. My first teacher left after a few weeks and Miss Thompson took her place. It really transformed my life at school. Miss Thompson was a great teacher. I felt at ease with her. I can remember when she really encouraged me and helped me take a main part in the school play. It really boosted my confidence. She was a lively, enthusiastic teacher. She took an interest in everyone and really encouraged people. She made learning an exciting experience and there was never a dull moment. She really encouraged you to work and try your hardest at everything you did.

Mr Grasp

I can recall my own teacher, Mr Grasp, a small thickset man. Even before I went into his class I was petrified at the very thought. This was a general feeling by pupils. The classroom was long and narrow with thirty-eight desks in straight lines. It really could have been something out of Charles Dickens! The times I sat, or so I thought, in relative safety at my desk two rows from the back, only to be spotted by Mr Grasp and hauled out to the front to answer questions on the board. I would not have minded, but I was considered a fairly intelligent, quiet and able pupil, who tried to be as insignificant as possible in class. When I found myself looking at the board with all eyes on me, I became a quivering wreck and was in no state to speak coherently. It was far safer to appear stupid and to say nothing, than to say the wrong thing and be further ridiculed.

Mr Passion

The teacher who really inspired me was someone called Mr Passion. He was a maths teacher who always looked you straight in the eye and was invariably polite. He was also very enthusiastic in his teaching but made it clear that it was okay to get things wrong and that I wasn't expected to be right all the time. He was a person that showed great empathy and was willing to spend time to help those who were finding things difficult. This teacher stands out in my mind because he was approachable and would talk to every child, even for a few seconds, to make sure that they were managing. It didn't seem to matter how many times I said that I was stuck on a question, Mr Passion would not only explain it again but had various ways of putting his teaching across. He would commend me on what I got right and help me to work on things that I hadn't.

Mr Passion made me feel valued and, most importantly, was not critical, so I was no longer afraid to try in case of failure. Mr Passion's attitude was entirely different from that of my parents! The fact that I want to be a teacher myself stems from the fact that I want to play an active and useful role in the lives of children, just as Mr Passion did for me.

Notice the key words in the first extract:

◆ encouraged
◆ transformed
◆ exciting.

Compare them with key words from the second extract:

◆ petrified
◆ quivering
◆ ridiculed.

And in the third:

◆ inspired
◆ approachable
◆ valued.

In Miss Thompson's case, she helped to stimulate a thirst for learning through her positive and imaginative teaching. She not only had confidence in the children's ability to achieve a lot but gave them self-belief that they were capable of doing it. Her lessons were characterized by a lively approach, relevant work and an interest in the child's welfare outside the immediacy of formal classroom interactions. Mr Grasp, on the other hand, used fear as a weapon. He seems only to have been interested in academic achievement and took little account of children's emotional well-being. Mr Passion was interested in each child and did his utmost to ensure that progress in learning was facilitated by patient explanations, understanding and constructive advice. We can imagine that whereas Miss Thompson and Mr Passion used children's mistakes and misconceptions as opportunities to promote learning, Mr Grasp considered them to be an indicator of personal inadequacy. Perhaps Mr Grasp's children gained the same sort of formal test results as those in Miss Thompson's and Mr Passion's classes, but it is not difficult to imagine which group of children were more highly motivated and developed a lifelong zest for learning. We should not base our teaching solely on nostalgia (Mitchell and Weber 1999) but it is undoubtedly the case that whatever theories of teaching and learning you may espouse as a teacher, they are largely worthless if you cannot motivate children and provide a secure learning environment. Children don't have to like a teacher in order to learn, but there does need to be an atmosphere of mutual respect and tolerance if optimum progress is to be made.

Chapter 6 has offered insights into the complex world of children's learning and used practical examples to demonstrate how their needs can be met more effectively. Chapter 7 now considers the process of lesson planning and the production of lesson plans as an essential contributor towards high quality learning.

Further reading

Goodwin, P. (ed.) (2002) *The Articulate Classroom*, London: David Fulton.

Moyles, J. and Robinson, G. (2002) *Beginning Teaching, Beginning Learning*, Buckingham: Open University Press.

Lesson plans and preparation

Lesson preparation

Imagine going on holiday with only a vague idea about where you were heading, carrying a few items thrown into a suitcase and a map of the general area in the hope that you could somehow find your way around. It is unlikely that the holiday would be a success and you would need to be unusually adept at thinking on your feet to survive to the end of the week! The same principles apply to lesson planning.

Lesson *plans* can be accessed from web sites, taken from one of the many books with lesson ideas or something supplied to you by the host school or a friend. However, the mere provision of a plan cannot substitute for the process of *planning*, in which you take account of the particular factors associated with the classroom situation, such as the number of pupils, availability of resources, size of teaching space, time available, ability of the children and their previous experience. Effective planning anticipates problems, foresees practical implications and makes suitable provision for them. The finished product of 'the plan' is, therefore, a product of a comprehensive and ongoing process. The better the planning, the greater the likelihood that the plan will fulfil its intended purpose, but every good plan must take account of the particular learning situation.

Lesson planning cannot anticipate everything that might happen during the session, but the more thoroughly the predictable elements have been thought through and prepared for, the easier it will be to cope with the unexpected. As a trainee, it is possible to fall into the trap of observing an experienced teacher at work and, on noticing how easily he or she deals with situations, to imagine that you will be able to do the same with a similar degree of preparation. This is far from the case. Teachers can only teach so smoothly and respond so adeptly to unexpected events because they have got other aspects of the lesson firmly under control, using skills gained from hard-earned experience.

Reece and Walker (2000) point out that experienced teachers make far less detailed plans than a trainee is expected to keep but stress the need for care in preparation. Thus:

If you observe experienced teachers you may find a wide variation in practice with regard to their approach to lesson plans. Some teachers have very detailed plans, while others appear to have little at all in the way of a plan. What is important is that the lesson is always planned with care.

(Reece and Walker 2000, p. 329)

Unlike trainees, experienced teachers are often able to cope without detailed plans for two reasons. First, they have tested and refined their plans over time and found what works in practice. Second, the best of them are constantly standing outside their lessons and reflecting on ways to improve them. Qualified teachers who prosper despite having little in the way of written plans are only able to do so because they can carry in their heads details that you, as a teacher at the beginning of your career, cannot possibly manage to do. There is little point in resenting the time that you have to put in to formal preparation when you compare yourself with the class teacher. You would not teach as effectively without making such an effort.

A lesson plan can be compared with a map of the underground. The purpose of the map is to take you from where you are to where you want to go in a series of carefully designed stages. In this analogy, the stages consist of a series of straight coloured lines drawn between stations. The map does not tell you anything about the state of the trains, the distance between stations, or the atmosphere in the tunnels; nor does it claim to do so. A lesson plan parallels some of these features. It sets out how to get from start to finish in such a way that the intended objectives and learning outcomes for the children are achieved. It does not contain details of how the children will behave, whether the equipment will be satisfactory or the nature of the classroom climate. It is not intended for such purposes. However, if your journey through the lesson is to be a success, you need more than a road map. Your lesson planning must anticipate

Comment

Advice on lesson planning is available electronically. For example, there is the standards' site for literacy at www.standards.dfee.gov.uk/literacy and guidance about planning from the DfES/OFSTED/QCA at www.teachernet.gov.uk/remodelling. The advice includes the need to establish clear objectives and to consider the impact of planning both on your teaching and children's learning. The availability of these (and related) sites highlights the fact that planning does not need to start from a blank piece of paper and that ICT can reduce planning time in the long term, though initially it may create additional work for you. It is also important to remember that most planning is now carried out in collaboration with colleagues and is not a solitary activity.

opportunities for learning, and likely snags and holdups, and take account of their impact. The success with which you handle the lesson will be reflected in the extent to which you are able to look ahead and build some flexibility into your approach.

Principles for lesson planning

Lessons are a means for helping children to organize their thinking, to practise skills and to understand concepts better, and all lesson planning must therefore take account of three factors:

1 What the children already know and understand
2 What the children need to know and understand
3 The best way to help them move from point 1 to point 2.

Lessons consist of a variety of different approaches. A formal lesson might involve the teacher doing nearly all of the talking and the pupils doing most of the listening, followed by a silent session in which the pupils work individually at tasks. At the other end of the scale, the lesson might be a 'big space' games session on the school field, where other factors need to be considered, such as health and safety and correct use of equipment. Regardless of the circumstances, however, there are some basic principles that apply to every lesson:

♦ Use a systematic approach, assisted by an outline lesson proforma (usually supplied by your college or the school)
♦ Concentrate on the things that you want the children to learn or experience
♦ Incorporate activities that will help to fulfil the lesson intentions
♦ Specify the links with the national curriculum (NC), Literacy Strategy (DfEE, 1998) or other relevant documentation
♦ Identify key vocabulary and questions (though recognize that the children may raise others)
♦ State how you intend to assess the children's progress
♦ Specify the resources that will be needed
♦ Write down the anticipated lesson process, step by step, including the introduction, the main body of the lesson and the conclusion
♦ Ensure that your plans take account of the learning needs of different children or groups, including the more able.

Some lessons that you teach, especially in shorter placements or early in a teaching practice, will be a one-off. In such cases, it is particularly important that you explain the purpose to the children, begin the lesson brightly and establish its relevance. The majority of lessons will lie somewhere within a sequence, so a lot depends on its place in the order. If it is the *first* lesson in a series, you will probably want to spend a lot of time introducing the topic, enthusing about it, and using your imagination to fix the children's interest. If it lies *midway* in a sequence, you can use the first few minutes of the session to remind the children of what has gone before, ask some questions to elicit how much they remember and remind them of some key points, before describing the content and purpose of the present lesson. If the lesson is the *final* one in a series, you will probably want to spend more time revising, reviewing and celebrating what has gone before. Nevertheless, a good quality lesson plan of any kind will consist of seven components:

1   The overall lesson objective(s) expressed in terms of what it is intended to achieve.
2   What you expect pupils will/could/should learn, expressed in one or more of four ways:
    ◆ the *knowledge* they should acquire or reinforce
    ◆ the *understanding* that they should develop
    ◆ the *skills* that they should acquire or refine
    ◆ the *attitudes* that they should develop.
3   Your role during the different phases of the lesson.
4   The activities and tasks that pupils will undertake to reinforce and extend their learning.
5   The resources required for pupils to complete their work.
6   Health and safety factors.
7   The assessment indicators that you will use to evaluate the extent of children's progress in the four elements listed under point 2 above.

Some lesson plans will emphasize certain components more than others. For instance, resources and safety aspects always figure strongly in a PE lesson using small-scale equipment. In an art lesson, drawing skills may be particularly significant. In a literacy session, the supporting activities and tasks will normally form an essential part of the learning process. In an enquiry-based science lesson, resources, time factors and the composition of the collaborative groups need careful organizing and monitoring. Every lesson requires, therefore, attention both to general principles (such as specifying learning objectives) and specific characteristics that relate to the particular subject or topic.

The lesson process

The teaching methods you intend to employ must be taken into account in your planning, and their nature will depend on what you are trying to achieve. For instance, the lesson may be largely concerned with introducing a new concept, demonstrating a skill, rehearsing some half-forgotten ideas or refining a familiar process. *Introducing a new concept* will often involve the teacher in a lot of direct talking to the class, the use of question and answer to establish what they already know and the use of visual aids. *Demonstrating a skill* will necessitate the teacher talking aloud about the processes that the children are observing. *Posing dilemmas* or describing a variety of scenarios to the children for discussion is likely to involve a great deal of interactive teaching and inviting pupil responses, with the teacher providing regular summaries of what has been said. Regardless of the particular circumstances, however, your teaching approach for most lessons will involve ten steps:

1   Reminding the children of what they have covered in previous lessons.
2   Finding out through question and answer what they remember and what they have forgotten or become confused about.
3   Introducing what they are going to be doing and learning in the lesson.
4   Giving them any necessary background information about the topic.
5   Explaining the way in which the session will be organized.
6   Discussing the standard of work that is expected.
7   Setting the children to work on the tasks and activities.
8   Monitoring their progress and establishing individual short-term targets.
9   Concluding and drawing the lesson to a close.
10 Clearing up and dismissing the children.

Of course, these steps are easier to write down than to execute, and each one requires a considerable degree of thought and planning. For instance, the amount of *time* spent on each step during the lesson has to be considered. When lessons are of specific duration (one hour, say) it is essential to have a clear idea about the length of each phase. It is also a challenge to keep the lesson on course when it becomes evident that the children are less secure in their understanding than you imagined or when they raise some genuine questions about issues that demand a lengthy explanation. On the whole, it is better to press on with the lesson as you intended rather than become sidetracked. However, it is important to find an opportunity in the immediate future to follow up the points, especially to clarify any lingering misconceptions, as wrong ideas can easily take root if not dealt with quickly.

It is never easy at the best of times to steer a lesson while trying to read your lesson notes, control the class, provide appropriate resources, monitor progress and keep an eye on the time. However, sloppy planning and unrealistic learning targets can result in the lesson being a shambles rather than the slick operation you had intended, so thoroughness of preparation is essential. Once you feel more confident about maintaining a lesson schedule, you can deviate slightly from your planned timing as the lesson unfolds. If you have not bothered to think about the timing, you will not have anything to deviate from!

On a practical note, there is no need to disguise your lesson plan from the children or feel that it is shameful to refer to it. If children ask what you are looking at, tell them plainly. Older children are often fascinated to gain an insight into what teachers do behind the scenes and will not view the plan as an indication of your inexperience. Some trainees have found it helpful to spend five minutes of preparation time writing out the broad outline of the lesson in bold pen on a large sheet of paper and temporarily pinning it to the wall opposite. In this way they do not need to worry so much about having to look down at the formal lesson plan so much. Other trainees use the same technique for reminding themselves of questions they intend to ask the children, key vocabulary or things to remember. One way or another it is essential to avoid the embarrassment of losing your way or getting flustered because you are trying to do too many things at once. There is a difference between maintaining an appropriate pace and rushing the lesson.

Comment

Laar *et al.* (1989) insist that teachers must know and understand what they are dealing with, how children learn best and, as a result, employ the most effective method to teach it.

> The effective teacher begins from a strong knowledge base, both knowledge of subject disciplines, as well as knowledge of how those disciplines are successfully learned and taught.
>
> (Laar *et al.* 1989, p. 35)

Teaching principle

Know what you are doing, what the children are doing, why they are doing it and how it will happen.

Differentiation

The term 'differentiation' has numerous definitions, but broadly speaking it is used to describe the process by which teaching and learning is made relevant to all abilities of children. Bearne (1996) argues that the term must denote flexibility in teaching approach to make learning accessible to every child.

Differentiated planning is a means whereby children of differing abilities and aptitude can engage meaningfully with work that takes account of their understanding, experience and maturity. As Proctor *et al.* (1995, p. 46) rightly remind us, 'children do not work at the same rate or in the same way. They need different sorts of instruction, different access to the subject matter, varying amounts of practice and reinforcement'. In other words, differentiation does not merely reside in the creation of a formal plan that takes account of children's abilities but in a careful consideration of methods of implementation during the process of teaching. This requires either that children are given different tasks according to their ability (differentiation by activity) or all the children work their way through a series of tasks, commencing with the most basic and working through at their own pace to tackle the harder challenges (differentiation by progression, see Figure 7.1). One way or another, tasks and activities need to be matched to the children's proficiencies but this should not mean that those with the potential to tackle bigger challenges are held back by the limitations of the work.

Differentiation also requires teachers to use appropriate teaching strategies, especially in four areas:

1   *The vocabulary and speed of speech when addressing children.* Less able children often have a more limited vocabulary than their more able classmates and absorb

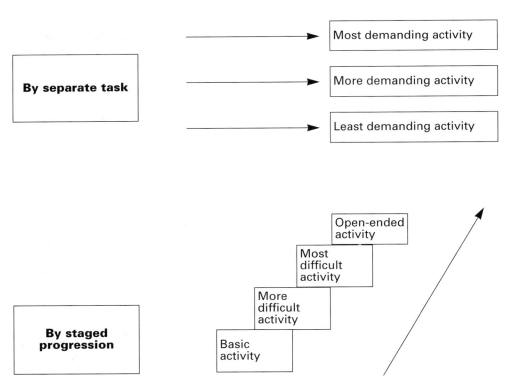

Figure 7.1 *Differentiated activities*

information more slowly. Consequently, teachers need to be careful that they explain specialist terms using appropriate language, repeat key points and allow short pauses between giving portions of information to allow the children's brains to process them. It is useful to ask children what they think you have just said as a means of checking whether or not they are keeping in touch with what you say.

2 *The questions they ask.* Some children, particularly the less able and under-confident ones, tend to be reluctant to answer questions for fear of saying something inappropriate and being ridiculed by their classmates. They may also struggle with a teacher's speculative questions that require them to evaluate situations, offer suggestions and predict outcomes. Nevertheless, teachers need to be careful that they do not ask only the brighter children and ignore those who are less confident. Inclusion can be enhanced by:

◆ Commencing with elementary questions that every child can feel confident to answer and choosing the less able children to do so

◆ Offering either/or questions and asking for a blanket response. The less able tend to follow the majority view and can share the teacher's approving comments

◆ Occasionally giving children thirty seconds to think about their answer in pairs before responding, as this allows for thinking time and reduces the likelihood of ill-considered spontaneous answers.

As we shall see in Chapter 8, the use of more open and speculative questions (rather than questions to which there is a single answer) makes learning more enjoyable both for children and teachers.

3 *The expectations for work outcomes.* Less able children may try hard to achieve a satisfactory result and yet attain a lower standard than their more able classmates. As with so many aspects of a teacher's working life, a balance has to be struck between maintaining high expectations and taking account of individual ability. Unreasonable expectations lead to children becoming demoralized owing to the unattainable target. Low expectation results in children becoming bored or disaffected with the work owing to the lack of challenge. Two children completing the same task may merit praise, despite the wide difference in quality of outcome, assuming that both of them have worked up to their potential.

4 *The use of enquiry-based learning.* Collaborative investigations and problem-solving enterprises offer opportunities for groups consisting of the less and more able children to work together. Although these groups are likely to be dominated by the brighter children, the less academic are able to contribute to the team effort and gain status from the successful outcome. Some children who are academically weak possess organizational and leadership skills that blossom during group sessions. The challenge for teachers is to empower children in such a way that they can function autonomously and gain satisfaction from their contribution.

Edwards (2000) insists that an essential part of every teacher's work is not only to plan in such a way that children's needs are met through appropriate teaching and activities, but to reflect carefully after the lesson has been taught. Thus: 'It is here that the teacher can analyse whether the differentiation has supported, stretched and enriched the children or challenged and motivated them by providing the best opportunity for learning' (Edwards 2000, p. 35). Differentiation is not a piece of educational jargon but a vital factor in lesson planning that will allow all children, within the constraints of the classroom system, to achieve well and feel positive about their ability to learn.

Comment

Dean (1999) underlines the importance of viewing differentiation as more than merely matching tasks to the ability of the children. Thorough preparation considers children's existing understanding and grasp of the knowledge and skills associated with the subject matter. Dean highlights the vital role of shared language, especially relevant when specialist terms are employed.

> In preparation the teacher can consider the experiences it is likely that the children have had and the experiences they will need in order to understand the new concepts involved. It is also helpful to consider the language that will be needed and the extent to which the children will have a similar understanding of it to that of the teacher.
>
> (Dean 1999, p. 64)

Inclusion

The NC2000 (DfEE/QCA, 1999) emphasizes the importance of inclusion and stresses the fact that all schools have a responsibility to provide a broad and balanced curriculum for all pupils. There are three principles that are considered essential in providing an inclusive curriculum (DfEE/QCA 1999, p. 30):

1   Setting suitable learning challenges
2   Responding to pupils' diverse learning needs
3   Overcoming potential barriers to learning and assessment for individuals and groups of pupils.

Setting suitable learning challenges must take account of high and low achieving pupils; for example, by planning in such a way that more able children are provided with challenges that encourage them to draw from different subjects across the curriculum and incorporate them into the work. Responding to the diversity of learning needs requires that teachers create a learning environment in which all children can thrive and plan lessons that motivate and inspire children from all walks of life. Overcoming potential barriers to learning and assessment is particularly relevant to children who have been identified as having physical, mental or emotional needs. Planning to meet these needs must take account of factors such as appropriate vocabulary, accessibility of resources and strategies for managing behaviour. For example, children with English as an additional language may require extra adult help or to be paired with a child who has a good command of the language. Children with physical disabilities may require extra space in which to operate, assistance with equipment or resources at a given height. They may tire more easily and need to have breaks built into their work pattern. Emotionally vulnerable children may need to have a variety of work that incorporates short-term goals and easily verifiable outcomes, and allows for some 'time out' from the intensity of the lesson. Lesson planning must take such matters into careful consideration, particularly in regard to the supportive use of other adults.

Providing appropriate and adequate resources is a vital element of lesson planning. If you intend to use specialized equipment (such as IT software or design and technology tools) then in addition to basic health and safety issues, and the need for proper training in their use, children should have equal access to them. As you plan your lessons, envisage how the allocation of resources will ensure that quiet and timid children will have as much opportunity as bolder ones. It is common for less confident children, even when offered opportunities to have their turn, to quickly hand over to a more assertive classmate rather than suffer the embarrassment of being at the centre of attention. It is your job to get alongside such children and encourage them to persist with their efforts, offering careful support and commendation wherever possible. Similarly, in group discussions, question-and-answer sessions and collaborative problem-solving, some children will tend to be marginalized and part of your time must be spent in clarifying boundaries and the rules of interaction if they are ever to become part of the enterprise. You may want to consider a form of positive discrimination such that timid children or those with limited English are given priority treatment.

Special educational needs

Advice about special educational needs is contained in a publication by the Department for Education and Skills (DfES 2001) commonly referred to by its sub-title, the Code of Practice. The Code consists of ten chapters and a lengthy annex, but only the first five chapters contain some information of interest to trainee teachers:

1   Principles and policies
2   Working in partnership with parents
3   Pupil participation
4   Identification, assessment and provision in early education settings
5   Identification, assessment and provision in the primary phase.

Children are identified as having a learning difficulty on the basis of having a significantly greater difficulty in learning than the majority of children of the same age or if they have a disability that prevents or hinders them from use of educational facilities. For example, a child in a wheelchair may not be able to use the sink because of its location. Similarly, a child with a muscular condition may experience problems unscrewing containers or pouring liquids. Legislation requires that the school liaises with the parent to ensure, as far as possible, that no child is further disadvantaged because of inadequate provision. Consequently, there has been an increase in adult support staff and attempts to ensure that the physical environment is adjusted to take account of the special needs.

The Code offers guidance about the signs that intervention is necessary; for example, that the children show a lack of progress in areas that have been targeted for special attention or demonstrate persistent behavioural difficulties. If children with sensory or physical problems continue to make little progress despite the provision of personal aids and equipment or have communication difficulties, then this also triggers action.

Comment

As well as planning single and multiple lessons with respect to diversity of ability and children's propensity for learning, your preparation and presentation must take account of the variety of children represented in the class. Thus, from NC2000 (DfEE/QCA 1999, p. 31):

> When planning, teachers should set high expectations and provide opportunities for all pupils to achieve, including boys and girls, pupils with special educational needs, pupils with disabilities, pupils from all social and cultural backgrounds, pupils of different ethnic groups, including travellers, refugees and asylum seekers, and those from diverse linguistic backgrounds.

It is worth noting that the term 'special needs' is sometimes referred to as 'additional needs'.

Activities

Trainee teachers are understandably anxious to have plenty of ideas for things to do with the children during lessons. However, it is important not only to provide activities but to consider what relevance they have in respect of the identified learning goals. The commonest reasons for giving the children tasks to do during a lesson include the following:

◆ The children need to reinforce what they already know something about, so the tasks extend their understanding of previous work
◆ The children need to learn something that they do not yet know or understand, so the tasks make them engage with new ideas
◆ The children need to learn and practise a particular skill, so the tasks include specific training and guidance from an informed adult
◆ The children need opportunities to discover things for themselves, so resources and time are made available to allow them to search and experiment
◆ The children need opportunities to work with others, so the tasks involve co-operation.

When planning, the key question for you to consider is to what extent the tasks contribute towards the learning goals, bearing in mind that some of them may be part of a *cumulative* set of objectives over several sessions. It is sometimes tempting to give children straightforward things (such as colouring) to keep them occupied or as a control device rather than setting tasks with learning objectives in mind, but these occasions should be kept to a minimum. Children may learn things other than those you anticipate from an activity, but this merely proves the amorphous character of learning. It is also a reminder that lesson objectives are intentions, not absolutes.

In planning activities to support and extend children's learning, you need to take account of four things. First, whether they are *suitable for the purpose*. For instance, if you were encouraging children to take personal responsibility for their environment as part of citizenship sessions, it would be appropriate for the children to spend time (say) organizing a rota for keeping the classroom tidy. If, on the other hand, you wanted the children to think hard about a whole school policy for keeping the environment pleasant, designing posters to display outside the classroom door or opportunities for children to contribute ideas with the aim of producing a ten-point set of rules would be more appropriate. The lesson intention would guide the activity.

Second, activities need to be *manageable*. It may help to reinforce children's understanding of warm air rising by building a hot air balloon in the playground, but if it is impractical the enterprise has the potential for being chaotic. You may have to settle for demonstrating to the class under tightly controlled conditions the way that the heat from a hair-drier creates a similar effect. Activities also need to be manageable in respect of the time that they take to complete. Inexperienced teachers often attempt to do far too much in a single lesson and end up swamping the children with tasks. It is far better to use fewer activities and spend some time discussing their implications with the children.

Third, activities should be *intellectually appropriate*. We have already noted that teachers must differentiate in the way they use vocabulary, ask questions and allocate responsibilities, such that all children have a chance to learn and progress. Similarly, designated tasks must allow children to understand what is required from them and have the capacity and experience to make progress, yet cause them to think, reason and extend their boundaries. One way to ensure that children are extended in this way is to provide them with a challenge as a component of the lesson. For example:

◆ Now make up three problems for a friend to solve
◆ Write down five other words that you might have used in the story
◆ Draw a picture to show what a miniature version of it would look like
◆ Write some sentences containing made-up verbs that sound as if they are real
◆ What would the instructions say if everyone were twice the size?

Fourth, activities must *serve a purpose* and incorporate children's existing knowledge whenever possible. If children perceive a task as isolated from past experiences and little to do with the future, it is far harder to enthuse them to do their best than if it has relevance and a place in the scheme of things.

Resources

A surprising number of lessons fail to achieve their potential owing to poor levels of resourcing. Although it is unnecessary to mention every small item that is required for the lesson in your written plan, it is wise to check and double-check that you have not overlooked some vital piece of equipment. In particular, it pays to give careful thought to the acquisition and use of resources in five ways:

1   Resources that *you* need, such as a whiteboard, demonstration materials, video cassettes and books.
2   Resources that the *children* will need, such as science equipment, art materials, worksheets, computer diskettes.
3   *Space resources*, ensuring that the children have sufficient room to carry out their work comfortably and efficiently.
4   *Time resources*, whereby there is adequate time to achieve the lesson objectives and give slower workers opportunity to complete tasks without undue pressure.
5   *Adult resources*, making certain that the assistants have been properly briefed about their role.

Sometimes the resources are stored away from the classroom and have to be collected in advance of the lesson (e.g. musical instruments). Your preparation must take account of the time involved in collecting and returning the equipment, as well as finding out where the key to the cupboard is kept! It is equally important to consider pupils' access to resources, the way that they will be distributed and what happens to them at the end of the lesson. For instance, the children may be asked to collect the item from trays previously set out on separate tables or at another collection point, in which case you will have to ensure that it is done in an orderly and sensible manner. The children may be working in groups on an investigation that involves the use of specialist equipment, so you will need to spend time showing them how to use it correctly. At the end of the lesson, it is quite common for some work to be incomplete, owing to the fact that some children progressed more slowly than expected or you misjudged the time they required. In such situations, you will have to decide whether to collect in the work, leave it until the next lesson for completion or organize two piles, one for completed and the other for uncompleted work. Teachers are frequently faced with a decision about the most appropriate strategy for dealing with incomplete work and have three options:

1   Accept the work as its stands and use the amount of progress made as an assessment indicator. Children receive feedback in the normal way.
2   Treat what has been done as work in progress and offer an opportunity at a later time to complete it. This option needs to take account of how the children who have completed their work will be occupied.
3   Use the plenary or a subsequent lesson to follow up in detail the issues arising from the session, with special emphasis on the incomplete elements.

The problem with option 1 is that slower workers do not ever have the opportunity to engage with the latter portion of the lesson. The additional problem with option 2 is finding a suitable time for completion in a busy timetable. The problem with option 3 is that the follow-up is almost invariably hurried when it deserves fuller attention. Some of these dilemmas can be offset by considering a *series* of lessons together and allowing the children to work through the content over several days and at their own pace. However, this requires great skill by the teacher to keep everyone suitably employed when the children are working at different rates. A second means of offsetting the difficulty in trying to produce a lesson plan that precisely fits the time available in a given session is to use large blocks of time (a half-day, say) for extended work in the same subject. One way and another, time constraints will always have to be considered in judging what is realistically achievable and deciding a cut-off point beyond which effort expended on the work is unproductive. Trainee teachers are, to a large extent, at the mercy of the existing system but there may be opportunity for you to discuss the options with the class teacher.

Teaching principle

In every aspect of planning, the details should be thought through before the lesson and not during it.

Sometimes it is helpful to use 'pupil monitors' to collect up the work, which itself requires close attention by you to ensure that the job is carried out sensibly and efficiently. For instance, a lot of aggravation is caused if a monitor tries to remove a piece of work when the child concerned is still trying to finish writing. Assisting the teacher should be viewed by monitors as a privilege and not something that is given to the mischievous children in the vain hope that it will keep them involved.

Assessment criteria

It is essential to consider assessment criteria as part of lesson preparation and incorporate them into your plans accordingly. Assessments are not for the purpose of catching out children or finding fault. They are an integral part of the teaching and learning cycle in which children's progress is evaluated in the hope and expectation that learning can be enhanced as a result. Assessments are normally based on one or more of the following forms of evidence:

◆ the quality of the children's written output
◆ the quality of the children's constructions, models or representations
◆ comments that the children make about their work
◆ the children's responses to your structured questions about the work
◆ the children's ability to demonstrate a skill (manual or cerebral)
◆ peer review and feedback (usually in pairs)
◆ formal testing procedures and examinations.

In identifying one or more of these assessment areas in your lesson plan, it is important to ensure that your objectives (what you want the children to learn and achieve) are closely linked with the assessment criteria. You must also distinguish between the *specific* assessment criteria for a particular lesson and *general* criteria (such as syntax) that apply to almost every situation. For instance, if the lesson objective is to promote imaginative use of verbs in free writing, it is inappropriate to use accurate spelling as a principal measure of quality, though it may become a more important assessment point when a final draft of the work is completed in a subsequent lesson.

After the session, a careful consideration of children's progress based on the assessment criteria that you established should inform your future lesson planning. Commonly, some children will not have coped with the tasks that you gave them to complete because they lacked sufficient experience in handling the concepts involved. In such cases, your future lesson plans will need to allocate time to rehearse and revise previous knowledge, help to clarify key points and sort out areas of confusion. Alternatively, some children may have completed the work with ease and finished earlier than expected, thereby putting pressure on you as you struggled to think of how you could keep them usefully occupied. In such cases, your future lesson plans will need to include some more challenging work for those pupils and, where appropriate, provide an open-ended investigative challenge for them to tackle. Some children may have underachieved through loss of interest, in which case you will need to give considerable thought to the content of the lesson and the manner in which you present it.

In carrying out assessments of children's achievements as part of the overall lesson evaluation, your decisions about their progress should not only take account of an individual's output and responses, but (for your own information) how much a child has achieved in comparison with the other children in the class. It is often the case that the same assessment criteria apply to a consecutive series of lessons, though the fine detail may vary. Assessment is dealt with more fully in Chapter 11.

Annotating plans

Regardless of how thoroughly you prepare, there will always be aspects of the lesson that could have been better. A useful and straightforward method of identifying and addressing the issues that emerge from a lesson is to annotate your original lesson plan using a different colour of ink. What you write down should be legible but does not need to be extensive. For instance, you may decide that the objectives were insufficiently focused, in which case you note on the plan the need to be more focused in future. Similarly, you may want to write that you 'gave insufficient advice about completing the tasks' or 'failed to give the low achievers as much attention as they needed' or 'left inadequate time for clearing up at the end'.

Once you have annotated your plan, you can extract the four or five handwritten comments that you have made and list them as your targets for future lessons. In doing so, it is helpful to indicate the way that improvements can be made. Thus, if you were unhappy with the lack of interest that a particular child showed for the work, your logged notes might look like this:

Issue: On-task behaviour of child X
Action: Provide shorter tasks that offer more immediate fulfilment.

Similarly, if you found that you spent too much time talking and the children became restless as a result:

> *Issue*: Concentration span of children
> *Action*: Intersperse my talk with speculative questions and visual aids.

After several more lessons, you can revisit these issues and include a third line about the outcome. For example, if you found that groups of children engaged on a practical task were constantly bickering about who did what, you may end up with the following notes in your log:

> *Issue*: Low level of co-operation in groups
> *Action*: Talk to children about fairness, allocate specific jobs to members of groups, make sure that too many assertive children are not together in a single group
> *Outcome*: Improvement in co-operation, decrease in noise level; however, some children appear to miss out on having a turn at the interesting bits
> *Further action*: Reduce group sizes from five to four and create an additional group out of the 'spare' children.

You may then discover that the additional group results in extra resource demands or classroom space becomes more of an issue, and these points form the next set of targets to take into account in future lesson planning. While annotating lesson plans and creating an agenda for improvement, two principles should be borne in mind: first, the system should be simple and easy to administer; second, the emphasis on areas for improvement should not detract from the many positive aspects of the lessons. There is a major difference between a thoughtful consideration of a lesson and negativity.

Enhancing the quality of the lesson

The earlier part of this chapter emphasized that lesson preparation is an integral component of successful teaching. Although some trainees can survive on their wits for a time, lesson quality is usually closely linked to the thoroughness of planning. Crucially, lesson planning must be translated into classroom practice and to increase the likelihood of success the following issues should be taken into account as you finalize your plans:

◆ *Get the lesson off to a good start* Be clear in your mind what the purpose is, settle the children quickly, know what you are going to say to them and the questions you will ask, insist upon their attention and delay starting until you have it, and introduce the lesson with a quiet enthusiasm.

◆ *Revise previous learning* Invite children to contribute what they remember, remind them of what has gone before, quote from a pupil's work or use it as a visual aid where appropriate, commend what has already been achieved and refer to any points of difficulty or confusion. It is also essential to show how the present lesson links with previous ones.

◆ *Clarify the tasks and activities* Explain their purpose, identify constraints and opportunities, specify whether the work is to be done individually or collaboratively, give a time limit for completion (or a reasonable amount of progress) and make it clear how much you are prepared to intervene and offer assistance. Don't be in too much of a hurry to send children off to do their tasks if they seem puzzled about what they have to do, but don't delay unduly either so that they become restless.

◆ *Make transitions between lesson phases as smooth as possible* Provide sufficient time for pupils to complete the task, give regular reminders to the class or group of the time and what remains to be done and what has to be done next. Great care over these transition phases will help you to remain calm and in control. Keep pupil movement to a minimum and anticipate logistical problems. Monitor health and safety issues if children have to move places or around the classroom.

◆ *Monitor progress effectively* Show an interest in what pupils are doing, get involved in their learning, encourage them to ask questions and offer appropriate support and feedback. Identify achievements by telling children what they have done well. Combat learned helplessness by expressing your confidence in children's abilities.

Comment

Atkinson (2000) argues that successful teaching depends on using both conscious, analytical thinking and intuition. He offers two extreme types of trainee teachers, one type relying too much on intuition in teaching and another type that suppresses intuitive behaviour for fear of deviating from the lesson plan. The first trainee type may jeopardize their chances of success due to the minimal written evidence they offer to support their achievement claims. They may also struggle to get a job because they have not analysed their teaching sufficiently well to explain their ideas to an interview panel. The second type of trainee tends to adopt a rigid approach to work.

> On teaching practice, such students work conscientiously to plan the perfect lesson and yet often produce uninspired and unimaginative learning experiences as they seek to implement ill-understood ideas that derive from the experience of others.
>
> (Atkinson 2000, p. 80)

Overall, have a decisive impact on the direction of learning without being suffocating.

◆ *Review learning* Give the children adequate warning of the lesson's conclusion, explain what they must do with their completed and incomplete work, allow time for recapping, remind them of what they have done and commend their achievements. Involve the children in clearing up and insist on continued good order after the formal conclusion of the session.

Not all these points can or should be written down on a plan, but it is important to include them in your overall planning and preparation. Mentally rehearsing the lesson in advance will soon highlight the areas for attention, rather than just seeing how it goes and making adjustments next time. Although every teaching session throws up fresh insights and points for improvement, a stitch in time saves nine!

Teaching principle

There is a lot more to lesson preparation than writing a plan.

This chapter has dealt with issues relating to lesson planning and the production of plans. In Chapter 8 we turn to the numerous skills and teaching strategies that all teachers have to master if they are to help children learn effectively and maintain good classroom control.

Further reading

Katz, L. G. and Chard, S. C. (2000) *Engaging Children's Minds*, Stamford, Connecticut: Ablex Publishing. See Chapter 6 of the book.
Kershner, R. and Miles, S. (1996) *'Thinking and talking about differentiation'*, in E. Bearne (ed.) *Differentiation and Diversity*, London: Routledge.

CHAPTER 8

Teaching skills and strategies

Teachers use a wide range of classroom teaching skills and strategies. The two terms can be distinguished in that whereas a *skill* is an ability by which means something can be successfully accomplished, a *strategy* is the method by which skills are employed to achieve it. Skills and strategies are refined through the practice of teaching, observing teachers in action and thoughtful perseverance.

In Chapter 7 it was emphasized that to improve your teaching effectiveness it is essential to prepare thoroughly, to be bold but realistic in what you can achieve, to rehearse each aspect of the lesson, to keep resources close at hand and to anticipate likely problems and opportunities. The effective employment of skills and strategies in teaching requires the utmost determination and, inevitably, it feels like swimming with one foot on the bottom for a time, but practice makes perfect, providing you are willing to learn from your mistakes. To help you refine your teaching, it is useful to take every opportunity to take note of those employed by a range of practitioners. This experience is not necessarily for the purpose of imitating their methods, and certainly not to do so unthinkingly, but to raise your awareness of the wealth of approaches that can be used by teachers.

The skill of communicating

Barnes (1975), who laid down a number of seminal principles in respect of language use in schools, stressed that communication principally involves the development of understanding between teacher and taught, and claimed that 'learning to communicate is at the heart of education' (Barnes 1975, p. 20). Thus the teacher's tone of voice, gestures and responses are significant in establishing the liberated social context that Barnes deems necessary to optimize shared understanding. The way that adult and child communicate and the way that pupils interpret the teacher's expectations and mood will reflect the quality of working relationships between them. The effort that teachers make in creating a trusting and safe social environment enhances the likelihood that learning will take place. Whether in formal teaching situations or more relaxed settings, the following principles of good communication apply (based on Stern 1995).

Set the boundaries

Some children have had unhappy experiences of adults in their lives and respond well to someone who is kind and considerate. As a trainee, you may even find that certain children relate themselves to you in a way that they find it hard to do with their regular teacher. Although you will no doubt welcome this level of trust, there is a danger of children becoming too dependent upon you so, while maintaining a sympathetic and generous attitude, it is necessary to avoid becoming emotionally involved. The ideal situation is a trusting relationship based upon mutual respect and acceptance of boundaries. The majority of children feel more secure when you show by your words and actions that although you want to be friendly, you are not requiring them to 'be friends'. It is also worth being aware that mischievous children may try to gain your favour, only to show their true colours after they have lulled you into a false sense of security and you have dropped your guard. Redressing this unsatisfactory situation is far from easy.

Value children's comments

Children want adults to understand them but may not have the vocabulary to express themselves clearly. It is tempting to brush children aside when you are busy and they are struggling to say something to you, but this approach can demoralize a hesitant child. It may sometimes be necessary to tell children that they should go away and think about what they are trying to say before resuming the conversation, especially when the situation arises at a critical moment in a lesson. Wherever possible, however, allow children to finish speaking before you interrupt, as it is one thing to assist children when they are struggling to find the right word but is quite another to complete what they are trying to say and deprive them of the opportunity to verbalize their thoughts. Occasionally, a talkative child will need to be more self-controlled and curb intrusive chatter. Using an outstretched palm towards the transgressor or finger to the lips, but without taking your eyes off the child who is grappling with ideas, is often a helpful strategy.

Consider children's feelings

Children may not always respond to what teachers say but this does not mean that the words have had no effect. Stinging condemnation hurts children, even if they appear to laugh it off. They are upset when they feel misunderstood or misrepresented. They are angry when they perceive that a situation is unfair and confused when they are treated inconsistently by adults. On the other hand, children are delighted when grown-ups share a small confidence with them and feel encouraged when they are warmly praised. They are motivated by a stimulating conversation and reassured by being accepted and liked. As children try to make sense of a complicated world, your sensitivity and awareness of their fragile emotions sends out a clear signal that they are special and important.

Encourage children to persevere

Some aspects of a teacher's role involve making difficult decisions about interpersonal situations, grievances and disputes. Other aspects of the role require a teacher to cope with unpromising areas of the curriculum and prepare children for tests and examinations for which they may have limited enthusiasm. You can help by explaining to children why it is necessary to do certain things, encourage and spur them on when the work is demanding, and offer them your support when they are struggling. Although you will sometimes have to insist that a task must be done and persuade reluctant children to do their best with unpopular activities, this is not the same as hectoring them at the first hint of protest. The most effective teachers listen to children's complaints rather than dismissing them out of hand. There is often a fine balance to be struck between insistence and sympathy, but it is one that you must achieve. The child who asks 'do we have to do this?' may be lazy or may be expressing a genuine grievance over a task that is perceived to be irrelevant. In such situations the best course of action is to reply as pleasantly as possible that 'yes, I'm afraid so, and the quicker you begin, the sooner you will finish', giving a hint of interesting things that lie ahead.

Make room for error in your judgement of the value of a situation

All adults who work in school have experienced the discomfort caused by misreading a situation, overreacting or jumping to unwarranted conclusions without first determining the truth. Due to the considerable number of decisions that teachers make every day, it is not surprising that they occasionally get things wrong. Children are remarkably forgiving and will tolerate being misjudged from time to time, but if you are to maintain open communication with them, it is essential to avoid making hasty decisions about questions of right and wrong before considering the evidence. Most misjudgements come as a result of teachers being under too much pressure and having insufficient space or time to think clearly. One way to minimize being in such a predicament is to be thoroughly prepared, properly organized and clear about the direction of the lesson.

Protect the voice

No teacher can be effective without paying close attention to the use of the voice, so spending time in learning how to speak effectively is vitally important. Care of the voice should be made a priority, as many problems are caused through inappropriate use that results in strain and tension. At the start of each day, it is important to exercise the lungs by spending a minute breathing slowly but steadily through the nostrils in a reasonably warm environment, holding the breath down in the lungs, and exhaling steadily through the mouth. Humming a popular tune, singing it to 'la' and practising speaking a short poem or rhyme (such as *Peter Piper*) that requires the free use of lips and tongue, also assists the warm-up process. Training yourself to speak in the middle register to avoid using a high pitch or whispering reduces strain on the voice. Consequently, control strategies that involve shouting, screeching or growling at children must be avoided for your own sake, let alone theirs.

The delivery side of teaching also demands the most assiduous attention. If the children struggle to hear you because you speak in a muffled tone or too quickly or slur your words, it is hardly surprising if they become restless. McGee (1998) suggests that the most common mistakes in speaking include:

◆ Insufficient preparation
◆ Shouting rather than projecting the voice
◆ A monotonous tone
◆ Mumbling
◆ Mispronunciations
◆ Fading away at the end of a sentence
◆ Using a contrived style.

A teacher's voice can be either soft or strong, but it must always be clear. Poor articulation makes it difficult for children to catch what you are saying and leads to confusion. Common failings include dropping the voice at the end of a sentence, slurring over longer words, speaking too quickly and using a monotone. As you consider your clarity of speech, it is equally crucial to take care over the use of terms and colloquial expressions that may be unfamiliar to the children. Tone of voice conveys a lot about your mood, such as whether you are calm, angry, pleased or dismayed. Approximately one quarter of your communicative power is located within voice tone (most of the remainder is associated with body language). It tells the children something about your confidence level, inspires them to work harder or to slacken their efforts, and reassures or alarms them. When voice tone has such a major impact on learning, it is worth allocating time towards improving and enhancing its effect.

A few hours spent rehearsing at home with a tape recorder will pay dividends as you seek to improve your enunciation and diction. One of the best methods of

---

Comment

The Roman orator and statesman, Cicero, contended that delivery is a sort of language of the body, since it consists of movements or gesture as well as of voice or speech. In other words, it is not just what emerges from our mouths but the conviction with which we say it.

---

improving your diction and clarity is through telling stories, especially those with several character parts where you can be creative with your voice. Storytelling is an important part of a teacher's repertoire anyway, so practising the skills necessary to do it effectively has a double benefit: giving pleasure to children and enhancing the quality of your speech.

Classroom teaching skills

Teaching skills encompass many aspects of interaction between teachers and pupils and the following list is a sample of those that all teachers must strive to acquire and cultivate. The skill of *questioning* is singularly significant and enjoys a section to itself later in the chapter.

Giving direct information and instructions to children

To ensure that children hear and understand what you are saying, it is important first to be clear in your own mind about what you want to convey, then to say it steadily and deliberately. There is a limit to the amount of information that children can hold in their minds at one time, so the use of visual supports such as a diagram or summary sheet is often useful. Allow opportunity for the children to ask you questions to clarify what you have said. Don't assume because they tell you they understand that they have actually done so. It goes without saying that there is little point in addressing the children if you do not have their full attention. Careful sequencing of points is important, especially for less able children.

Responding to children's questions about the work

Children tend to ask two types of questions about the work they are asked to do. By far the most common questions are about procedures: do we have to do this or that? It is important to remember that most children who ask for clarification do so because they are anxious to confirm what they already know, so resist the temptation to become irritable with them for not understanding. If you get a reputation for telling children off when they ask you procedural questions, less confident ones will panic and prefer to struggle on uncertainly rather than risk your wrath. The more effectively you give information and instructions in the first place, the less of a need there will be to spend time reiterating what you have said. A large sheet pinned to the wall with a list of instructions, prepared in advance, or individual cards with instructions for each table, are often advantageous as a supporting device but cannot substitute for explicit directions. The second type of explanation relates to children's lack of understanding about concepts or their inability to employ skills (such as using a dictionary). Teachers are often faced with the choice about whether to tell children or encourage them to work things out for themselves, and the quality of their judgement in these matters is often a yardstick for the effectiveness of their teaching. It will soon become obvious if the work is conceptually too demanding, and in such instances you will just have to do the best you can to support children through the present lesson and make appropriate adjustments in future ones.

Demonstrating techniques to the children

The use of demonstration as a teaching strategy is often seen as a poor substitute for hands-on experiential learning. There are, however, a number of instances when a teacher demonstrating techniques or showing the way that something is done can be a highly effective way of introducing ideas, reinforcing learning and motivating the children. Commonly, a demonstration and explanation of the correct usage and limitations of equipment or resources is often necessary in advance of a practical lesson. Demonstrations that *introduce ideas* benefit from a systematic yet lively presentation. Demonstrations for *reinforcing learning* should, where possible, be linked with the children's wider experiences, especially everyday examples from outside school. Demonstrations that need to *motivate* children should be short, sharp and spectacular. If a demonstration requires the use of specialist equipment or is potentially hazardous, then health and safety considerations are of paramount importance. For instance, sharp objects should be kept out of children's reach and secured from prying fingers. Technology also provides many opportunities for demonstration. For instance, showing variations in syntax through the use of an interactive whiteboard. Once the demonstration is completed, you have to decide how to develop the lesson. This can be done in one or more of three ways:

1   Children to use the same or a similar piece of equipment (e.g. in artwork);
2   Children write, draw or create something based on the process that they have observed (e.g. an experiment);
3   Children practise the skills associated with the demonstration (e.g. a gymnastic movement).

Keeping children on task

Time on task does not necessarily equate with the quality of work produced. Like adults, children benefit from moments of respite and the challenge for teachers is to achieve a balance between insisting that children focus on the work in hand and relaxing their grip on a situation to allow moments of relaxation. Some trainees find that they are inclined to be draconian in their insistence on the children's total application to the task for fear that the situation may get out of hand if they ease up. In keeping children on task, however, it is necessary to be aware that motivation, appropriateness of the tasks and sensible pacing of the lesson contribute to a successful outcome as much as teacher dominance. The quality of work is almost always better when children are enjoying what they are doing. A sure sign of a successful session is when the children complain when told to stop. The challenge is to maintain a firm hold without crushing the life out of the lesson, so occasional light moments (such as sharing the humour in a situation) are valuable.

Maintaining order and handling disorder

As alluded to earlier, one of the greatest worries that trainee teachers have is about class control, so much so that many books have been written that are solely dedicated to the topic (see Chapter 10). Trainee teachers have no influence over the standard of behaviour that they find on their arrival in the classes to which they are allocated but they can soon make a considerable impact, for better or for worse. Maintaining classroom order is invariably difficult for a new teacher, regardless of ability and previous successes, and involves a complex blend of factors: appropriate lesson material, effective relationships with the children, relevant activities, engaging personality and so forth. There are important principles that should underpin your actions, but even the best intentions can be eroded by a child who cannot, or will not, comply with your demands. You may wonder why the class teacher can usually exercise control so easily when you struggle to do so in similar circumstances. There are three reasons. First, he or she has spent a lot of time training the children to respond appropriately to his or her wishes and priorities. Second, the teacher and the children have learned to compromise over what is allowable. Third, the teacher is familiar with the children's idiosyncrasies and backgrounds, and instinctively knows when to insist and when to desist. It is also important for you to remember that the settled classroom environment has not been achieved without a lot of trial, error and perseverance. If you ask the teacher what the class was like at the start of the school year, you may be surprised at what you hear! The faster you become aware of the prevailing classroom norms, the easier it will be to maintain order without employing authoritarian measures.

Offering feedback with the child present

In your first few days in a new school placement, the children may use you principally as a source of information and only occasionally ask your advice about what they are doing. As you gain their trust and respect, they may invite your comments about the quality of their work. These invitations are usually signs that you are being accepted as an insider. On the whole it is better to be quietly approving of children's efforts and gently encouraging until you have established yourself in the classroom. Children can be surprisingly coy about receiving praise or suggestions from a stranger. Once this initiation period is over, your feedback should comprise three elements. First, to ascertain what the child thinks; second, to say what you think; third, to suggest the next step. If you need to reprove children or make stern comments about the quality of their work, be sensitive to their status among the rest of the class. This is particularly true when dealing with top juniors, as they will be concerned about the reaction of their peers to your remarks. It is always useful to encourage children to think about their own work and evaluate its merit, though the less able and insecure may abuse this opportunity by making casual remarks or distorted claims about its quality. In such cases, it is worth following up by asking the children concerned to give reasons for their comments and not allowing them to get away with a dismissive 'because it is' explanation. It is also worth remembering how you feel when getting feedback about your teaching from a teacher or a tutor, so err on the approving side if the child seems to have made a genuine effort.

Concluding a lesson

The introduction of a literacy hour in schools has alerted teachers to the potential usefulness of allocating the end period of a lesson to a plenary (a term that is defined as 'all members being present'). A plenary is for the purpose of summarizing the lesson's content, celebrating children's achievements and forging links with future lessons. It should never be protracted. As children work at different speeds and vary in their ability to bring their work to a halt, it is essential to give several reminders of the time remaining before the deadline. The lesson conclusion makes heavy demands upon a teacher, for even when the children have completed the task and are paying attention, it requires some quick thinking on your part to determine the most appropriate way of finishing. Although the design of the plenary should be registered on the lesson plan, there are still spontaneous decisions that need to be made about its precise composition. The best plenary allows time to review what has taken place during the lesson, point out examples of good work (indicating their special qualities), congratulate those who have tried hard and offer a glimpse of what will follow. Using the plenary to lament children's lack of effort or poor behaviour should be resisted. If a lesson is one in a closely-knit series, it is often sufficient to spend just a few moments reviewing it. The plenary is best conducted in a calm but buoyant atmosphere and it should not try to replicate the pace and ebullience of the lesson's opening phase.

Assessing work without the child present

Every school has a marking policy that teachers are asked to follow. The purpose of marking or grading work evokes a lot of controversy, as some teachers feel that it serves to highlight the divide between children of differing abilities and detracts from the effort that less able children make. Teachers also argue that assessing progress without the child being present serves little purpose. As with every strategy, it is essential to be clear about the principle underpinning the action. Sometimes a few large ticks and a hand-drawn smiling face is appropriate for a child who has tried hard, even if the end result of the work does not compare favourably with others in the group. On the other hand, you may want to offer some rapid verbal feedback, in which case a short sentence at the end of the work might be better. In the latter case, you also need to weigh up the time that individual approaches take. In Chapter 5 we saw how trainee teacher Nadia wrestled with maintaining the agreed school policy on marking and implementing her own priorities. The most common reason for marking the work *away* from the child is a lack of time to do so during the lesson. However, you may also need to compare and contrast the work of different children, grade a formal task or deliberate over the nature of children's mistakes and misconceptions as the basis for future planning. Whatever the reason, you should consider how you will go about returning the work to the children and how you will deal with the subsequent queries, explanations and follow-up that result (see also Chapter 11).

Using teaching aids

Teaching aids cover a range of resources, from the sophisticated use of Powerpoint and interactive white boards to the humble felt pen. Selection of the aid depends upon three basic factors:

◆ The availability of the resource
◆ The suitability of the resource
◆ The manageability of the resource.

Aids are intended to aid! If the benefits outweigh the disadvantages the aid serves a useful purpose. If they take up too much of your time or prove difficult to handle, then the advantages are probably insufficient to justify their use. To improve efficiency, ensure that resources are within reach and physically secure. The last thing you want is an easel collapsing in the middle of your literacy lesson!

Questioning skills

Asking questions and responding to children's answers is a particularly important teaching skill, as it opens up areas of learning that would otherwise remain concealed. Generally speaking, the younger the children, the more literally they interpret questions, so the use of rhetorical questions is rarely effective with infants and usually results in an explosion of unwanted answers. As children get older, their attitude towards teachers' questions not only depends upon their knowledge of the subject but also whether they feel confident to answer. Children will understandably prefer to say nothing if they feel that their responses will be overlooked or ignored, or if they fear being patronized. It is part of your role to encourage all children to participate and show an interest in every opinion that is genuinely expressed. As in so many teaching situations, careful listening and affirming comments are prerequisites for successful interaction.

Questions can be broadly categorized into 'closed' and 'open' types. Closed questions have a single correct answer and teachers normally ask them as a means of reminding children of previous work or assessing their knowledge and understanding. Open questions require children to speculate and evaluate alternatives, and teachers use them as a means of stirring interest, stimulating discussion and extending children's thinking. Both open and closed forms of questioning are widely used in teaching, though there is a tendency for teachers to use far more closed than open ones. Fisher (1990) suggests that there are five principal forms of question that teachers use, and the following typology of question types is based on his analysis (Fisher 1990, pp. 76–7):

1   *Questions that focus attention* (observations)
    ◆ Have you seen?
    ◆ Do you notice?
2   *Questions that force comparisons* (comparing like with like, classifying, ordering)
    ◆ How many?
    ◆ How long?
    ◆ How often?
3   *Questions that seek clarification* (making sure)
    ◆ What do you mean by . . . ?
    ◆ Can you show me . . . ?
    ◆ Can you explain further . . . ?
4   *Questions that invite enquiry* (probing deeper)
    ◆ How can we find out . . . ?
    ◆ Can you find a way to . . . ?
    ◆ What would happen if . . . ?
5   *Questions that seek reasons* (requiring explanations)
◆   Why did you say that?

- What are your reasons for . . . ?
- What is your evidence for . . . ?

Fisher also argues that teachers should strive to encourage a questioning attitude among the children and can foster this type of learning environment in four ways:

1   By encouraging children to ask questions themselves.
2   By stimulating the children's curiosity.
3   By encouraging children to bring in items of interest.
4   By using open-ended, provocative questions.

The fourth strategy is difficult for trainee teachers to employ because such questions are difficult to think of and children's responses are harder to manage. A question that requires a single correct answer is relatively straightforward to handle, as incorrect answers can be rejected and correct ones accepted. Children raise their hands when they think they know the answer and leave them down when they do not, so apart from insisting on children not calling out, the teacher has merely to choose a respondent. By contrast, the open-ended, provocative question requires children to think more widely and yields a variety of answers. The teacher not only has to select a child to give his or her response but also has to *evaluate* the quality and appropriateness of the reply. This process requires alertness, careful listening to what children say and sensitivity when trying to encourage responses from less secure children.

Another important issue concerns the length of time that teachers are prepared to wait for answers to the questions. Some children think slowly and deeply, while others are more spontaneous and willing to risk making mistakes for the pleasure of being chosen by the teacher to give the answer. Owing to the emphasis on maintaining pace in lessons, a lot of teachers are nervous about silence and giving children time to consider their replies. However, allowing children to cogitate for longer improves the quality of their answers, whereas peppering questions at them in the expectation of immediate responses tends to lead to superficiality. It is, therefore, essential to be clear in your mind as to the *purpose* that the questions are serving and to adjust the type of questioning accordingly.

Children's self-confidence is another factor that must be taken into account during question-and-answer sessions. Whereas timid children keep their hands firmly in their laps, bolder children are constantly throwing up their arms and volunteering an answer. To avoid marginalizing the less able and less confident children, a number of unusual strategies can occasionally be employed:

- Offer an either/or pair of answers and ask children to wink at you with one eye if they agree with the first and both eyes if they agree with the second
- Ask a question but only allow responses from a defined group of children

◆ Ask a question, give the children thirty seconds to whisper what they think in their neighbour's ear, reveal the answer, then ask them to raise their hands if their neighbours were correct.

As Kerry (1998) argues, the classroom environment has to be conducive to questioning, where children feel secure and not intimidated by the prospect of making a mistake. Kerry insists that the children must be convinced that the aim is to share knowledge and ideas within a supportive framework where each serious comment is valued. The creation of a learning environment in which children are encouraged to respond to open questions and teachers display a genuine interest in their answers is therefore essential. Harlen (2000) claims that this supportive style of teaching motivates children to answer questions without fear attached to being wrong. In this way, misunderstandings can be used constructively as a basis for formative assessment and adjusting the way that future lessons are presented.

Teaching principle

Teachers should avoid asking questions that necessitate children reading their minds. Children who say little may be thinking much.

Strategies to promote learning

To respond more effectively to children involves a careful consideration of their capability, attitude and potential, and adjusting your teaching approach accordingly. Regardless of their particular learning needs, however, there are at least six techniques that can be employed in achieving the highest standards when working with all types of children:

Take account of the child's physical and emotional needs

Children's learning will suffer if they are fidgety, unhappy or feeling vulnerable. It is part of the teacher's job to ensure that children are seated comfortably, treated considerately and made to feel that they are significant. Children who are physically satisfied and emotionally at ease are more likely to achieve their academic potential than those who are not.

Relate past experiences to current ones

It is always worth reminding children of what they have already achieved, experienced and discovered before launching into a new lesson. Children do not compartmentalize knowledge in the way that adults tend to do, so the more that you can alert them to the continuity of their learning, the more that the things they are presently doing will seem relevant.

Reflect out loud on what the children are doing

Effective teachers not only monitor what children do, but also put their thoughts into words. For instance:

- *Well done to underline your heading, Roxanne*
- *I like the way that you have shown every stage of your working, Imogene*
- *Ijaaz, that's very kind of you to share your eraser with Jack*
- *Ocean, I'm so pleased that you are remembering your finger spacing.*

Public comment on children's work and progress not only affirms for the child your satisfaction, but also transmits important messages to others about the standards that you are expecting from them.

Demonstrate and suggest new possibilities

In addition to reflecting out loud, it is useful as part of the formative process to suggest new ways of working and direction. In general, it is helpful to combine your reflective comments with some practical suggestions. Thus, using the above examples:

- Well done to underline your heading, Roxanne. I wonder if it would be better to use a coloured pencil rather than a pen, to stop the ink smudging.
- I like the way that you have shown every stage of your working, Imogene. Do you think that it would be better to keep all the working on the right hand side of the page so that it doesn't get mixed up with the rest of the sum?
- Ijaaz, that's very kind of you to share your eraser with Donald. Perhaps if the table rubber were always returned to the box there would be no need for Donald to keep asking you for yours.
- Ocean, I'm so pleased that you are remembering your finger spacing! Let's see if you can keep your letters about the same size and straight across the page when you write the next line.

There will be some occasions when you will need to insist on children conforming or following set procedures and other times (such as the above examples) when it is appropriate to offer them some choice in the matter and thereby encourage them to take responsibility for their own learning. Of course, you must accept that if you offer them a choice, your advice may not be heeded, so if your invitation is, in reality, a command, make this clear to the child.

Give the children time and space to explore their interests

Flexibility to follow up children's spontaneous interests is limited in school, as most of the curriculum is closely regulated and does not leave much room for deviating from the main subject content. Trainee teachers are normally advised to adhere closely to the lesson plan and stated learning objectives. However, there are occasions when children ask questions that did not occur to you or offer insights that surprise you. It is unwise to allow yourself to become distracted by casual and random comments but it makes good educational sense to 'scratch where it itches' and seek ways to encourage children who are hungry for particular knowledge or want to share and explore ideas. It may be possible to examine some of these issues during the plenary phase of the lesson or, subsequently, during 'circle-time'. Where possible, it is useful to have a small notebook handy so that you can scribble a reminder for yourself.

Encourage children to think for themselves

Well-intentioned teachers tend to guard the curriculum closely and may fail to allow children sufficient opportunities to try things out, make mistakes and engage deeply with learning. It is important to make it clear when the children have to conform to the task that is set before them and when they have liberty to adjust and modify things. In all circumstances it pays to stimulate children's interest by asking speculative questions and encouraging them to raise ones of their own. The start of such questions might begin with phrases such as:

◆ Imagine if we . . . ?
◆ Suppose that we took . . . ?
◆ What if we could not . . . ?
◆ Can you think of different ways . . . ?
◆ Is it possible to . . . ?
◆ Did you notice how . . . ?

The best teachers are always looking for ways to help children make connections with other areas of knowledge, alerting them to interesting details and sharpening their sense of awe and wonder.

Celebrate achievement

The amount of work displayed in school has diminished in recent years owing to other priorities. Putting up and servicing a display is time-consuming, so some teachers make use of a classroom assistant or parent. Others find shortcuts to reduce the time spent. For instance:

◆ Putting an attractive semi-permanent 'frame' in place around the perimeter of the display board
◆ Using good quality backing material that does not require constant replacement
◆ Using small pins with rounded heads for fixing that are easy to pull out.

Displays can easily be enhanced by:

◆ Draping some attractive material from a top corner and around the base of the board
◆ Printing labels using computer technology
◆ Creating 3D effects by pinning only two diagonal corners of a sheet of paper such that it stands away from the wall
◆ Stapling a few shallow boxes on to the board and attaching display items to them so that they stand proud of the wall.

Some displays are for the purpose of celebrating children's achievements, in which case the selection should be done with great care, especially in respect of which items are chosen. Sometimes a compromise involves displaying a small sample of work and placing the remainder in a 'class book' made by stapling together sheets of thin card and pasting an attractive cover page on the front. Children should be encouraged to produce their own nametags for their work, either using bold pens, material or computer-generated labels. Other displays are intended to stimulate interest, whet children's appetites for learning and create a focal point for conversation. They may consist of a poster, some interesting objects and a few boldly written questions. It is possible to be more versatile with displays if a small table is placed at the foot of the vertical board for three-dimensional objects and question cards. All displays should be interactive in the sense that they cause children to think, feel and react. Some displays, especially those that are science-based, encourage children to interact through physically responding: touching, smelling, testing (though be aware of potential hazards). However, such displays invariably become untidy and require a lot of supervising. Be careful, too, that work is not out of date, as young children in particular make such rapid progress over the period of a term that their writing and drawing can improve markedly over that time. A visitor examining an old display, especially a parent, may thereby gain a false impression of a child's ability and the standard of work in the class.

Strategies for working with groups

It is common in most primary classrooms to divide children into groups for at least part of each lesson to work co-operatively or collaboratively on tasks or activities. During your first week or two in a new placement school, it is usual to assist with groups of children whose work has been planned and organized by the class teacher and given responsibility for monitoring the work of a single group. This apparently straightforward task is challenging because:

◆ You have no ownership of the lesson plans
◆ You do not know much about their previous experience or knowledge
◆ Having close encounters with children is tiring and intensive.

Dealing with just four or five children sounds idyllic but can be quite strenuous for three reasons. First, the interaction is at close quarters, which means that it is difficult to stand back owing to some children's insatiable appetite for asking questions and requesting help. Second, you feel obliged to keep the children on task at all times, which is a pressure that some children find hard to accommodate. Children (and trainees) who struggle to concentrate for long periods of time and need moments of respite from the demands of the work find the intensity of the exchanges too much to handle and may become restless. Third, the temptation is to be highly prescriptive and authoritarian about what the children do and how they go about it. This approach tends to increase the level of the children's compliance but also increases the likelihood that you will get exhausted owing to the intensity of the occasion. Ideally, your involvement with a single group should reflect the way that you would behave with the whole class (see below). That is, to explain the purpose of the session, organize resources, give children sufficient information about the task, offer help and support where necessary as they do the activity, and make sure that they have opportunity to think, discuss and make suggestions. It is also important to bear in mind that if the children finish sooner than expected, they may not be able to disperse and gain access to other resources owing to other nearby groups still being quietly occupied. It always pays to have a straightforward holding activity available, such as a picture to draw, a cloze passage for filling in missing words or a word search. One way and another you should avoid the embarrassing situation where you are desperately trying to contain a group of restless, inactive children.

As you become more confident and experienced, you will take more responsibility for planning lessons and supervising several groups or the whole class, making use of a teaching assistant, parent or the class teacher to supervise a group or individuals. Taking responsibility for several groups of children places more demands on you:

1   You have to take account of the varying needs of children in different groups.
2   You have to clarify that the assistants know their roles.

3   You need to adopt a 'crow's nest' mentality as you monitor conditions throughout the room.

Whether you are supervising one or several groups, it is important to ensure that:

◆ The children are suitably seated (with adequate light and space)
◆ The children have easy access to adequate resources
◆ Each child is given an appropriate amount of support and encouragement
◆ Every child has opportunity to be involved in the group task
◆ The noise is at a suitable level.

If you have responsibility for several groups or all the children in the classroom, the following factors need to be carefully considered:

Be aware of what is happening across the rest of the class

It is all too easy to become immersed in your interaction with a few children and forget to look up, scan the room, check that the children are on-task and offer a few words of encouragement or direction.

Give each group a fair share of your time

If you are the supporting adult for a single group then you will, of necessity, give them your full attention for much of the time. On other occasions, make sure that you spread yourself evenly around the room and avoid spending too much time with anxious or fussy children.

Draw the threads of the lesson together carefully

The more diverse the range of activities, the longer it takes to draw matters to a close, summarize what has been happening and celebrate successes. You need to be particularly active and vigilant when resources are being returned, tables cleared and work handed in. It pays to be brisk and businesslike with your instructions and behaviour management.

It is also important to be aware of whether or not you intend a group of children to work individually, co-operatively or collaboratively. Many teachers view group work as a means of enhancing children's social skills or giving them opportunity to discuss issues. As important as these aims are, they should not be confused with collaborative work. If you intend that the task should involve each child in a combined effort to achieve a solution, this requires a different form of organization and management from one in which the children merely sit together, doing the same task. Truly collaborative tasks normally involve an element of problem-solving and necessitate that each member of the group plays an active role. If you have responsibility for several groups of children, each group carrying out collaborative work, then allow time at the end of the session or sessions for feedback and sharing. Collaboration almost invariably extends the time required for a solution, but the quality of the end product is normally far higher than when each child tackles the problem individually.

Whole class teaching strategies

Working with a large number of children requires thorough organization, voice clarity, strong body language and good interactive skills. The larger the space in which you are working and the more dispersed the children around the room, the slower and more deliberate your speech should be. Dean (1999) describes the importance of the interaction between teachers and children, and supports the use of more whole class teaching as an opportunity to enhance learning.

> Learning and achievement are strongly linked to the amount of interaction there is between teacher and child. Where a great deal of work is individual, there is only a limited amount of time a teacher can spend with each child, and research suggests that this interaction is very brief and not at a very high or demanding level. More interaction between teacher and children occurs in whole class activity, and this is why the national projects in both literacy and numeracy suggest that there should be a considerable amount of work daily where the teacher works with the whole class.
>
> (Dean 1999, p. 60)

Teaching skills that enhance your effectiveness include:

◆ Talking *to* the children, not *at* them
◆ Directing your speech such that all the children can hear
◆ Varying your tone, volume and voice inflection to keep children alert and attentive
◆ Using eye contact and gestures to exercise control.

Working with large numbers of children also needs to take close account of organizational and management issues (see Chapter 9) and consider:

◆ The amount of noise generated by activities
◆ The number of individual queries raised about what to do and how to do it
◆ The demands of monitoring progress during the lesson
◆ The evaluation and marking of work after the lesson
◆ The need for an orderly dismissal.

One of the most striking contrasts between teaching a group of four and a class of thirty-four is rooted in the number of interactions between teacher and children. Although it is important to treat every child as significant, whether in a small or large scale setting, it is not sensible to try to view a whole class session merely as a magnified version of the small group session. Nevertheless, the principles of effective teaching are the same regardless of group size: careful preparation and planning, clear learning objectives, appropriate resources, careful explanations, tasks that match children's capabilities, decisiveness and sound discipline.

Whole class responsibility comes in many forms and presents an exciting challenge for every trainee. It may involve telling a story, setting a test, organizing groups that are supervised by assistants or monitoring several different activities on your own. In their imagination, some trainees wonder if they can cope with thirty lively children and have visions of uncontrollable hordes running wild! It is important to recognize that the ability to manage the whole class well is the *ultimate* aim of teaching experience and to do so effectively will be the pinnacle of success. All whole class teaching necessitates careful organization, the use of a clear voice when addressing the children, close monitoring of what is happening in the room both in terms of the work and behaviour and learning to do many things simultaneously. For instance, you have to talk to the children using appropriate vocabulary, maintain their attention, write on the board, ask pertinent questions, offer informed comment, incorporate children's responses, explain the activities and emphasize your expectations. When the children are working on activities, you have to monitor their progress, answer questions, spend time with individuals, keep a close eye on the time, assess the quality of work, encourage and praise good effort, exhort reluctant learners to apply themselves, draw the lesson to a firm conclusion, collect and store work, and leave the room tidy. It is little wonder that many trainees struggle to handle the range of demands and need a lot of practice, guidance and support while they learn to manage the situation.

There are three broad 'direct teaching' approaches that teachers commonly use when addressing the whole class: direct transmission, participative and interactive teaching. Each demands the employment of particular skills:

Direct transmission teaching (DTT)

This is the most straightforward in that the teacher initiates and sustains the momentum of the talk. Pupils are not expected to respond verbally other than to confirm that they understand. DTT is characterized by the following:

◆ The teacher provides information and pupils receive it
◆ Children do not offer opinion or comment
◆ There is an absence of question-and-answer technique
◆ Visual aids and the board are frequently used
◆ The teacher uses an imaginative delivery style to maintain interest.

It is important to remember that DTT is a form of *teaching*. It should not be confused with times when you make announcements or give directions. DTT should be used sparingly, as children have to sit still and may become restless if left inactive for too long or expected to absorb too much knowledge in a short time. It is frequently necessary to repeat or rehearse facts or to ask the children to tell you what you have just told them.

Participative teaching (PT)

This is similar to DTT but invites children to make responses at appropriate times as determined by the teacher. PT is probably the most commonly used form of whole-class teaching and requires careful structuring, preparation of information and predetermined questions. PT is characterized by the following:

◆ The teacher controls the situation closely
◆ Pupils respond to the teacher's questions when invited
◆ Visual aids are occasionally used
◆ Questions include both *direct* types (to test knowledge) and *speculative* (to get children thinking)
◆ The teacher tries to involve all the children, not merely the confident ones
◆ Children normally go on to complete tasks and activities set by the teacher.

Thus, PT invites pupil participation in a controlled setting, managed closely by the teacher. In contrast to DTT, however, children take a more active part in the lesson.

Interactive teaching (INT)

This method encourages participation from the children and requires a considerable amount of teaching skill. The teacher's role is equivalent to being an orchestra conductor, so it is essential to make sure you are confident and in control before attempting it. During INT, children can ask questions, contribute ideas and initiate fresh ways of approaching problems or issues. The teacher still retains overall control but encourages a free flow of contributions as far as possible, while summarizing and reviewing the learning that is taking place. INT is often used:

◆ To discuss issues and find solutions
◆ To make class decisions
◆ To encourage a large number of children to contribute
◆ To explore complex problems.

Interactive teaching is one of the hardest skills to master, not least because some children may be inclined to call out, interrupt, refuse to participate or not take things seriously. The following points will help to improve your skill in this sphere of teaching:

1   Practise the session in your mind beforehand and anticipate how you will deal with children who behave inappropriately.
2   Clarify with the children the rules that govern answering questions and enforce them.
3   Maintain good eye contact and a lively manner throughout.
4   Keep the lesson moving purposefully but avoid a sense of rush.
5   Speak naturally but forcefully.
6   Distinguish between deliberately silly comments that children make and inoffensive ones.
7   Give affirmative approval for good responses.
8   Allow a few brief pauses when children sit quietly and/or close their eyes to order their thoughts.
9   Ensure that all the children have heard the responses from others by repeating them. For instance: 'Yes, that's right Julie, well done! Julie has reminded us that we can add 98 to a number by adding 100 and subtracting two at the end. It's much easier that way. Can anyone give us another example?'

It is essential that INT be conducted in a calm atmosphere, where the rules of engagement are clear to everyone. For instance, there has to be agreement about not calling out or mocking other children's contributions. Older children can become quite animated on occasions and need a firm hand. Children who attempt to dominate proceedings may have to be curtailed by imposing a time limit or number of occasions when any one person can speak.

Comment

The National Numeracy Strategy (DfEE 1999) encourages teachers to use their professional judgement in determining the activities, timing and organization of each part of the lesson, but accepts that some lessons will involve more direct, whole-class teaching than others.

> In the main part of the lesson, in particular, there is scope for considerable variety and creativity, with a different mix of work with the whole class, groups, pairs and individuals on different days, although each lesson should include direct teaching and interaction with the pupils, and activities or exercises that pupils do.
>
> (DfEE 1999, p. 15)

Teaching principle

Regardless of class size, it is the individual learning experience of each child that matters.

A means to an end

Teaching skills are not fragmented, mechanical portions of a teacher's repertoire that can be rehearsed and fused effortlessly into effective practice, nor do they emerge spontaneously through regular contact with children in the classroom. Skilful teachers learn to use questioning, explaining, monitoring and evaluating progress as a means of enhancing children's learning. They refine these individual skills, not as an end in themselves, but as tools to promote children's creativity and intelligent application to the work. As Wragg (1993, p. 190) reminds us:

> It requires immense professional skill to create, or elicit from pupils, tasks which are not only appropriate to the age, intelligence and previous experience of the child and the field being studied, but which extend the imagination and stimulate thought and action.

This is the challenge for every aspiring teacher.

In this chapter the basic skills and strategies commonly used by teachers have been outlined. Chapter 9 now explores what is meant by the difficult concept of effective teaching.

Further reading

Merry, R. (1998) *Successful Teaching, Successful Learning*, Buckingham: Open University Press.

Wyse, D. (2002) *Becoming a Primary School Teacher*, London: RoutledgeFalmer.

Effective teaching

The need for effectiveness has underpinned a lot of government policy about teaching over the past few decades, and provided the climate for an evidence-based profession in which primary teachers are required to demonstrate that they have raised standards, particularly in literacy and numeracy. Promotion and salary increases now depend to a large extent upon teachers' ability to prove that they have been instrumental in directly enhancing children's measurable progress. Although many practitioners are uncomfortable with the imposition of these quantitative measures, they generally accept the situation and do their best to conform. For schools, too, there is a need to show that overall standards are improving year upon year. To be deemed effective, therefore, every teacher has to spend a considerable amount of time monitoring and assessing children to provide verifiable measures of attainment. This is not the whole story, however.

Engaging with young minds

The essence of effective teaching lies in an ability to understand how children think and learn. All effective teachers must be keen observers of pupils as the children undertake classroom activities, respond to questions, interact with their peers, relate to adults, persevere with tasks, follow procedures, collaborate and co-operate, modify their behaviour and react to the unexpected. Teachers have the fascinating task of noting each child's responses and aptitude in these areas and adjusting their teaching approaches accordingly. Although final work outcomes give a lot of information about children's ability, it is also necessary to take note of their enthusiasm, application to task, willingness to attempt something new and assist others to do the same. Consequently, knowing *about* a child is not the same as *knowing* the child, and teachers need to utilize that knowledge to advantage in planning lessons and teaching. Test results and grades offer important insights into a child's knowledge and understanding, but they only give a snapshot in time and under specific conditions. As a teacher, the most valuable qualities that you can offer to the children in your class consist in being available to them when they need you, explaining things carefully and allowing them space and time to gain knowledge and grasp concepts.

In terms of children's academic learning, teachers must use any records of past achievement that are available and spend time discussing the progress of individuals with the previous teacher. It is also useful to discover something of children's background and factors that might intrude upon their learning and attitude to school, though it is unwise to jump to conclusions on the basis of the information you receive. For instance, children from rough and ready home situations must not be written off as inevitable failures; children arriving from overseas with limited English must not be treated as if they were unintelligent. Similarly, not all well-groomed children are helpful and co-operative; not every cultivated child excels as a member of a group, and so on. Nevertheless, background knowledge can help you to interpret and explain the vagaries in children's behaviour and academic performance and respond more effectively to their learning and social needs.

A further important aspect of the teacher's role is to evaluate each child's *potential* for learning, bearing in mind that a child may learn all kinds of things that cannot be identified through formal assessments. For instance, a low achiever may prove to be articulate, aware of world events, artistically creative, adaptable and reliable. It is surprising how children who struggle (say) with conventional mathematics and structured forms of writing know about a favourite hobby or pastime, and how they can employ irregular yet effective techniques to solve problems. Some children, who appear to be unenthusiastic about learning and scornful of your attempts to motivate them with the regular curriculum, spring into life when they are allowed to share their interests with you and the class. While you will always want to help children to achieve success in measurable components of the curriculum, part of your skill as a teacher is to recognize, encourage and celebrate other expressions of a child's capability.

Comment

Packard and Race (2000) observe that strong relationships between the teacher and child lie at the heart of effective teaching.

> Children need to feel safe in your care. If you don't have their trust, getting them to make progress in your class is going to be an uphill struggle. It's not a question of wrapping them up in cotton wool, however. Ideally, you would want every child to feel comfortable in the classroom from day one, but building this relationship can take time with some children.
>
> (Packard and Race 2000, p. 124)

Effective teachers have a responsibility to encourage children to become independent and self-motivated learners. Although children, and younger children in particular, often need close guidance, this is not to imply that they should be suffocated by well-intentioned adults who end up doing most of the thinking for them. As you get to know the children in the class better, you will be able to achieve a balance between the situation where they become too reliant on your support and help, and that of them being expected to cope with insufficient direction and advice. Striking this particular balance is one of many challenges facing you as a teacher. It is, perhaps, too much to expect children to be always highly motivated and enthusiastic about learning, but releasing them into a greater measure of independence is a big step towards achieving that goal.

Born or bred?

Some people appear to have a natural way with children and fit easily into the classroom environment. Others struggle to find their feet and may never seem wholly at ease during the training period yet blossom once they have their own classes. The majority of people possess some natural abilities and have to work hard to improve their weaker areas. One way and another, whether a person is a 'born teacher' or not, every trainee should strive to regularly evaluate his or her progress and tackle resolutely the areas that require attention. Regardless of whether you consider yourself to be a natural teacher, the quality of your lesson preparation, classroom management and ability to relate to children is crucial to teaching success. If you do not consider yourself to possess a lot of natural ability, don't fall into the trap of believing that you are somehow inadequate or will never compete with your more illustrious peers. Remember the story of the hare and the tortoise!

Teaching effectiveness is difficult to measure and for the trainee teacher is often a question of how you perceive things rather than the way they really are. In fact,

---

Comment

Wilson and Cameron (1996) traced how trainee teachers moved from a *teacher-centred* perspective to a *pupil-centred* view of instruction, from a *personal* to a *professional* view of relationships with pupils and from a *controlling* to a *management* approach in securing a positive classroom climate. It is typical over time for trainees to see teaching increasingly from the child's perspective, become less emotionally affected by classroom encounters and see discipline more in terms of good management and relevant teaching than adopting strategies for exercising rigid control.

although your progress as a teacher is likely to be unpredictable, enigmatic and inconsistent, you are probably doing much better than you realize. Experienced teachers will tell you that feelings about how well the lesson went are strongly influenced by the children's behaviour and your inner sense of well-being. The co-operative and orderly class that produces neat and careful work may or may not have learnt more than an unco-operative class with its casual attitude. Trainee teachers who are prepared to persevere, ask questions, think deeply about their work and seek advice, always do better in the long run than those who rely on easy solutions and simplistic theories.

The route to improvement

Progress as a teacher involves regular study to ensure that you are well informed and knowledgeable about subjects and teaching strategies. In addition to good communication skills, you will need to develop a determination to complete tasks efficiently and an awareness of research findings that offer fresh insights into classroom and school life. You will also want to forge strong links with more experienced colleagues who can guide and direct you. Regrettably, a small minority of trainees are unwilling to learn from their mistakes and adopt an attitude of 'let me get on with it and leave me alone'. Their behaviour is perceived by staff in school as disdain rather than self-sufficiency and serves to alienate them from teachers and tutors. If a trainee is not willing to learn as well as teach, it eventually results in stale and lifeless classroom practice.

The most effective trainee teachers are committed to doing their best, learning from others, thinking carefully about their classroom practice, mastering time management and providing a positive role model to the children. It is also helpful if they have a sunny disposition, excellent subject knowledge, a thoughtful attitude and a propensity for hard work. It's quite a challenge! However, the situation is not straightforward. For instance, it is obviously an advantage to have good subject knowledge when you are trying to teach, but if it is weak it can be rectified by some serious study. On the other hand, a feeble personality is less easily changed. Again, poor time management can be improved by becoming more systematic and taking advice from colleagues but a lack of commitment to the job is difficult to remedy and is extremely annoying to the host teachers. Having a pleasant disposition gives a distinct advantage over those who tend to be gloomy but without having strong teaching skills your cheery manner may be viewed by tutors as a sign of superficiality: all froth and no substance.

One way in which you can improve your chances of doing well in teaching is to develop good, effective classroom practices early on in your training so that you have a firm foundation on which to build. If you allow poor habits to take root (e.g. shouting at children, speaking too quickly, highlighting children's weaknesses, failing

| Hard working |
| Well informed about the subject |
| Committed to doing their best |
| Thoughtful about classroom practice |
| Willing to learn from others |
| Positive role models for pupils |
| Engaging personality |

Figure 9.1 *Characteristics of effective trainee teachers*

to explain what you expect children to do) they are hard to dislodge and can hinder your effectiveness in the long as well as the short term (see Figure 9.1).

Perseverance is an attribute enjoyed by all successful teachers. Some trainee teachers begin in a trail of glory and end up crawling over the finishing line. Others start slowly and end strongly. The majority takes a bumpy path that has its ups and downs but ultimately leads them, somewhat battered and bruised, to the summit. Only a very small number of trainees become competent teachers in a smooth, unhindered way that continues into their first teaching posts. It is natural for you to compare and contrast your progress with that of fellow trainees, but comparisons are difficult due to the many variations that typify any cohort. The person you so admire, who seems to have everything under control and is competent at everything, may secretly have the same opinion of you!

Teaching principle

Getting better at teaching is like hill climbing: just when you think you've reached the summit, another peak appears!

Some teachers have a lot of charisma and project their personalities strongly in the classroom but may be less confident about their subject knowledge. Other teachers are well versed in what they have to teach but struggle when employing classroom management and teaching skills. However, without having the necessary subject knowledge *and* skills, you will never prosper in teaching, regardless of how enthusiastic you are about doing the job. Some teachers ('Performers') sparkle in front of the children but owing to their poor organization or weak subject knowledge, fail to carry through their good intentions. Other teachers ('Pedants') are knowledgeable about the subject and the curriculum but lack the creativity to motivate children to learn. The best teachers ('Inspirers') are able to combine all the qualities, and this should be your aim, too (see Figure 9.2).

The relationship between teaching and learning is complex. A teacher can be technically competent yet fail to make a significant impact upon the children. Another teacher can have a profound effect on children's learning over a few lessons but fail to maintain the momentum in the longer term. Children may improve their formal test scores yet make little progress in respect of their love for learning and enthusiasm for gaining knowledge. The very best teachers have the ability to help children develop a love for learning *and* do well in their tests.

Type of teacher	Characteristics	Impact on children	Effect on children's learning
Performer	Strong presentational skills Weaker subject knowledge	Inspiring but little depth in the teaching	Children enjoy school but tend to underachieve
Pedant	Weak presentational skills Strong subject knowledge	Profound insights but little ability to motivate	Predictable, bland and unspectacular
Inspirer	Strong presentational skills Strong subject knowledge	Positive impact on children's motivation and understanding	Children make optimum progress

Figure 9.2 *Three types of teacher*

Comment

Calderhead and Shorrock (1997) make the important point that teaching is not only concerned with the technical competence involved in planning and presenting lessons. The best teachers are constantly thinking about the purpose of education and endeavouring to translate this understanding into meaningful and relevant experiences for the children.

> Obviously, learning to teach does involve the acquisition of certain knowledge and skills that are essential to adequate classroom performance. It is also the case, however, that learning to teach involves being able to reason about one's own actions, being able to justify particular strategies, understanding the subject matter, children and their ways of learning, and having a conception of the purposes of education and the ways in which schools operate in order to promote education.
>
> (Calderhead and Shorrock 1997, p. 192)

Organization and management

Lesson organization and management is at the heart of successful teaching. Organization is most significant *before* the lesson begins, and in clearing up at the end, though some minor adjustments to the organization are frequently required as the session unfolds. Management is essentially dealing with what takes place *during* the lesson. In practice, organizing and managing are interrelated, as good organization facilitates effective management. Issues concerning organization and management will form the basis for most discussions with the class teacher and mentor and shape your ideas for when you have responsibility for your own classroom during your NQT induction year (see Chapter 13). In its simplest terms, to *organize* entails providing a structure for what is taking place during a lesson. It has two broad, though interrelated, strands:

- ◆ General classroom organization
- ◆ Lesson organization.

General classroom organization

This form of organization underpins the daily operation of the classroom, including the arrangements of tables and chairs, procedures for pupils entering and leaving the room, storage of consumables and equipment, and other ongoing resource issues. The class teacher will already have established a general system to which you must adhere, so your initial task is to help maintain the physical orderliness of the room and basic procedures, taking careful account of the teacher's preferences and priorities. Later in the placement, the teacher may allow you to modify some aspects of the general organization but otherwise you have to work within the existing framework.

Lesson organization

This will vary according to the particular lesson requirements and from session to session. For example, an investigative science lesson will involve a different form of organization from one on handwriting. The science lesson will almost invariably involve group activities, whereas the handwriting will be individually based. As noted in Chapter 7, lesson organization is a key consideration in lesson planning. A well-organized lesson optimizes your chances of teaching effectively, both in respect of successfully managing the lesson and the confidence it gives you in knowing that everything is under control. Organizing efficiently will not only streamline your lessons but also provide you with more authority as you deal with the children. To enhance the chances of a lesson running successfully, it is especially important to ensure that resources (both physical and human) are in place, and procedures understood by everyone before the lesson begins. To assist this process, the following simple but important considerations facilitate the smooth running of the session:

Preparing visual aids

As visual aids need to be seen by every child, factors such as clarity and size of print, ease of handling, and manageability have to be taken into account when selecting, producing and using them. The management of the lesson is greatly enhanced if the aids are within comfortable reach.

Checking that basic resources are fit for use

It is frustrating and unsettling to have children complain during the lesson about blunt pencils, the lack of sharpeners and erasers, dried-up felt pens and so forth, so it is always worth checking them carefully beforehand or asking an assistant to do so.

Checking that equipment is working

If equipment is needed for the lesson, particularly in PE or a practical activity, it is potentially disrupting if it proves unserviceable. A few moments spent checking the items earlier in the day or the night before is amply rewarded by avoiding spending precious time sorting out the problem.

Providing worksheets

A worksheet is only as useful as its appropriateness to the needs of the children and the learning objectives. It is not intended to be a means of keeping children quiet while teachers attend to more pressing matters. On the other hand, a sufficient number of well-designed sheets can be of considerable benefit to a busy teacher, especially when dealing with a large number of children. The golden rule is to ensure that they are not overloaded with words and facts. If sheets are published ones, you may need to modify them for your group of children, as they are not necessarily appropriate as they stand.

Deciding how children will be grouped

If children have to be split into pairs or groups, it is normally better to sort things out in advance of the lesson rather than during it. Although in sessions such as team games (especially with older children) the choosing of team members can form part of the fun and excitement, it can also be a source of conflict. You have to decide whether to exert your authority over selections or allow the children to gain experience in dealing with this type of social situation.

Ensuring that classroom assistants are properly informed

Teachers can improve the morale and satisfaction of general assistants and learning support assistants by ensuring that they are informed about their involvement, particularly if there is going to be a deviation from the normal routine. While most lessons follow a predictable routine, the introduction of sudden, unannounced changes is unfair to support staff and the source of considerable angst.

Comment

Pinder (1987) captures the essence of how poor organization not only damages the lesson but also has the potential to annoy other staff:

> Classrooms have to be carefully organized so that everything the children will need to complete their tasks is available to them. While the odd piece of equipment could be borrowed from another class, colleagues would not be very happy to have a constant stream of children arriving at intervals because their class teacher had not been able to organize them earlier. The inability to organize adequately is probably the greatest cause of failure among young teachers. Luckily, most learn this fairly quickly.

> (Pinder 1987, p. 46)

Involving children

Ainscow and Tweddle (1988, p. 62) point out that 'classroom arrangements that facilitate greater pupil involvement can be a useful means of releasing the teacher to carry out more significant duties'. Where possible, it is helpful to promote pupil involvement in organizing the classroom. Many children love being monitors and helping the teacher, and everyone should be encouraged to make a contribution to the learning enterprise. The creation of a supportive and reliable set of children can be an immense help in maintaining daily routines and allowing the main job of learning to take place unhindered by trivial tasks.

Management

The word *management* is based on the root 'manage', which has several shades of meaning, such as being in charge of an enterprise, succeeding in carrying something through to completion and effectively controlling a situation. Successful lesson management therefore involves:

- Using lesson plans effectively
- Promoting learning and maintaining discipline
- Monitoring the direction of the lesson and children's progress to a satisfactory conclusion.

Lesson management needs to be *efficient* in the sense that things are well run and *effective* in that it has the desired impact on children's learning. A lesson might be efficient in as much as it is thoroughly planned and painstakingly prepared, yet ineffective owing to a variety of other factors, such as uninspiring presentation or unsuitable activities. It is not often that an inefficient lesson proves effective. Difficulties with lesson management occur because of weak organization, poor resources, unsuitable content, confusing explanations, vague expectations, ill-considered procedures, unhelpful responses to children's queries, bad timing, or a combination of these factors. However, there are particular moments when management is more likely to break down and these require close attention:

- When children are settling . . . so bring them to order quickly and get the lesson underway with minimum delay
- Changing from one activity to another . . . so be precise in explaining what has to happen and your expectations
- When resources are inadequate or badly located . . . so ensure that they are in proper order and sufficient in number
- When pupils are confused about what to do . . . so explain things thoroughly to save them having to ask you endless questions of clarification

◆ When you are tied up for too long with specific children . . . so don't bury yourself for too long in one corner or ignore what is happening around you

◆ When they are leaving the room for playtime . . . so control their exit, preferably standing at or near the door while they leave.

Ayers and Gray (1998) recommend that teachers need to actively teach pupils how to follow appropriate directions by the use of positive recognition, such as mentally noting which children are doing what they have been told, identifying this publicly and restating the direction as a reminder to the others. In particular, they suggest that teachers should always look for opportunities to praise children who are normally non-conformists. The average primary school pupil has to cope with hundreds of non-academic and academic routines in an average school week. Little wonder that they, and trainee teachers, sometimes get confused!

Time management

The way that you manage your time and order priorities will have a major influence on the success of your school placement. Effective time management involves keeping abreast of events and being aware of deadlines. It also requires that tasks are dealt with promptly, paperwork is kept up to date and meetings with host teachers and tutors are used effectively. It helps to plan your schedule with reference to *fixed* times (conforming to a timetable) and *flexible* times where there is a degree of choice. The predictable and regular events that characterize the *fixed* times mean that tasks and activities associated with them can be pre-planned. Examples of fixed times are the start and end of the school day, the location of particular lessons and break times. Sometimes, however, even so-called fixed times vary. For example, assemblies are prolonged, break times are extended, hall sessions are cancelled at the last moment, and the regular timetable is suspended owing (say) to the visit of a theatre company or a sports' day. Your host teachers will expect you to grin and bear the situation just as they have to, even on the occasions when you are the last one to be informed about the alterations.

Many aspects of a teacher's working day are unpredictable and need to be reacted to rather than planned in advance. On such occasions your ability to make rapid decisions and cope with irregular amounts of time has a considerable impact upon your working life and effectiveness. While fixed times usually require conforming to set arrangements, the flexible times require you to make decisions about priorities. For instance, whether you:

◆ Spend time in the playground after school making informal contact with parents or talk to the teacher next door about a shared concern

◆ Write up your diary or visit the staff room and chat informally

- Help with an extra-curricular activity or mark books
- Assist a colleague with bus duty or put up a display
- Prepare your own resources for a literacy lesson or spend time searching web sites for them, and so forth.

To help you make wise choices it is useful to make a determined effort to categorize the tasks under one of the following four headings:

1 Tasks that are NOT URGENT and UNIMPORTANT
2 Tasks that are URGENT but UNIMPORTANT
3 Tasks that are URGENT and IMPORTANT
4 Tasks that are NOT URGENT but IMPORTANT.

As you do so, consider the following points:

1 Don't waste time on things that are neither urgent nor important, even if they interest you. For example, you may enjoy spending hours pondering different ways in which the children might be grouped for various activities, but unless there is a crisis situation, such tasks do not warrant priority status.
2 Urgent tasks that are relatively unimportant should be dealt with as quickly as possible without worrying about detail. Don't try to be a perfectionist. For example, you may suddenly remember that you need to prepare a visual aid for the next day. It is far better to spend a few minutes making something adequate by using a bold pen and large sheet of paper, than to spend hours meticulously creating a masterpiece to the neglect of (say) assessing children's work or getting some much-needed sleep!
3 If something is urgent and important it obviously has to be done as soon as possible. For example, if just as you are leaving school one evening, the teacher tells you that the head has asked staff for a list of the software they use to support core subject teaching *by tomorrow morning*, the fact that you have a hundred other things to do cannot be used as an excuse for inaction. You simply have to spend less time on other tasks (such as marking and lesson preparation) and respond to the new priority. However, in the majority of cases, the important tasks (such as completing reports for parents) require quality time and should not be forced into an inadequate space. Take advice from your mentor if you are suddenly faced with an urgent task and feel overwhelmed owing to insufficient time.
4 Much of a teacher's work is ongoing. For example, you may need to complete some detailed profiles of children for your assessment file. These important but non-urgent tasks have deadlines, of course, but they are usually some way off and it is tempting to put them out of your mind until nearer the time. This is not a wise strategy, however, for all too often the deadline creeps up on you unexpectedly. Using a *planner* with interim targets is essential if you are to avoid last-minute

panic. In the case of child profiles, it is important to take notes and gather evidence about their work as soon as practically possible, well in advance of the final assessment.

Another way to monitor your use of time is to use a priority checklist as a basis for 'must do now' tasks and 'it can wait' tasks, and thinking ahead as you do so, such that circumstances do not find you unprepared. Some open-ended jobs, such as putting up displays, are enjoyable but time-consuming, and have to be subordinated to the essentials (especially planning, assessing and recording). You can gain greater control over your time by regularly asking yourself:

◆ What needs to checked out *first thing* in the morning?
◆ What needs to be done at *break* or dinnertime?
◆ What must be done *before you go home* this evening?
◆ What is best left until you *get home* tonight?
◆ What can be left until *tomorrow*?
◆ What can you *delegate* to other adults or children?
◆ What are *longer-term* needs?
◆ What things *don't really need doing* at all!

Some teachers like to get their work done while they are in school, even if it means staying behind until quite late in the evening. Other teachers prefer to work at home. Yet others have specific days of the week when they make a major effort to complete tasks and leave other days more flexible. If your life is one of unrelenting pressure, you will benefit considerably from stepping back and examining alternative ways of arranging your time.

Completing forms, filling-in lists and other administrative tasks have a greater significance than you may realize at the time. Your colleagues will advise you about priorities and the categorization listed earlier will help you to negotiate them. However, there are always unexpected demands being made of teachers, and you need to ensure that you don't get submerged in paperwork through a lack of forward planning and allow tasks to build up until they become a burdensome chore.

Teaching principle

Thinking ahead is the best preparation for thinking on your feet.

Making classroom decisions

Teachers have to make hundreds of decisions every day, and the ability to make appropriate ones is a crucial element of successful teaching. One of the criteria used by tutors and mentors to assess the capability of trainee teachers is their level of decisiveness, so refining the necessary skills to become a more effective decision-maker is a priority. There are two main categories of decisions that trainees have to deal with:

- Those that are planned and prepared for in advance.
- Those that are impromptu (unplanned) and a spontaneous response to particular circumstances.

In school, *planned* decisions tend to be of the 'yes, we will' or 'no, we will not' variety and are often based on whole school policies or agreement that has been reached between groups of teachers. In addition, an important part of being a thinking and learning teacher is to spend time pondering the appropriate parameters for all sorts of decisions associated with the intricacies of classroom practice. For trainee teachers, these planned decisions typically relate to class discipline, teaching style and selection of resources. *Unplanned* decisions are, by definition, more difficult to manage because of their unpredictability. However, the larger number of planned decisions that are in place, the easier it becomes to cope with the unexpected. One of the advantages for trainees in observing more experienced teachers at work is to take note of the way they deal with unforeseen situations and imagining themselves to be in the teacher's place. Mental rehearsal of potential reactions to unplanned decisions should form a major component of your deliberations, as such decisions usually rely on a confident, decisive reaction, while taking close account of existing school and classroom norms.

Planned decisions

There are numerous planned (predetermined) decisions that can be made in advance of the teaching session:

Decisions to do with the lesson
- Identifying the lesson purpose
- Being clear about what information, knowledge and understanding forms the heart of the lesson
- Specifying the resources that are needed
- Planning the overall lesson structure
- Listing the assessment criteria to gauge the extent of children's learning.

Decisions to do with teaching method
◆ The place of discursive (direct transmission) treatment of the subject content
◆ Whether or how soon to introduce an interactive element
◆ At what point to allocate tasks and activities
◆ The best means of concluding the lesson.

Decisions to do with learning
◆ The extent of individual or group work
◆ The time to spend on problem-solving or investigative approaches
◆ The amount of teacher or peer support to make available
◆ Opportunities for feedback and review.

Decisions to do with pupil behaviour
◆ Ways to promote enthusiasm and motivation
◆ Actions that will not be tolerated
◆ Strategies to minimize disruptive behaviour
◆ Sanctions that will be employed where necessary.

In particular, planned decisions about pupils' behaviour always have to be weighed against practicalities, as the best-laid plan flounders when children behave unpredictably. In such cases, impromptu decisions have to be made about whether, for instance, to ignore the behaviour, react in a particular way, give a warning, or use the occasion to remind the whole class of the standard that you expect.

Unplanned decisions

The ability to make rapid, well judged unplanned decisions is essential for effective teaching. There are likely to be at least four areas in which planned decisions are superseded by unplanned decisions: lesson content, teaching style, children's learning and behaviour.

The planned *lesson content* may have to be modified following the introduction, when it becomes apparent to you that pupils do not possess the anticipated knowledge or understanding on which the lesson plan is based. Time must then be spent revising and reinforcing the areas of uncertainty. On the other hand, children may be more familiar with the ideas and concepts than expected. Consequently, you are left with the option of reducing the amount of time that you originally intended to spend on the introduction and allocating more time to other phases of the lesson.

The planned *teaching style* may initially be interactive but, due to the number of interruptions from pupils or obvious gaps in their knowledge, you may make an on the spot decision to revert to a more formal and prescribed approach. The opposite may also occur.

Planned decisions about *pupil learning* may need to be modified due to a variety of in-class factors, especially the way in which children respond to the tasks. For instance, a closely defined method that the whole class has to follow in science may be modified into a more investigative form as it becomes apparent that pupils have an appetite to discover more and the ability to push the boundaries beyond the predetermined plan.

The planned way to deal with *behaviour* during the lesson involving (say) writing names of transgressors on the board may have to be adjusted if the children are disdainful of such an approach. Instead, you may decide to implement tighter control of movement around the room, the curtailing of collaborative practice and the introduction of a more individualized approach. On the other hand, your planned strategy for 'ruling with a rod of iron' might be softened if it is evident from the children's enthusiasm and responsible attitude that a more relaxed approach would be more beneficial to learning.

As an inexperienced teacher, it is often difficult to judge how much flexibility to employ and how much to modify ideas and decisions during the lesson. For example, you may decide in advance that children who have not completed their work must stay in during break time to finish, and warn the class accordingly. You may feel pleased with your decisiveness until you realize that you have failed to take into account a number of complications, such as children who do not complete the work because:

◆ They find the work genuinely difficult
◆ They are naturally slow in their work
◆ They have an important commitment during the break (such as a sport practice) and were distracted during the lesson as a result
◆ They feel unwell and have not only struggled with the task but need to go outside for some fresh air.

If your lesson is being observed, you may be reluctant to make even minor modifications for fear of being criticized for a lack of precision in your teaching, even though the situation cries out for changes. On the other hand, to adopt a rigid position without taking account of the realities of a situation might indicate inflexibility rather than signalling determination. There are no easy answers and you must trust your informed instincts to guide you, but it is essential that you explore the issues with the class teacher at every opportunity. Do not assume that because the teacher makes no comment that he or she understands what you are doing and is in sympathy with it. Some class teachers store up their concerns and suddenly confront you with them, just as you thought everything was going smoothly.

Not surprisingly, trainee teachers find unplanned decisions particularly difficult early on in the placement, as they do not have the experience, confidence, familiarity with the situation or knowledge of the routines to exercise sound judgement. This can lead to them feeling vulnerable and give them the sense of being unable to cope. As noted in Chapters 3 and 5, some trainee teachers who had been successful in a previous placement doubted their teaching ability when placed in a new one. However, with perseverance and advice, these feelings of inadequacy quickly passed. As you settle into the school and take more responsibility for teaching and learning, you are called upon to make an increasingly large number of decisions, shaped in the first instance by the existing norms. For instance:

- *Customs*, such as 'let's begin the day as usual by answering the register in French'.
- *Health and safety*, such as 'walk along the corridor, don't run'.
- *Procedures*, such as 'only one person can go to the toilet at a time'.
- *Learning patterns*, such as 'make sure you always rule a line at the end of your work'.
- *Organizational factors*, such as 'walk down the corridor in pairs'.
- *Control issues*, such as 'no-one goes out to play until the room is tidy'.

You may initially struggle when asked to conform to decisions that have already been made about school or classroom policy requirements because you were not present

Comment

Furlong and Maynard (1995) claim that trainee teachers can only learn some aspects of the teacher's role by experiencing it for themselves. For example, it is not possible to assess the mood of a class until coming face to face with them. They write as follows about a group of trainees' initial responses to the classroom situation:

> Once the student teachers began their school experience, their idealism appeared rapidly to fade in the face of the realities of the classroom and they became obsessed with their own personal survival.

> (Furlong and Maynard 1995, p. 76)

It is important to note that 'survival' is not a dirty word. Try telling that to a mountaineer! The important point is that you should quickly move beyond the obsession stage referred to in the quotation and get on with the job. Although your ideals may pale somewhat in the heat of classroom practice, it is important to remind yourself of the sort of teacher you want to be and the kind of classroom environment for which you intend to strive. After all, if you do not have a dream, how is your dream ever going to come true?

when they were developed and do not have any ownership of them. Some teachers are very happy for you to try out your innovations with their classes, while others will be reluctant to allow you to experiment. Although you may be bursting to try your ideas, there are constraints operating that might frustrate your intentions. For example, in the period preceding national tests and examinations, teachers are too preoccupied with preparing the children for these important events to accommodate the whims of a trainee teacher.

When you have your own class you will discover that even the most carefully considered decisions have to be modified in the light of circumstances, so don't be too hard on class teachers who don't conform fully to your idealized model of decision-making effectiveness.

Teaching principle

The better your planned decisions, the easier it becomes to make appropriate unplanned changes.

Modelling

As a means of increasing their effectiveness, trainee teachers are asked to consider the appropriateness of modelling their teaching on that of an experienced teacher. Modelling is a valuable strategy for improving classroom practice but it has to be undertaken in a constructively critical manner. Teachers differ in their approach and priorities, so you need to use your judgement to determine what aspects should be adopted, replicated, modified or ignored. This task requires a lot of thought, discussion and wisdom, so to help you improve your competence, compare and contrast the approaches of these two teachers and see what you can discern about their educational values. Brett teaches year 6 and Jenny teaches year 2.

Organization

Brett: Brett likes the children to get down to work quickly, and uses a lot of duplicated sheets and textbooks. He prefers to do a brisk lively introduction to the whole class and subsequently deal with children on a one-to-one basis. All the children tend to be given the same task, though it is graded so that the work gradually becomes more challenging.

Jenny: Jenny likes to organize children in groups and speaks to the whole class when they sit together on the carpet. She uses historical names (such as Vikings, Saxons) for groups. She gives different tasks depending on the ability of the groups. She makes sure that the children have an extension task when the main work is completed.

Management

Brett: The lesson begins well but noise levels soon rise. Children who find the task hard make heavy demands upon his time and queues sometimes form. He tends to muddle through and rely on his instincts to sort out problems.

Jenny: Jenny perseveres to ensure that the children understand procedures. Because the activities are appropriate for the children's ability, there is less need for her to answer a series of similar questions.

Control

Brett: Though normally quite cheerful with the children, Brett sometimes resorts to harsher comments and rebukes as the lesson develops. The children know exactly where they stand with him and most of them seem to be immune to the rather caustic remarks he makes on occasions.

Jenny: Jenny tends to appeal to the children's sense of responsibility and only makes firm comments if there is a lack of response on their part. The relationship between teacher and taught is sufficiently secure such that the need for admonition is minimized; she uses mainly eye contact and arm signals to restore order. Some children take longer to get themselves organized than would be the case if Jenny were more directly controlling. One particularly restless girl is allowed to roam the classroom freely, as Jenny believes that insistence would result in confrontation and create more problems than it solved.

Children's learning

Brett: Brett believes that children should get on with the task rather than spend a lot of time discussing it. The children tend to rely heavily on him for guidance. Although the children work enthusiastically, the final product is sometimes poorly presented. Brett spends only a very small amount of time on the plenary session.

Jenny: Jenny believes that learning should be enjoyable and cultivates a light but purposeful atmosphere. Jenny likes children to work collaboratively whenever possible and sometimes pairs less and more able children.

Lesson outcomes

Brett: The work is completed by most of the children. More able children tend to finish early and are encouraged to finish off work from earlier lessons. Brett provides a lot of active support for less able children to enable them to complete the work successfully.

Jenny: The work matches the children's ability closely. The children find the tasks fulfilling. Expectations are explicit so children know what they are expected to achieve and work towards that end.

Generally

Brett tends to be at the hub of classroom life and has a bold presence. He is quite loud and tends to be domineering but he can also be caring and humorous. His teaching is task-centred and he is vaguely dismissive of target setting and maintaining detailed records. He encourages talk and active questioning but insists on making most of the final decisions. The children both adore and fear him. Brett is well known and respected by the children throughout the school because of his sporting prowess. Parents consider him to be a bit enigmatic but recognize that underneath the bluster, Brett is passionate about his work and cares deeply for the children.

Jenny has a more low-key personality and promotes an orderly classroom in which the children are encouraged to take responsibility for their own actions. She plans thoroughly and keeps very detailed records. Jenny is highly conscious of the need to

---

Comment

In recent years there has been a tendency to consider teaching effectiveness largely in terms of measurable academic performance. Gradually, however, there has been an acknowledgement that working effectively with children requires a more profound knowledge of them as unique and special individuals. The following quotation encourages teachers to consider educating the 'whole child':

> All young people have different capacities, aptitudes and biographies. They have different pasts and different futures. One of the roles of education is to help them find their future and understand their pasts. This begins by helping them to discover their own strengths, passions and sensibilities. Young people spend their most formative and impressionable years at school. Their needs are not only academic. They are social, spiritual and emotional. All young people need an education that helps them to find meaning and to make sense of themselves and their lives.
>
> (DfEE/QCA 1999, p. 23)

maintain and raise standards in basic skills. Consequently, she spends a lot of time explaining to the children what she expects from them and how they can improve their work. A strong feature of Jenny's teaching is the length of the sharing times in which achievements are celebrated. Jenny is adored by her children and has the complete trust of parents.

This chapter has described a range of issues that impinge upon effective teaching. In Chapter 10 we look at the area of school life that is often of greatest concern to trainee teachers because it hinders effectiveness, namely, classroom discipline and pupil behaviour.

Further reading

Hayes, L., Nikolic, V. and Cabaj, H. (2000) *Am I Teaching Well?* Exeter: Learning Matters.

Stringer, J. and Powell, R. (1998) *Raising Achievement in the Primary School*, Stafford: Robert Powell Publications.

CHAPTER 10

Classroom discipline and behaviour

Classroom discipline is one of the most pressing concerns for nearly all trainee teachers, despite the fact that most of them are placed in quiet, orderly classrooms where the teacher has already done the hard work in settling the children and inculcating efficient procedures and good habits. The majority of trainees who enter these pleasant environments generally only need to maintain the teacher's existing approach to ensure that such harmony continues. It is a paradox that many children feel more, not less, secure when you are very firm with them about their work and conduct. It is possible to be friendly and chatty with children who show a willingness to persevere and behave themselves, while being resolutely tough with those who do not. At the same time, you will want to avoid giving the impression that your strictness is due to personal animosity towards a child. A small number of trainees arrive in school to find that the class is very challenging and even the teacher is struggling to maintain control. Occasionally, a trainee teacher is eventually just as successful with a difficult class as the permanent teacher has been.

Basic principles

A settled classroom environment depends upon many factors, not least the teacher's ability to establish a good working relationship with the children. This relationship must consist of mutual respect and a clear demarcation of boundaries. The establishment of effective relationships cannot be hurried and is only secured when children are convinced that the teacher can be trusted and is for them, not against them. Trainee teachers take time to move through this initiation process and must persevere to show that they are worthy to receive the children's full confidence.

Well-organized classrooms are usually the most productive, but this is not the same as being fussy about everything or trying to make the classroom look like a palace. Good organization covers a variety of practicalities, such as having lesson plans in place, thinking about presenting and leading the session through, and ensuring that children have enough resources and space to carry out their tasks. Poor organization has an adverse effect on the management of the lesson and children's behaviour. Gill (1998) rightly comments that 'getting organized will pay off for you in a number of ways. Your [pupils] will have confidence in what you are teaching because you have an agenda and know where you are going' (1998, p. 27).

There are a number of principles that all teachers have to keep in mind when grappling with issues of control and discipline. First, children are happiest when they are interested in the work and find it satisfying. This fundamental truth needs to be balanced against the fact that some types of work will, inevitably, be less exciting than others are. Children have to be encouraged to attend to the task, even when they do not particularly enjoy what they are doing. On the other hand, the more appealing and relevant lessons are to children, the more they will be keen to engage with them and do their best. Second, children behave well largely because they want to do so, not because they are forced to do so. Being stern and insistent is sometimes necessary but it is a poor substitute for children exercising *self*-discipline and does little to promote classroom harmony. Third, children who behave well for one teacher will not necessarily do so for another. As far as the children are concerned, a trainee teacher is just another adult to be tried and tested before being accorded 'real teacher' status. Don't court popularity. Be the person you are and try to exude self-belief (see Figure 10.1). Assume that the children will do as they are told and you greatly increase the chances that they will.

Most of teachers' control strategies are based on the belief that *indiscipline* occurs when children know what they are doing and choose not to do it. Bad behaviour occurs when children don't know *how* to behave, in which case it is pointless to tell a child to behave unless he or she is clear about what behaving well means. Inappropriate behaviour sometimes signals that the child has an underlying problem that requires attention (such as a neurological disorder, a disturbed background or a deviant personality) but may also indicate that something is wrong with the lesson. It is helpful to have a rule framework to which the teacher can refer when necessary, so that pupil infringements can be checked against the agreed behaviour code. Children need to be gradually inculcated into an understanding that they have both the right and the responsibility to take control over events and circumstances in their

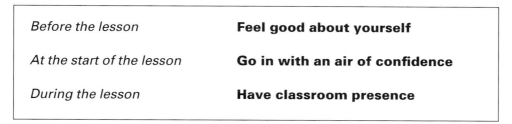

Before the lesson	**Feel good about yourself**
At the start of the lesson	**Go in with an air of confidence**
During the lesson	**Have classroom presence**

Figure 10.1 *Exuding self-belief*

own lives. Porter (1999) identifies a key characteristic of pupils who are reluctant to accept that they can or need to make an effort to improve: 'These children think that external forces control them, rather than believing that they can make a difference in their own lives' (1999, p. 177). It is part of the challenge for every teacher to convince them otherwise.

Teachers understandably interpret unacceptable behaviour as a challenge or threat to them personally, and a reflection upon their ability to cope or provide appropriate and interesting lessons. Nevertheless, the majority of children want to behave well and please their teachers, so it is important to clarify with children what you mean by acceptable behaviour. Classroom control is greatly assisted when children see that you are being firm (not harsh), fair (not favouring a chosen few), tolerant (not patronizing), natural (not condescending), and sincere (yet not overly serious). By emphasizing positive behaviour, you are setting high expectations of the pupils that are important because doing so has, as Smith and Laslett (1993, p. 15) observe, 'a powerful influence in helping or hindering the development of the pupils' self-image as competent or incompetent learners'. Consequently, teachers have an important role in boosting children's confidence in themselves by affirming their ability to achieve highly, and this has an impact on their behaviour.

When a trainee teacher first meets the class, the children are weighing up the newcomer by asking themselves a number of questions. In particular, they ask whether this teacher will:

◆ Be strict
◆ Teach interesting lessons
◆ Smile and see the funny side of life
◆ Take a personal interest in them
◆ Control the naughty children
◆ Explain things to them if they do not understand
◆ Get frustrated if they ask questions
◆ Think the best or worst about them.

If you find it puzzling that children behave so differently for you compared to the way they respond to the regular teachers, much of it is explained by the fact that they are trying to discover answers to the sorts of questions noted above. Children can only find out about you by watching and listening to the way that you speak, act and the way that you respond to them in a variety of situations. It seems to be an inviolable rule that they assume that trainee teachers are *not* strict unless they prove otherwise, so be warned! Although it is generally better to begin by being firm and insistent, this approach should not be confused with being negative or intimidating. Children like to know where they stand but will react badly towards an adult whom they perceive to be bullying or unreasonable. It is far from easy to strike a proper balance, especially when you do not know the children, so some errors of judgement are inevitable. Be assured that occasional lapses do not signal the end of your teaching career!

When teaching, some account must be taken of the child's maturity, social skills and previous learning experiences. Younger children usually respond well to a measured but lively approach, supported by a variety of visual aids. Older children often like to work collaboratively and are invariably curious. All children should be encouraged to contribute ideas, discuss issues and be actively involved in learning through play, drama, discussion and problem-solving whenever possible. Creative teachers who are willing to be innovative normally have fewer discipline problems than those who insist on a constant diet of pencil and paper exercises.

Behaviour and control

A popular view of the ability to exercise control over children is that it needs to be internalized rather than externally forced upon them, as they will revert to their former behaviour as soon as the constraints are lifted. As noted earlier, this interpretation is subject to the proviso that the child understands how to control his or her own behaviour in the first place and has the strategies, willpower or grasp of conventions to effect change. It is possible for a teacher to become increasingly exasperated with children's apparent obstinacy and berate them by repeating the demand to behave without giving them the skills with which to do so. Directing children to sit up, keep hands still, look directly at the teacher, and so forth, are not authoritarian regulations to terrorize hapless youngsters, but to offer them a framework for ensuring a reasonable level of conformity across the whole class. Ultimately, children have to make the conscious decision to behave appropriately, but in the process of doing so they require a fair and consistent set of rules within which they can gradually strengthen their self-control. As every teacher knows, however, some children need more externally constraining than others do!

There are particular times during a lesson when poor behaviour is more likely, especially when resources are being distributed, transitions from one type of activity to another are taking place, and during the clearing-up phase (see later in this chapter). It goes without saying that if the work is tedious, few children will sit passively, hanging onto the teacher's every word! If they are kept on the carpet for too long or made to complete work when they are weary of doing it, it is hardly surprising if they become fidgety. It is on such occasions that you need to work swiftly and efficiently, be a visible presence around the room and give clear orders or advice. Disaffection has its roots in a variety of factors. The work may be uninteresting, the room may be too stuffy or the lesson may be too long and tiring. Think of how *you* feel about some lectures in college and how you cannot wait to escape at the end! It is also important, however, for children to understand the value of perseverance. Effective teachers promote such a learning climate by instilling a 'have a go' attitude in the children. Judging the amount of time that children should be asked to sit still or continue to do a certain task is difficult, but tell-tale signs such as glazed eyes and distraction behaviour (such as twizzling the hair of the child in front) give fair warning that your peroration should cease.

Minor instances of misbehaviour are usually due to tedium, irrelevance of task or poor classroom management, and are best taken care of by issuing a quiet but firm reminder than by exploding or making a public issue out of the matter (see pp. 216–18 later in this chapter). Nevertheless, if such irritating behaviour occurs, it is important to reflect on the following three points *after* the lesson as part of the lesson evaluation:

◆ The action you might have taken to prevent the behaviour happening in the first place
◆ What the action tells you about the individual child or the class mood
◆ Future strategies to improve the situation.

Children quickly realize that what they cannot get away with when taught by one teacher, they can with a different less experienced teacher. As with so many other features of classroom life, therefore, advice from a wiser and more experienced colleague is invaluable and should be sought unhesitatingly.

Teaching principle

Never leave a control issue unresolved.

Management and control

A lesson cannot run smoothly if it is punctuated by stops-and-starts to deal with poor behaviour. Not only does it disrupt the lesson but it exhausts the teacher and creates a tense classroom climate. Many control problems can be avoided through good preparation and mentally envisaging in detail the phases of the session. As Robertson (1996, p. 82) points out: 'It is in such skills as organizing, presenting, communicating and monitoring that teachers' actual authority rests. Without them they will fail to capture the interest of their (pupils) or to gain their respect.' There are three occasions in which the opportunities for naughtiness are greater than usual. It is worth thinking about how some of these potential problems can be pre-empted and managed more satisfactorily.

The start of a session

Carpet sessions are commonplace in primary classrooms, especially with younger children. They allow direct interaction between you and the pupils but also provide an environment for messing about if the session is tedious or you insist that they stay seated for too long. Although even the youngest children can concentrate for a surprising length of time, it is best to keep the time to around twenty minutes maximum. There are some occasions when it is easier to manage the situation if the children are sitting on their chairs, such as when it is difficult to see a visual aid from the floor. At the start of the day or after an exciting lesson or a wet playtime, children are often more unsettled and animated than usual. It is worth having a simple individual task ready for them to do for the first few minutes, such as copying, drawing, completing missing words, etc, or a simple response game, such as 'Do this, do that'. After they have calmed down, the prepared lesson can begin.

Moving from the classroom to another place

Children often have to leave the room for another venue; for instance, going to a maths' set, additional reading, PE lessons and assemblies. The key principle in maintaining order at such times is to be consistent and specific about the way things are done. For example, releasing children a few at a time while you stand by the door to monitor behaviour, walking at the front of the queue during a 'crocodile' (single file) excursion, insisting that no child should overtake you and watching out for silliness at the back of the line. With a crocodile file, it is important to walk quite slowly and stop from time to time so that the line does not straggle too far. Beware, though, of stopping abruptly and children deliberately bumping into the person in front!

The end of the session

Despite the temptation to get rid of the children as quickly as possible and flop into the nearest chair, the end of the session is crucially important in ensuring that the lesson concludes positively and that you maintain your hard-won authority. Be careful that you do not extend the main body of the lesson too far and therefore have to hurry the final moments, but never let a child exit until you are satisfied that everything is in proper order. If the children are leaving the room to go to break, stand by the door and monitor their departure. If you are moving the class on to the next lesson, allow some time for them to adjust from those things that have been occupying them in the previous one. Some children seem to think that playtime begins at the end of the lesson. In fact, the break starts when they reach the playground, so it pays to be very firm and set high expectations for their behaviour while they are inside the building.

Reasons for misbehaviour

Although some children have trouble exercising self-control, conforming to classroom routines and responding to teachers' expectations, misbehaviour occurs in the majority for one or more of a number of reasons (based on Kyriacou 1991):

Uncertainty

It is essential to explain carefully to children what has to be completed and the standard to which they should aspire. This requires that you give the children specific guidance about how they should go about the work, while encouraging them to think for themselves or collaborate or experiment. Children who are unsure will sometimes appear sullen or declare that the work is boring rather than admit to their failure to grasp what has to be done.

Monotony

Children who are prone to restlessness, quickly become distracted unless they receive close monitoring from an adult and regular stimuli. Being imaginative in your lesson presentation, making sure that the work matches the children's abilities and offering them short-term successes, all help to reduce apathy and increase motivation. The lesson should not be allowed to drag, but racing through too quickly and losing the children's attention is equally damaging. In theory every child should receive an equal proportion of a teacher's attention. In reality the restless children often claim the lion's share, so be careful not to starve the well-behaved children of your time.

Prolonged mental effort

Although children must learn to persevere, it is counterproductive to insist that they plough on regardless of circumstances, especially when it is obvious that they have lost interest. On the other hand, setting the achievement level so low that children can do the work effortlessly results in lethargy. An occasional inquiry to ask if everything is going smoothly gives a child with a short attention span a valid excuse for momentary distraction and helps to ease the lesson along. Every child needs some moments to daydream as this allows the brain to process information and recharge.

Social chat

Casual talking is habitual for some children, so they must be trained to concentrate, take their work more seriously and think differently about classroom life. Of course, pupil talk may be fruitful and task-related or otherwise, but even the most conscientious children require some help to refocus and get back on track. Lesson targets help to keep children on task and give you a yardstick by which to judge their progress and it is useful to attach the target to a time limit so that there is an easily verifiable criterion available. If necessary, persistent talkers should be sat apart from their friends for a while until they can prove their reliability. Avoid allowing queues of children to form because they provide the ideal environment for informal chatter.

Low academic self-esteem

Both low and high achieving children can suffer from low self-esteem or anxiety. They need to be set achievable tasks so that they can gain some immediate satisfaction from their endeavours. Be careful that in an effort to assist the children who struggle to achieve their goal, you do not give them such simple work that the child is teased by classmates. Self-confidence is fragile and your careful approach, commending attitude and reassuring comments will give worried children the support they need. Even loud and outwardly assertive children are often insecure and require just as much sensitivity as timid ones, despite the fact that you may not always feel so sympathetic towards them!

Emotional difficulties

It is difficult for children to concentrate on schoolwork when other aspects of their lives are in a mess. Even short-term issues, such as not being invited to a birthday party by a member of the peer group, can have a powerful negative effect upon a child. Despite their inappropriate behaviour on occasions, school may actually be a haven for emotionally distressed children. You have the privilege and responsibility of being a caring adult in a chaotic world.

Poor attitude

A small percentage of children have a very poor attitude towards school and learning. Others are unwilling to compromise and 'toe the line', insisting instead upon pursuing their own agenda, regardless of how this may affect others and their own progress. There are, alas, no quick solutions to the problem. However, your enthusiasm, encouragement and willingness to get alongside such children can make a substantial difference to their attitude *over time*. You should not blame yourself for their persistently unsatisfactory behaviour. It may be that unknown to you there is a history of mental health problems in the family or negative parental attitudes are having a detrimental effect. You simply have to persevere and accept that change comes gradually. When it feels as if you are fighting a losing battle it may be some consolation to know that for deeply disturbed children your influence will be one of the most positive. You can only do your best, be consistent, fair and firm, and demonstrate through your words and actions that you want the best for each child.

Lack of concern about consequences

It is a sad fact that a very small number of children are largely indifferent to sanctions that result from their poor behaviour. They may come from tough backgrounds or may have become cynical about school and education generally. No matter how much effort you make to ensure that they conform, they seem to be able to shrug it all off and carry on in much the same way as before. The involvement of parents is important in the process but even this does not always provide a solution. This very small minority of children should already be receiving additional support and adult intervention. In the unlikely event that it is not, you should discuss the situation urgently with your tutor.

Responding to minor disruption

One of the most powerful strategies that teachers can develop is to remain calm at all times, as children tend to behave more erratically when they sense that a teacher is becoming exasperated. The incidence of petty classroom misbehaviour may also increase if teachers become too animated and make the children overexcited, so before doing so make certain that you have the ability to bring the children to order. Minor irritants take various forms, but examples include:

◆ Talking when you are speaking
◆ Tapping an object on the table
◆ Leaning back on a chair
◆ Giggling instead of concentrating
◆ Making silly comments at inappropriate times
◆ Chatting with a neighbour
◆ Wandering aimlessly around the room.

These minor annoyances can, if left unchecked, assume far greater significance than they would do if dealt with promptly. Minor disruption is annoying but should not be allowed to disturb the equilibrium of lessons. In most instances, it is better to conceal from the children that it is upsetting you and to deal decisively with the situation. There are at least eight possible responses that you can make when children irritate you by their naughtiness. The list is not intended to provide a checklist for action but to offer a sequence of strategies with which to combat unacceptable behaviour, starting with the least intrusive tactic and ending with the most severe. You have the challenging task of deciding which is appropriate for a particular instance . . .

1   *Inert response* You ignore the behaviour and continue as if it hadn't happened. If the behaviour ceases, then a quiet word to the child later in the lesson suffices.

2   *Mute reaction* You make no comment but look directly at the child while continuing with the lesson. In most cases, this curbs the behaviour, otherwise try strategy 3 or 4.

3   *Calm directive* Using a relaxed tone, you briefly ask the child to stop showing off and pay attention, then immediately continue with the lesson, disregarding any feigned protest.

4   *Rebuke* You speak the pupil's name sharply without looking at him or her or deviating from what you are saying, and with minimal effect on the flow of the lesson. If the behaviour continues, use strategy 5.

5   *Reorientate* You ask the child to stop the behaviour and state specifically what must be done (e.g. 'keep your hands together in your lap'). If the inappropriate behaviour is repeated, try strategy 6.

6   *Relocate* Move the child to a different part of the room, initially for a short probationary period of (say) ten minutes. The child is allowed to move back after demonstrating that he or she has made progress. It is surprising how often the child prefers to stay in the new location.

7   *Redirect* If the misdemeanour persists, do not make a fuss about it, but rather divert the child's attention into a different sphere of activity (e.g. 'Duggie, please check that we have enough dictionaries for one between two and tidy the shelf. Thanks.'). This is a useful strategy for children who have short attention spans or who appear to be winding up towards more serious disruptive behaviour. It is worth noting that a commonly used acronym to describe a failure for children to pay attention is ADD, which stands for attention-deficit disorder. If children also exhibit impulsive tendencies, such as shouting out answers or wandering about the room, this is sometimes referred to as ADHD, which stands for attention-deficit and hyperactivity disorder. Although children's poor behaviour should not necessarily be excused on the grounds that they seem to possess one of these disorders, it may provide a starting point for addressing the problem in consultation with other staff members.

8   *Punish* Where all other methods have failed, impose a sanction on the spot without apology, looking and sounding resolute. Exceptionally, it is necessary to punish a persistent offender before exhausting the other possibilities listed above (1–7). This action is normally undesirable except in instances where you feel it is needed to show the child that you are capable of being very tough if required or if the poor behaviour has continued throughout the day. Administering sanctions is sometimes more stressful for the trainee than the pupil but if it is necessary then it should be enforced without fear or favour. The support of the class teacher is important but you must eventually show that you are capable of handling the situation alone.

You will note that the list does not contain any reference to invective, denunciation, mockery or sarcasm. Speak firmly and clearly but avoid using an affected tone.

Children need to know that you mean business but your response should be in proportion to the nature of the offence. For example, sending a child out of the class for throwing a rubber across the table would be ridiculous. If you overreact in response to a minor incident, you are left with little in the way of strategies should more severe behaviour occur. While you will want to act decisively, it is important to remain calm and in control of your reactions, and not be dragged into unnecessary confrontations.

Judging which of the above approaches to use comes through classroom experience. If the strategy you select does not have the desired effect, it is normal to use the next one in the sequence and not jump several steps ahead. However, children who display a wilful defiance, offer deliberate cheek or are contemptuous of your status cannot expect to be handled with kid gloves and must be firmly dealt with by being reported to the class teacher immediately.

Whatever strategies you use, it is important to ensure that you also *commend* appropriate behaviour regularly but not ostentatiously. Studies show that teachers tend to make more negative than positive comments to children, so the more that you can foster a climate of approval, the greater the chance that children will want to behave that way. If a child responds to your command as requested, it is normal to briefly acknowledge the fact courteously.

Comment

Curwin and Mendler (1988) carried out experiments on the effectiveness of different teacher voices in maintaining control. They discovered that the softer the voice and the closer the teacher to the individual child, the more effective the discipline.

Teaching principle

The disruption created by the teacher's intervention should be in proportion to the severity of the offence.

Developing a settled climate

As effective teaching relies on establishing and maintaining a settled and purposeful classroom climate, it is important to think carefully about the principles that support actions rather than relying purely on your instincts. Although no two teaching situations are alike, the way that a teacher handles class control and responds to circumstances will be random without an underlying structure of values. The following propositions (based on Hayes 1999b) provide a basis for your classroom practice as you decide what kind of teacher you are trying to be and work with determination to attain your ideals:

◆ Keep situations in proportion and do not overreact.
◆ Win pupils' co-operation.
◆ Accept that children make mistakes.
◆ Celebrate children's achievements.
◆ Encourage effort and praise good results.
◆ Explain things calmly when asked.
◆ Help children to make responsible choices and accept the consequences of their actions.
◆ Take time to discover the facts before making accusations.
◆ Apply sanctions only when a child has wilfully broken the rules.
◆ Adopt a steady and unflappable manner when interrogating children about an incident lest fear may tempt them to lie.
◆ Deal with incidents without humiliating children or causing loss of face.
◆ Set an excellent example to the children in your personal conduct.

In particular, you will want to give children opportunities to develop their self-sufficiency and self-discipline, a point underlined by Thody *et al.* (2000, p. 19):

> If pupils are constantly ordered about and controlled, they will never learn to be self-effective. To demonstrate responsibility, pupils should be given opportunities to practise. We all need to understand that we choose our own behaviour. Behaviour is the result of our own decisions, and pupils need to learn the skill of making decisions and reflecting on the effects of their choice.

It is important to note that the writers are not recommending a sloppy approach in allowing children to do what they want, when they feel like it, or thoughtlessly disregarding rules. Rather, they are advising that children have to understand *why* certain forms of behaviour are unacceptable. Teachers who exert unyielding and rigid control over the class will never gain children's willing co-operation. On the other hand, those who adopt a casual approach will struggle when they find it necessary to insist that children behave in a certain way. Although there are occasions when children simply have to do what they are told, whether or not they understand the reason, it is generally better to explain, but not justify, your decisions.

It is an axiom that regardless of how experienced, confident and knowledgeable you are, the children will never respond positively to your attempts to teach them if they do not respect you. It is very unsettling to be in a position in which the children are only grudgingly compliant rather than enthusiastic, and there are four approaches that contribute towards the establishment and maintenance of a healthy, happy and co-operative learning climate:

Make children feel special

◆ By knowing about them. Children want to feel that you are interested in them as individuals, not merely as a member of the class. It is important to listen for snippets of conversation between children to get an idea of what interests them and current fads.

◆ By accepting what they say. A lot of children are not used to having adults believe them, so your willingness to respond positively is appreciated by the children and helps to build their self-esteem.

◆ By acknowledging their feelings, beliefs and preferences. Because some children do not say much, it is possible to imagine that life is passing over their heads. In fact the majority of them have far stronger feelings and beliefs about issues than may be immediately obvious. Valuing opinions is a powerful antidote to low self-confidence.

Model acceptable behaviour

◆ By the way you speak and act. If you are courteous, pleasant and fair, children will tend to orientate towards your standards.

◆ By your reactions under stress. If you snap every time there is a problem or a situation that you find a bit threatening, children become either fractious or subdued.

◆ By expressing your feelings about the behaviour, not about the child. Even the most hard-headed miscreant wants to feel accepted and loved. In fact, a lot of poor behaviour is due to a child's lack of these fundamental human needs.

Visually celebrate their achievements

◆ By displaying work. Packard and Race (2000, p. 126) point out that 'displaying a piece of work by mounting it and putting it on the wall can be an extremely good way of praising work and helping to build self-esteem'. Display work has been neglected in recent years due to the many other demands upon a teacher's time. Thankfully, the situation is slowly being redressed. A classroom assistant is frequently involved in putting up and maintaining displays but the teacher normally determines its design. Providing it is of good quality, seeing their work put on display motivates nearly all children. All parents look for their own child's work and are disappointed if they never see any displayed.

◆ By making the classroom/unit look interesting. The classroom should resemble a well-ordered workshop rather than a waiting room!

Take account of their life outside school

◆ By acknowledging special events, such as birthdays. Children look forward to their birthdays for months in advance and are delighted if adults express an interest.
◆ By asking questions about their out-of-school activities. Even children with limited academic ability have lots to say about their hobbies and pastimes.
◆ By allowing time for them to share important things with others. The familiar 'sharing time' at the start of the day has become less common in recent years owing to curriculum pressures. It is, however, well worth spending a few minutes encouraging children to talk about their favourite things as a means of fostering a closely-knit classroom community.

Wachter (1999) makes the point that the uniqueness of each child offers opportunities for teachers to exploit their diversity as a means of enriching the learning climate.

> Your class is made up of a combination of unique individuals. Each has special strengths and needs. If that were not enough of a challenge, the youngsters in your class also vary in their learning styles. Instead of shaking your sanity, this diversity can be reason for celebration if you handle the situation with effective techniques.
>
> (Wachter 1999, p. 33)

It is possible to win individual battles with children by employing extreme methods, but these 'victories' are usually short term, as the resentment that builds up leads to a deterioration of relationships and a decline in the quality of the learning environment. Bassey (1987) points out that it is difficult to find a balance between being assertive and being authoritarian. He refers to the issue of dominance in the classroom as being a concept that, in practice, requires a considerable degree of sensitivity and care, and something with which all teachers need to persevere if they want to achieve a productive learning environment. The following strategies are typical of those that might help to win a battle but eventually lose the war:

◆ Shouting at the children
◆ Dismissing children's opinions and protests
◆ Telling children that they are naughty for not understanding the work
◆ Nagging instead of explaining.

Sanctions such as keeping children in at playtime, depriving them of a treat and moving one child away from a friend have a short-term impact but fail to deal with the root cause of the problem. Whereas some of the strategies may be justified on occasions, they are not useful as regular methods of maintaining discipline, as children become immune to their impact or resentful of a perceived injustice. When sanctions *are* necessary, it should happen because other control strategies have been unsuccessful.

Establishing and maintaining a settled learning environment is neither straightforward nor guaranteed. It requires patient perseverance, supported by a thoughtful appraisal of each lesson and liaison with the class teacher. While you will want to take account of prevailing conditions and see where adjustments need to be made to your approach, it is extremely important not to compromise your basic beliefs about teaching because of the poor attitude of a minority of children. Short-term strict measures are sometimes necessary to arrest a disruptive situation, but they should be the exception rather than the rule.

Teaching principle

The classroom should be a learning zone, not a war zone!

Discipline and your emotions

Providing that you have established the rules with the children, you are entitled to expect them to respond positively to your teaching. Most of the time this is precisely what happens but on those occasions when problems occur, it can be demoralizing and even cause some trainee teachers to doubt their vocation. When children misbehave, the following feelings are commonly experienced:

◆ Bewilderment about why a few children should seek to ruin the lesson for everyone else
◆ Disappointment that some children gain more enjoyment from the disruption than from the lesson
◆ Annoyance that they should test your patience when you are doing your best for them
◆ Frustration that your legitimate strategies for retaining control are not successful
◆ Distress about your own feelings of impotence, despite telling yourself that testing is a natural part of the process
◆ Irritation that it is taking such a long time to gain control of the class
◆ Anxiety that it might be your personal inadequacies that are to blame.

Regardless of the circumstances, it is important to preserve your own well-being and handle your emotions positively rather than resigning yourself to them. Aspire to do the following:

- Remind yourself that it takes time to get things right.
- Share your concerns with a trusted colleague and take advice.
- Write down or verbally rehearse your strategies.
- Inform the children about the necessary changes (e.g. 'Last time we had a story some of you were very fidgety, so we're going to try sitting with arms folded to see if it helps us all to concentrate better.')
- Make behaving well a cool thing to do rather than always associating it with submissive pupils.
- Avoid grumbling and praise co-operation.

It is important to get into the habit of talking up the lesson, getting children curious and activating the 'tingle factor'. Children rarely misbehave because they don't like you or are out to make your life miserable. It is normally because you lack experience in managing a lesson or the children sense your insecurity. Remind yourself that the host teachers, who seem to cope so easily, have all been in your position once. They coped, and so will you. You may like to refer to the case studies in Chapter 3.

Teaching principle

Concentrate on motivating children and most behaviour issues will take care of themselves.

Case studies: What do I do now?

The four accounts below are examples of commonly asked questions that trainee teachers have put to their tutors during school placements. In each case, the trainee's uncertainty about appropriate action has generated the question: What do I do now?

1 *My class of six and seven year olds listened attentively when they were sitting on the carpet, receiving my instructions, but once they were sitting at their tables doing the activities, the noise level kept rising. I kept telling the class to keep quiet, and the noise reduced for a short time, but it soon became as bad as before. What can I do to prevent this behaviour happening during every lesson?*

It is natural for young children to talk to their friends when they are sitting together. Indeed, socialization is an important dimension of child development and maturation. The challenge for teachers is twofold: first, to see that the children concentrate on their work; second, that when they speak it is about the task and at an appropriate volume. You can foster concentration by planning interesting and relevant activities, setting achievement targets for the lesson and insisting that a certain amount of work is covered before the end of the session. The problem is that some children work extremely slowly, others need very short-term goals and a few seem incapable of applying themselves without close adult supervision. As the teacher, you have to persevere on all of these fronts before the situation begins to improve. Loud talking is, in many ways, more difficult to combat. You can promote a policy of whispering rather than shouting, but some young children have genuine difficulty in controlling their volume of speech. You can separate tables so that pairs of children sit together, but this seems to negate the positive social development that you are trying to establish. You can have a simple signal, such as a small tinkling bell, to indicate that you consider that the noise level is too high. As with most classroom situations, a lot depends on what you are trying to achieve during the session. If you are *primarily* interested in enhancing the children's social development, it is sensible to place tables together and tolerate a slightly higher noise level. If strictly academic outcomes are more important, then it is reasonable to separate the tables so that, for example, the children sit in pairs and work more quietly. Most classrooms have an agreed set of rules or a code of conduct and it is useful to remind the children about the agreement to speak quietly to their neighbours. Some teachers have a special flag and/or reward for the table that has tried hardest to concentrate and speak quietly, allocated at the end of each day. Finally, in the short term, it is better to speak to children on individual tables about the noise level, than to add to the cacophony by telling off the whole class in a booming voice. As with all issues relating to classroom order, it is often a combination of strategies that works best.

2 I took my reception class into the hall for PE. They did the warm-up phase in pairs very sensibly and I felt pleased, but then I tried to bring them to order, and that's when the problems began. All I did was to ask them whether they had finished what they were doing and were ready for the next task. My question triggered an outburst of responses. Children shouted 'yes' at the tops of their voices. Some of them even screamed! I couldn't make myself heard and felt as if I had lost control. Their shouting went on for what seemed like an eternity and left me feeling so demoralized that the supply teacher had to take the rest of the lesson. Where did I go wrong?

The large space in a hall has the same sort of effect on a young child as any other open area, such as a field or park. It is therefore essential to prepare the lesson meticulously, incorporating individual, pairs and group activities, with a problem-solving dimension towards the end, such as making up their own game or developing a small piece of dramatic movement. If you find yourself constantly having to drive the lesson and ending up exhausted and breathless, you have probably failed to give the children sufficient opportunity to explore ideas for themselves. It is also important to consider basic health and safety factors. Children who are given the opportunity to charge around and let off steam are liable to get injured and apart from the damage to the child, other children are unsupervised while you are dealing with the consequences. The unexpectedly fervent reaction from the children when asked if they were ready could not have been anticipated but, after all, they were only answering the question! A more satisfactory outcome would have been achieved by approaching the situation differently. For example, you could have told the class to sit down with their arms folded to show that they were ready to go on to the next task. You could have said that they had one minute left to complete what they were doing, and after this time counted down rapidly from ten to zero, by which time the children must 'freeze'. Your question to the children invited a vocal response and did not require them to do anything that you could monitor. By contrast, the 'show me that you are ready by doing' approach has observable consequences that places control in your hands and not in the children's. It is useful to take a tambourine into the hall for every PE lesson as it can be used to produce a signal for stopping and starting, thereby reducing strain on the voice. For instance, you can shake the tambourine for about five seconds to indicate that time to complete the task is coming to an end, followed by a single loud tap when you want them to stand still.

3   *I was monitoring the work of the eight Year 3 children who were trying to draw a pattern to show mirror symmetry. I helped the less capable ones by drawing part of the pattern for them, but gently insisted that they do the rest themselves. One boy with learning difficulties required a lot of help from me before he would do anything for himself. As I moved around the group, an able child told me that she could not do the task either. I tried to cajole her into persevering but she became adamant that the task was beyond her. As I knew full well that she was more than capable of doing it, I said that I was not prepared to help until she had at least made an effort. She suddenly pointed at the little boy with learning difficulties and, in floods of tears, claimed that as I had helped him, I should be helping her. I didn't know what to say or do. If I helped her then I was worried that she would become dependent on me and think that she could get her own way by crying. If I refused to help then she might get even more upset. I could imagine that she might go home that night and tell her mother that the teacher (me!) had been horrible to her. In the end I agreed to help her, but no sooner had I begun to do so than she took the pencil out of my hand and completed the task within minutes. She then thrust her work under my nose and had the audacity to tell me that it was too easy for her! Did I do the right thing?*

It is very disconcerting when children become upset. Trainees feel vulnerable and anxious that they have unwittingly caused the problem. In most cases, the tears dry up quickly and a little word of reassurance is sufficient. You seem to have handled the situation well. The girl completed her work and you offered an appropriate level of support in the circumstances. Helping vulnerable children to work independently takes time and persistence. Despite her intelligence, the girl is clearly lacking self-confidence, so using the same amount of encouragement and praise that you would employ for a less able child is the best strategy. It may be worth finding opportunities for the girl to assist her less able classmate as a means of enhancing her sense of worth. The girl's apparent audacity was, in fact, an expression of relief on her part and should have received the same appreciative comment from you as if she had not received help. Interpreting her behaviour as audacity is to unfairly attribute to her a sophistication that she is unlikely to possess at her age.

4 *I was teaching a literacy hour to my Year 5 class. At first they listened quite well, but two of the boys started getting silly and restless. I tried to ignore them but their antics were distracting the others. Then a few more children began to whisper together and giggle. I told them off and tried to sound stern but the impact of my words only lasted for a short time before they started again. I could hear myself getting cross and the pitch of my voice rising due to my anxiety, but the harder I worked at gaining their attention, the worse it became. By the time I sent them to work at tables, I was feeling a bit desperate and slightly humiliated. Later in the lesson I sent one of the children to another class for what was, quite honestly, a fairly minor misdemeanour, but I was at the end of my tether. How did things get to such a state, especially when I had planned so thoroughly and had such a good lesson last time?*

Teaching is full of high points and low points. Just when you think everything is going along smoothly, there is an unexpected setback. When you are speaking to children and have said that you do not want to be interrupted, but find that they persist in doing so, write down their names on the board each time it happens. Do so without looking in their direction or making a comment. The children will almost certainly ask why you have taken the action. You can answer simply that they broke the rule but refuse to say any more or argue about the matter. If, by the end of the day, a name is written down three times, then a sanction is imposed. At the start of the next day, the names are erased. If you persevere and do not get angry or agitated about the interruptions, the strategy will almost certainly ensure that children's behaviour improves dramatically. In the short term it would have been worth moving one of the boys out of eye contact with his friend, stopping the lesson briefly to insist that the whole class sat up and paid attention, while briefly stiffening your tone of voice and body language. Your overreaction at a later time happened because your emotional distress was out of proportion to the events of the lesson. Your perception of the lesson's apparent failure was probably not a true reflection of what was, from the children's point of view, an unexceptional session. On the other hand you may want to review the lesson carefully to identify the point at which it began to falter. The children were not naughty from the moment you started, so carrying out a post-mortem on what triggered their restlessness part way through will help to identify the cause.

Exceptional cases: trainee teachers' experiences

All trainees have to learn to cope with the demands of classroom life, through a combination of hard experience, advice and thoughtful reflection. The following selection of stories from school experience, recounted by trainee teachers, indicates the extreme range of challenges that they faced in school and strategies that they developed for handling them. It is very important to note that while individual children presented challenging behaviour, the vast majority of the class was well behaved, so while the situation had to be dealt with, it was important that the rest of the class did not suffer as a result.

Nursery class

Marty, a four-year old boy in the nursery required constant supervision for his own safety and that of the rest of the children. If Marty couldn't get his own way he would throw tantrums, shout and try to hurt someone close by. One morning he came into the nursery quite happily and sat down next to the toy train track. After a few minutes other children decided they wanted to play with the trains but by this time Marty had all the trains attached in a long line. The other children asked politely if they could have just one train and carriage but he retorted that 'they are mine'. He became angrier and angrier as the other children attempted to unhook a train to play with. I went across and asked what was going on in a strong, sharp tone. I bent down and lowered my voice so that they had to be quiet to hear what I was saying. Marty was able to explain his side of the situation and then I asked the other children what they were doing. In this way, all parties had an opportunity to give their views. Although Marty was still shouting, I felt more in control of the situation and initiated a game with the trains that would involve all the children. I talked to the children about using please and thank you and the need to share equipment. The rest of the children and I began our game and gradually Marty stopped his tantrum and took an interest in what we were doing. Once he started to co-operate I was able to praise him and draw him in. I was pleased that although I had not foreseen the possible difficulties created by the trains, especially the large amount of floor space they needed, I was able to stay calm in the situation and find ways to commend Marty's good behaviour.

Key points

- ◆ Marty's problems stemmed from immaturity and poor social skills
- ◆ Angry children need calm adults
- ◆ Improved organization helps to offset inappropriate behaviour.

Year 1 class

Joe was unpopular with the teachers and feared by the other children. He came across as a surly child with a huge chip on his shoulder. Joe seemed to feel that everything that happened was unfair and that nothing was his responsibility. He was on the fringe of boys who were the rough-and-tumble types that charged around the playground and played football. Joe wanted to be with this group but bullied them too often to be really welcome. He would work grudgingly and many times I saw him mouth the answers to questions but refuse to give them openly.

All of the children had a straw in their trays with which to have a drink from a cup. None of the children were given free access to the sink to obtain water unless given permission by the teacher, and even when they were allowed, the rule was that it was only one person at a time. One day, when it was very hot, I gave the children permission to get a drink if they needed to, and reminded them about the 'one at a time' rule. One child immediately got up and went to the sink. Almost before I had finished asking the class to resume working, Joe got out of his seat and followed the first child. I was stunned at his blatant disobedience and asked him in quite a loud voice and in front of everyone if he had heard what I had said. He glared at me and said that yes, he had heard me. I asked him to state the rule, and when he did so I asked him why he had gone against my instructions. He gave me a withering look and shrugged his shoulders. Joe often contravened rules in this way.

In the short term I dealt as best I could with the situation but there was a wider issue to address with Joe. He was very disaffected with school and this manifested itself in boredom, anger and disobedience. He appeared to lack motivation and was very under-challenged by the work that was set. Joe would sometimes finish his work very quickly, and to a high standard, then bother the other children on his table who were still finishing.

Joe's almost total lack of desire to please the teacher was strange and unsettling. I have never seen a young child act so belligerently. It seemed that there were issues of control and power that were being resolved between him and adults. I tried to encourage Joe by giving him extension work in mathematics (particularly) and used circle time to develop his social skills, build his self-esteem and make him feel that there was more to be gained from co-operating and fitting in than from being alienated. I made a point of sitting next to Joe sometimes, and although he eyed me suspiciously, I was able to affirm publicly how impressed I was with his work in mathematics and his understanding of the subject. The class teacher said later that she observed that his eyes lit up and he grew at least three inches in stature!

Key points

◆ Joe's problems stemmed from a lack of motivation
◆ Joe's low self-concept manifested itself in antisocial behaviour
◆ Even naughty children need encouragement.

Year 2 class

Mustafa often looked unhappy. One day in the playground he hurried over to me and complained that Arun had just sworn at him. I quickly tried to determine the most effective and appropriate way to deal with the situation, especially as I had not witnessed the incident. I decided that a tactful approach without immediately accusing Arun might be the best approach. I went across to Arun and told him that although I did not know for sure whether he had used bad language, I would be disappointed if it were true and expected better from him. I reminded both the children of the rules and how we should be kind to one another, stressing that if I heard such language I would have to take action. I also said that as I did not know the truth about the incident, I was not telling them off but reminding them of the agreement the whole class had made to speak kindly to one another. I spoke to them in a soft voice, at their height (almost kneeling down) and with strong eye contact.

I knew that Arun had a tendency to get upset easily at times and tended to react forcibly to the actions of others. I was also aware that Mustafa had the knack of upsetting children due to his domineering attitude. I could imagine what had happened: Mustafa initially interrupting something that Arun was doing and receiving a mouthful of abuse for his pains! In the end, I asked the children to apologize to each other and advised them to play separately for a while to diffuse any ill feeling between them. I still don't know if I made the right decision but it seemed to work.

Key points

◆ Playground bullying takes many forms
◆ Teachers need to check the facts before jumping to conclusions
◆ Deep-seated problems need long-term strategies.

Year 4 class

While the majority of the class listened and participated during lessons, the weakest academic children constantly fiddled and argued about pencils, complained about being stared at by others, kicked each other under the desk, and so forth. They not only disrupted the rest of the class but soaked up a lot of teacher attention. Although the experienced class teacher dealt with the situation firmly, it took time for me to develop my own strategies. I made sure that each child had a pencil to avoid them squabbling at the start of the activity and separated the two children who were the principal troublemakers. Finally, I made them miss their playtime. However, all these strategies had only a temporary effect, so I separated the cluster of tables so that they were sitting in a row rather than facing each other. I took advice from the class teacher and told this group of children that there were good and bad choices in life, so every decision reinforced one or the other. They could make a good choice by not disrupting the lesson, in which case everyone would be happy, or a bad choice by continuing their current behaviour and suffer the consequences.

In addition to taking these preventative actions, I wanted to get to the root cause of the problem and find out why the children were misbehaving in the first place. I was concerned that the work I was giving to them was too advanced, so I spent some time working closely with them to get a better feel of their capability. I also tried to give these children less public attention as I felt that this was unhelpful. On the teacher's advice I practised using my natural voice at closer range to the child rather than shouting across the room and this strategy was very effective.

Key points

◆ A combination of short and long-term strategies is best
◆ Unobtrusive personal attention benefits low-ability children
◆ Advice from an experienced teacher is invaluable.

Year 6 class

Mary and Ramona kept talking while I was talking, not concentrating on the task, and trying to drag other girls into their conversations. Mary had a history of intermittent bad behaviour and could get very sulky. As it was early in the placement, I did not know the children well and my response to their behaviour was therefore not as good as it might have been. I followed the school's disciplinary procedure and gave three warnings but there was no improvement. I became rattled by their disturbing antics, which they could plainly see, and as a result they carried on misbehaving. My public reprimands had little effect and whatever I said to them would be met with each of them accusing the others of being the perpetrators and getting louder and more assertive as they did so. Although I tried pointing out the consequences of their behaviour to the two of them, they lacked motivation and incentive. They had recently completed their end of key stage tests and were transferring to secondary school after the summer break, so as far as they were concerned, their poor behaviour did not have any serious consequences. I did not have any other strategies in my repertoire to deal with the situation, so I tried my best to ignore them and carry on with the lesson. By the end of the session I felt humiliated and angry, both with the girls for inflicting their behaviour on me, and with myself for being unable to stop them.

On reflection I realized that I should have adopted a different approach. Instead of telling them off in front of the class and giving them an audience for their antics, I should have gone across to them and privately delivered a soft reprimand. I also needed to be more consistent in my ways. Sometimes I chose to ignore minor misdemeanours and let them go until they became too noticeable to other pupils for me to ignore. On other occasions I would be watching a particular child, ready to pounce if he or she showed signs of the slightest naughtiness. With minor, repetitive behaviour I learned to ignore it but to monitor the situation closely. If a reprimand were necessary, I would wait until the child was about to misbehave in the same way again rather than at the end of the previous episode. In this way, the reprimand was associated with the temptation to misbehave, not the pleasure of doing so.

Key points

◆ Consistency of approach is vital
◆ Public attention feeds unruly behaviour
◆ Potential problems need to be nipped in the bud.

Case studies: developing effective strategies

Earlier examples of the ways in which trainee teachers dealt with challenging situations underlined the importance of the need to think carefully about methods to combat unsatisfactory behaviour. The six situations described below are typical of those found in primary classrooms. Consider how you would develop strategies to address the fundamental issues in terms of the following three points:

◆ The source of the problem
◆ The range of options available to you
◆ The implications for future adult/child relationships.

---

1 Wendy, a six-year old girl in Year 1 is not willing to apply herself to her writing. You have tried persuasion and various kinds of encouragement but nothing seems to work. You suspect that Wendy could perform the task but for some reason chooses not to do so. You are becoming frustrated at her lack of progress and apparent unwillingness to try, so you find yourself pressurizing her. This approach produces only a grudging effort by Wendy, who complains miserably that she doesn't understand what to do.

Pointers
◆ Give Wendy some starting phrases for her work
◆ Set short-term attainable goals
◆ Adopt a more upbeat approach to her ability to complete tasks.

Establishing and maintaining a settled classroom relies principally on the teacher and pupils feeling secure and confident, the relevance of work and the way that adults and children coexist. If mutually supportive relationships exist, then the atmosphere is one where success is celebrated, mistakes are accepted, viewpoints are tolerated and learning happens naturally. In particular, as McNamara and Moreton (2001, p. 44) remind us:

> The relationship that pupils have with their teachers is crucial for the way in which they behave in the classroom. On the most basic level, children will try to succeed with their behaviour or their work for a teacher they feel comfortable with and whom they like.

---

2 David, a seven year-old boy, is overactive, non-conforming, impulsive and lacks self-control. He experiences learning difficulties and has very poor attention skills. He often exhibits a high level of attention seeking. In the past, David has received a lot of attention for his 'odd' behaviour and his mother openly laughs at his antics when she meets him after school. The amount of work he produces is minimal, which is hardly surprising as he spends a lot of time off-task, staring at the ceiling or at other children and wandering about. The usual reward system seems to make little difference to his attitude.

Pointers
- Commend David when he is good
- Involve him in setting targets for his own behaviour
- Have realistic but not low expectations.

---

3 Philip and Wolf, aged eight years, seem incapable of remaining in their seats during group work. As a result, Philip interferes with other children's work around the room and Wolf regularly underachieves. They both find all sorts of reasons, like the need to find a book, for not getting on with their work. They are not outwardly defiant, but are born wanderers and lack concentration. They set a poor example to others in the class and you find it hard not to get angry with them. You feel rather threatened by their subtle defiance and secretly wonder if they are contemptuous of your authority.

Pointers
- Establish time limits for completion of work
- Check that resources are close at hand
- Reassure yourself that their behaviour is not personal to you.

4 Four-year old Kelly does not seem willing to try hard with her work. She stares at the page but won't actively do anything unless prompted. She sometimes gets part way through a task and gives up. Several times she has deliberately crumpled up her work or scribbled on it. Most recently you found several items of other children's work torn up and thrown in the bin. Kelly denies that she is responsible but you are almost sure that she is the culprit.

Pointers
- ◆ Permit Kelly to do more of what she enjoys doing
- ◆ Prominently display several pieces of her work
- ◆ Encourage her to assist other children.

5 Brigita, aged eleven years, has a bright, engaging personality and is usually the first to volunteer for jobs. She relates easily to adults but is not popular with her peers. She is academically slow and uses every excuse to avoid working. When challenged she pleads helplessness and, following your patient explanation, assures you that she understands. However, things never seem to improve.

Pointers
- ◆ Accept Brigita for the person she is
- ◆ Channel her enthusiasm rather than suppress it
- ◆ Give her an opportunity to gain public recognition in other ways (e.g. during an assembly).

This chapter has explored issues and practical situations relating to children's behaviour and to the employment of appropriate discipline strategies. Part 3 concludes with Chapter 11, where the complex but important procedures relating to pupil assessment are scrutinized.

CHAPTER 11

Assessing children's progress

Assessments

Assessing children's progress in learning is a challenge for every teacher, especially if the class is large and varied. The vivid description provided by Acker (1999) of a Year 4 classroom scene indicates the diversity of ability and disposition found in most groups:

> In general, the children were cooperative and there was a buzz of activity. In every group, there were always some children who put in little effort or did not do the work at all. Some children were frequently in this mode, others from time to time. The large ability span in each group was the reason for this situation . . . two other boys could not do the regular work at all; one of these children was tiny and could have been taken for a 5-year old. Four or five others were seriously below average in their ability to read and do other schoolwork. There were also children at the top end of the spectrum.
>
> (Acker 1999, p. 57)

At one level, regular teaching contact with children means that it is almost impossible *not* to assess their academic and social learning progress to some extent. However, like every other teaching skill, assessment can be carried out well or badly, the difference being that effective assessment supports learning whereas poor assessment does not. There are at least four reasons why the assessment of children's work is important:

1 It helps to shape lesson preparation and make it more relevant to children's needs.
2 It gives insights into what and how a child is learning.
3 It offers benchmarks to judge academic progress.
4 It allows learning problems to be more effectively identified and subsequently remedied.

Assessment relies largely on *evidence*. While your own intuition and close familiarity with children's work can act as a general guide in evaluating their progress, it is less exact than using specific measures. Drummond (1993) offers a timely warning that 'assumptions about a child's ability are sometimes based on superficial impressions rather than evidence. A poorly produced piece of work may say more about motivation, misunderstanding or uncertainty about the task, than a lack of understanding' (1993, p. 158). Assessment evidence needs, therefore, to be accumulated over a period of time rather than based on a single piece of work or test result. Most evidence comes from one or more of four sources:

◆ What children say about their work
◆ What children write down as a result of their work
◆ The way children respond to questions concerning the work
◆ Children's ability to transfer knowledge to new situations.

Children are often concerned more about the procedural aspects of their work than the substance. Consequently, questions directed towards the teacher usually concern what they have to do and how they must go about it, rather than inquisitiveness about the issues or discussion of the concepts. It is difficult for teachers to find time to talk to children individually to ascertain their understanding and grasp of detail but it requires determination to promote deeper learning as opposed to superficial learning (see Chapter 7). Instances of superficiality are commonly found in everyday life. For instance, consider how often it is possible to read the name of a place on a road sign yet be unable to spell it, or to travel a certain way every day for years, but be incapable of naming the roads and streets that form the route. The reason for this phenomenon is that the main purpose of the journey is to get from point A to point B and not to improve spelling or memorize a street map. If, however, you travelled the same route with the express purpose of mastering these details, the journey would take on a completely different perspective. Similarly children can 'follow the path' that you set before them in lessons by, for example, completing activity sheets and spending time on tasks without really focusing intently on the things that need to be understood and mastered. Fisher (1995) comments that focusing is part of what he refers to as 'cognitive coaching' that encourages the child to engage 'thinkingly' with the work. 'Where there is no challenge, no mental effort, then no new learning will take place' (Fisher 1995, p. 111). There is, therefore, not only a close relationship between assessment and children's learning, but between assessment and the *quality of your teaching*. If you succeed in making work relevant and interesting for children by raising good questions, speculating aloud, pointing out details and offering them opportunities to explore and create, then the quality of learning outcomes will be enriched. On the basis of this principle, assessment of children's attainment is not merely a functional procedure to discover what children know and understand, but is directly related to the skill with which you present and provide a productive learning milieu for them. To put it bluntly, if children do not appear to have learned much, the explanation has its roots in your teaching as much as in their ability or aptitude.

Assessment evidence is not only useful to assist lesson planning but also to inform other people who have an interest in the child's progress, especially teachers and parents. All teachers should therefore be asking how their assessments help them to meet pupils' learning needs more effectively and how written records of progress are best recorded, stored and translated into reports that are of use to others (see Figure 11.1).

Assessment is intended to be value-free. In other words, it is a mechanism to evaluate children's progress and discern ways in which they can be helped to do better. It is not intended to be used as a threat to force children to work harder, as a means of preferment or a measure of a child's individual worth. The danger that assessment can act as a further lowering of less able children's self-esteem and self-confidence is one that should cause you to approach this important area of your work thoughtfully.

The assessment evidence used (*tick as many as appropriate*)

◆ Written work completed

◆ Other completed work (not written)

◆ Children reading aloud from their work

◆ Children giving oral feedback about their work

◆ Results from group tasks

◆ Presentations by individual children

◆ Presentations by pairs or groups of children

◆ Demonstrations by individual children

◆ Demonstrations by pairs or groups of children

◆ Other (state)
  Names of children who struggled:
  The nature of their difficulties:
  Strategies to address the problems:
  Names of children who were under-challenged:
  Strategies to address the problems:

Figure 11.1 *Assessment proforma*

MARRA

MARRA is an acronym that stands for monitoring, assessing, recording, reporting and accountability. The acronym is more likely to be heard on teacher training and education courses than it is in school staff rooms. Teachers tend to use the term 'formative assessment' when they are referring to an evaluation of children's work during lessons and 'summative assessment' when referring to a formal evaluation of work at the conclusion of the task. Definitions for each letter of the MARRA acronym are broadly as follows:

◆ *Monitoring*: the regulating of children's work and progress during lessons
◆ *Assessing*: a general term associated with judgements about the quality of children's work
◆ *Recording*: the formal written record of children's progress using grades, marks or written descriptions
◆ *Reporting*: the process of transmitting information to colleagues and parents about a child's academic progress and achievement
◆ *Accountability*: a responsibility imposed on every teacher to set children appropriate targets for learning and work that reflects their ability.

One of the anomalies of the MARRA acronym is that the first letter 'A' (assessment) is the same word as the one that is used to describe the overall process. An alternative is MIRRA, using an 'I' instead of an A, to refer to the key skill of *intervention* in support of children's learning, whereby teachers provide help and encouragement during lessons, assist children to understand concepts, guide them to master skills and refocus their attention on the task. Thus, the MIRRA acronym stands for monitoring, intervening, recording, reporting and accountability, which together comprise the complete process of assessment (see Figure 11.2).

Yet another way of viewing the MARRA acronym is to interpret the final 'A' as achievement instead of accountability, linked to the four words of MARR. Thus:

◆ Monitoring achievement
◆ Assessing achievement
◆ Recording achievement
◆ Reporting achievement.

Assessment methods

Assessment of progress relies on having a reasonably clear idea about a child's present level of knowledge, skills and understanding that can feed into the detailed lesson plans and production of supporting activities. Five approaches are most commonly employed to elicit basic information about children's *existing* knowledge:

Monitoring	Monitoring
Assessing	Intervening
Recording	Recording
Reporting	Reporting
Accountability	Accountability

Figure 11.2 MARRA and MIRRA

Comment

The most recent guidance in respect of the standards that have to be achieved before QTS can be awarded (TTA 2002b) include three statements that directly relate to assessment, namely:

S3.2.1: Make appropriate use of a range of monitoring and assessment strategies to evaluate pupils' progress towards planned learning objectives, and use this information to improve their own planning and teaching.

S3.2.2: Monitor and assess as they teach, giving immediate and constructive feedback to support pupils as they learn . . . involve pupils in reflecting on, evaluating and improving their own performance.

S3.2.3: Able to assess pupil's progress accurately using . . . assessment frameworks or objectives from the national strategies. [Trainee teachers] may have guidance from an experienced teacher where appropriate.

Teaching principle

Assessments should enhance the quality of your teaching and the children's learning.

---

1   Children are encouraged to tell the teacher about the things they know. With older children, allowing them to talk in small groups first and report back to the rest of the class can facilitate this process. (This is a good teaching strategy at any time.)

2   Children are asked to draw or in some way represent the scope of their ideas by using a series of pictures, a chart, diagram or table. Younger children may need to work with a teaching assistant to complete this task.

3   The teacher writes down a number of key words and phrases about a topic with which the children may be familiar. In pairs or small groups they allocate them to three categories: *well known, slightly known, not known*. More capable children can add their own words and phrases to the list.

4   Children are organized into groups to design their own spider diagrams (sometimes referred to as concept maps) linking up the key words and phrases described in item 3 above. Where appropriate, you may want to distribute overhead projector transparencies and pens so that the final products can be shared visually with the whole class.

5   Children are placed in groups, each with a large blank sheet of paper, given the topic headings and asked to design a poster with differing features, such as key words and pictures that can be displayed around the room. ICT can be also used to produce the posters.

Once the information has been collated, the next stage of the process is to discuss with the children what has been produced and allow them opportunity to talk openly about the topic or subject area. Beard and Lloyd (1995) stress the need for teachers to listen to what children say as a means of assessing their understanding. 'Opportunities to listen to children talking in a variety of situations – alone in groups, during problem solving activities, in fantasy play, in the playground and in structured classroom environment – are a crucial part of assessment' (Beard and Lloyd 1995, p. 6). By listening carefully and asking gentle, probing questions, you can help to promote a dialogue, gain children's trust and discover more about the extent of their understanding and knowledge. As a principle, it is good practice to encourage children to review their own learning regularly, highlighting areas for celebration and improvement, and identifying where gaps and misunderstandings in their knowledge exist. The establishment of a child's present knowledge, skills and understanding is referred to as *baseline assessment*, though this term was originally used in respect of new school entrants (see Lindsay and Desforges 1998).

Clemson and Clemson (1996, p. 67) suggest that there are ten basic steps involved in making any type of assessment (my emphases):

1   What is the assessment *of*?
2   What is the assessment *for*?
3   What *resources* are needed?
4   What do the children actually *do*?
5   What *information* do I need to collect?
6   How am I going to *collect* it?
7   How shall I *collate* the information?

8   What are the possible *judgements* I can make?
9   What shall I do with the *outcomes*?
10   What happens *after* the assessment?

These ten steps provide a useful structure for the way that you go about assessing children's learning.

First, you need to be clear as to precisely what aspect of the children's work you are assessing. It may be something basic like spelling or specific like the ability to use speech marks. It may be quantitative in nature, resulting in a score, or qualitative in nature, reflecting qualities such as the ability to persevere with a problem. With formative assessment that happens during lessons you will instinctively be on the lookout for ways in which you can draw children's attention to improving their general work practices. Such practices might include neatness, layout, conforming to procedures and correct handling of equipment. In addition, however, you will want to make a more considered and thorough summative scrutiny to find out whether children understand a particular aspect of the work. This is often accomplished by setting them a task that will help to pinpoint specific aspects that have been grasped and those that remain doubtful.

Second, the assessment may be for the purpose of evaluating the progress of certain target children (a high, average and low attainer, for instance) to give you an indication of the class's overall progress or it might be an assessment of every child (e.g. through setting an identical, time-limited task) for purposes of comparison. Assessments may be to gain data for a formal report or (more likely for trainees) to guide future differentiation of activities. For example, if the assessment showed that the majority of children completed work too quickly, it suggests that either the task was too easy, the time allowed was too long, the explanation from you about what had to be done was inadequate or the work was conceptually too advanced. These points can form the basis for your lesson evaluation.

Third, the resources needed will be influenced by the purpose of the assessment. If you are only interested in gaining a superficial view of 'how things are going', the resources merely consist of a sharp pair of eyes and a means of recording your observations. If the assessment is more formal and systematic, you may require photocopies of the test and (for older children) sufficient space in the room so that they can carry out the work undisturbed. It is particularly important to have all the necessary equipment for test purposes as it is difficult to leave the room once the session has commenced.

Knowledge of the conditions under which the work being assessed takes place has to be taken into account when making a formal assessment of it. For instance, there is a considerable difference between the quality of work that would be expected between a task that was being attempted for the first time and one that was familiar to the children. Similarly, the judgements that are made about the finished product must be subject to factors such as the amount of adult or peer help that was received, the time available to complete the task and the amount of information given beforehand. Children may be engaged in a practical activity in which availability of resources and dexterity are significant, or a pen-and-paper exercise in which being systematic and well organized have a profound influence on outcomes. For example, a child with poor fine motor skills may be intellectually capable of separating a miscellany of items on the basis of their characteristics but fail to do so properly owing to clumsiness or slow pace of working. Similarly, a child with a sharp mind may make unnecessary errors in mathematical calculation due to poor layout of work or poor time management. Assessment is not, therefore, a detached activity based on supposed objective measures but a process that is influenced by a familiarity with the classroom context and individual circumstances. Your lack of awareness of these factors when you arrive is one reason why you should be cautious about making judgements about children's ability too soon in the placement.

The information required to assess attainment depends on what you are trying to find out. If your assessment criteria for a lesson or series of lessons are sufficiently well defined, then the assessment criteria will closely match them. For instance, if you are interested in whether children can use a particular writing frame, the content of your lesson(s) will already have addressed the sorts of issues associated with the best way to go about it. You will probably have given examples, allowed the class to practise the techniques, commented on drafts and offered constructive feedback. You have to determine the most appropriate time to check whether the children have properly grasped what you have been teaching them either by:

1   Using the work that they have been carrying out during the lessons as primary data.
2   Setting up a specific and distinct written task for them to carry out separately soon after the end of the lesson or series of lessons, take the work in at the end and grade it.

As a trainee teacher option 1 is likely to be the main source of information, as the immediacy of the data will give you a broad idea about the overall success of the lesson. However, unless you evaluate each child's output closely, you may not accumulate much evidence about the progress of *individuals*. Once you take greater responsibility for the teaching, you may want to use the second approach (option 2) occasionally to make a more formal assessment of target children or of each child in the group/class. The assessment of younger children more often depends upon verbal interaction between teacher and pupil than relying on written evidence. In such cases, the nature of your questions will obviously have to reflect what it is you are interested in finding out. Some less confident children require a lot of coaxing before they expose the full extent of their knowledge and understanding. Discussing the work with several children at one time can be successful, providing the dominant ones don't so all the talking! The more that children contribute towards the assessment procedures by offering their views about their own progress, the richer and more relevant for them the process of learning becomes.

Collating the information is challenging for every teacher owing to the time it takes and deciding what to include. Some teachers like to keep a 'mark book' with children's names listed down the left hand side and the grades or comments written alongside. Others use a notebook with a separate page for every child and record both quantitative scores and accompanying qualitative comment. For instance, Yahia might score nine out of ten for his mathematics test and the comment might read: 'Worked better independently than expected'. Some schools have assessment proformas that each teacher has to use as part of an agreed policy. If schools use end-of-year optional tests as well as the statutory end-of-key-stage tests, the procedures for testing and recording are well established. In other cases, the rule of thumb should be to record only those facts that (a) cannot be committed to memory, (b) assist in planning future work, (c) contribute towards a formal record (such as a report to parents). From your perspective, the second of these alternatives is particularly relevant. Consequently, your judgements about the quality of work and level of pupil comprehension are very important in respect of matching your lesson plans to children's ability and normally fall under one of three categories:

1   The child completed the work satisfactorily and is ready to move on to new or slightly more complex work.
2   The child did not complete the work satisfactorily, or with considerable adult support, and will require revision and reinforcement.
3   The child completed the work too easily and can cope with more advanced tasks.

Decisions about which of the three categories pertain are normally quite straight-forward on the basis of your observations about how the children deal with the set tasks and respond to your questions, but the *action* required is more challenging. If all the children completed the work satisfactorily, planning the next lesson or lessons can proceed as anticipated. However, if a small number of children struggle or fail to achieve to an acceptable level (as judged by you) a number of possibilities are open to you:

1   Spend time explaining and rehearsing points with them outside the lesson time
2   Get the children to repeat some of the work at the next convenient opportunity
3   Include a less difficult element as part of the next lesson so that the less confident children can find success with some of the work
4   Allocate the work for homework.

None of these options is problem-free. Option (1) normally has to be carried out during a break (recess) or, to avoid children missing their play time, extracting them from a lesson. Option (2) means that they have less time to do the work for the present lesson, which will result in them falling further behind. Option (3) involves differentiating tasks more precisely. Option (4) may be perceived as a punishment rather than a helpful method of remedying the problem and there may not be a knowledgeable adult available at home to offer support. To reduce the need to implement any of these 'catching up' strategies it pays to be more careful in the initial allocation of tasks, so that children don't endlessly struggle to keep pace and thereby lose heart.

Although it is a good policy to make the earlier tasks straightforward to give children the chance for immediate success, there is little to be learned about their ability by giving them work that offers little or no challenge. Children who struggle with a demanding task deserve to be commended, even if the final product is threadbare. Even with the most assiduous attention to differentiation, there are occasions when some children struggle to cope. There are also absences from class that disrupt proceedings, as when the child returns you have to carve out small pieces of time for 'catching up'.

Foundation Stage assessment

The original national framework for baseline assessment for new school entrants (SCAA 1997) embodied principles of equal entitlement and the provision of sufficient detail to identify specific learning needs and was designed so that children's later progress could be effectively monitored. The handbook of guidance (TTA 2002b) notes that trainees will be able to demonstrate that they meet this stage through familiarity with the structure and uses of the Foundation Stage profile. Details of the profile are available on the QCA web site: www.qca.org.uk.

The use of the term 'profile' in the latest legislation is significant, as it reflects a fresh approach to the assessment of young children based on what a child actually knows and is capable of doing with respect to the early learning goals and the foundation curriculum. The use of a profile avoids the need for the children to take tests and perform tasks. Instead, it is built over time and relies on the teacher's observations, perceptions and garnering of evidence through regular interaction with the children. The curriculum provided is intended to build towards the early learning goals.

The *Curriculum Guidance for the Foundation Stage* (DfEE 2000) provides stepping stones of progress towards the early learning goals that help teachers to identify the knowledge, skills, understanding and attitudes that children need to achieve the goals. The stepping stones are not supposed to be age-related but broadly speaking the yellow band applies to three year olds, the blue to four year olds and the green to five year olds. The early learning goals are underpinned by the stepping stones and are organized in six areas of learning:

◆ Personal, social and emotional well-being
◆ Communication, language and literacy

◆ Mathematical development
◆ Knowledge and understanding of the world
◆ Physical development
◆ Creative development.

The value of this holistic approach is that it reduces unnecessary formality, though there has to be a particular emphasis on language and literacy and mathematical development throughout the foundation stage. The disadvantage of the approach is that it may tempt teachers to measure characteristics of children that do not lend themselves to quantitative treatment. For example, it is one thing to describe a child's attitude in terms of being 'immature' or 'mature'; it is quite another thing to allocate a grade for it! Information about children's social development is important because it can help to explain their behaviour and application to work, which in turn influences both lesson preparation and your attitude to them in sessions.

Monitoring and intervention

Monitoring and intervening, in which a teacher's comments, questions and advice help children to know, do and understand better, is an integral part of the formative dimension of assessment that takes place during the lesson. *Monitoring* involves keeping a close eye on how children are coping with the practical application of the work. It is a term that is also applied to classroom management, especially supervising children's behaviour (see Chapter 10), but from an assessment perspective it refers specifically to safeguarding the quality of attainment. *Intervention* is the process of active encounter with children to acknowledge progress, correct their misunderstandings and redirect their thinking. Intervention not only supports teaching but provides a lot of information about how children are coping with the work and the different challenges that they face. Monitoring should provide clues about where and how to intervene. However, the act of intervening can distract you from monitoring the rest of the class if you become too immersed in the learning needs of a small number of children and ignore everyone else.

As monitoring and assessing often takes place when children are dealing with tasks and activities that have been set for them, interventions should be as discreet as possible to avoid embarrassing sensitive children. Older children especially do not want others in the class to be aware that they are struggling with the work, so tact is essential when responding to their requests for help or offering advice about improvement. On the other hand, examples of good work and innovative ideas should be shared with the rest of the children, either immediately or in the plenary phase. The following eight principles should guide your intervention strategy:

1   Note and commend the child's ability to recall and utilize previous knowledge and experience.

2   Affirm what the child is saying through approving facial expression and body language.
3   Encourage children to make choices and decisions for themselves, rather than merely telling them what to do and think.
4   Support children who decide to take risks and openly praise their willingness to try.
5   Stand alongside the children as they delve into new experiences by prompting, offering suggestions and praising their endeavour.
6   Generate an adventurous spirit of enquiry by offering innovative suggestions of your own.
7   Take particular care over vocabulary, use of specialist terms and adult expressions that young children may not grasp.
8   Use verbal praise, ticks and brief approving comments on the children's work to affirm their progress.

Marking and feedback

Years ago, marking normally consisted of giving a piece of work a score to indicate its worth. A piece of work considered by the teacher to be poor would receive, say, four out of ten or a grade E. Similarly, a piece of work considered to be good would receive nine out of ten or grade A, and so on. As mentioned earlier, however, marking is more worthwhile if it takes account of five factors:

◆ The appropriateness of the task
◆ The time given for the task
◆ The extent of adult or peer assistance
◆ The children's understanding about what the teacher expects from them
◆ Children's interpretation of the teacher's comments and grades.

In an ideal world, individual feedback would be given to every child about his or her work *during* the session, as it is far better to discuss issues with the child present than (say) writing an evaluative comment at the bottom of the work while sitting in the staff room. Clarke (2001) makes the point that marking away from the child (distance marking) particularly disadvantages less confident children, as only the most confident and able are willing to ask the teacher to explain the meaning of comments on their work. However, the practicalities of school life and large classes ensure that some work *has* to be marked away from the classroom, in which case it is important to consider the amount of time that you have at your disposal. Marking can become a wearisome chore and occupy a lot of time if you allow it to do so. Consider, too, the impact that your evaluation of the work will have upon children's enthusiasm for learning. Scrawled comments across the page, written in the late evening when you are feeling exhausted, can have a damaging effect when viewed by a child in the fresh light of day. Ironically, many children enjoy a simple 'well done' or a smiley face, even though it does not offer them any suggestions about improving the work. A combination of a brief written comment and a fuller explanation when you return the work to the child is an effective and manageable means of communicating your ideas about its merit and potential.

Marking for younger and older primary children will differ in type. Very young children may not comprehend long sentences, so written comments should be necessarily short and pointed. Alternatively, a 'good work' sticker/stamp or equivalent can be used. Older primary children may prefer a summary sentence and, in some cases, a numerical mark or grade. Some schools have marking policies that require teachers to write a comment about each major piece of work, in the hope and expectation that the child will respond by writing something in return or saying something directly to the teacher. This process can make a powerful contribution to learning but is extremely time-consuming and, inevitably, you have to be selective about the work that merits such treatment.

Other than when you are assessing a formally completed test, there is little point in spending a lot of time evaluating work unless it has a positive influence on a child's progress. Assessments should, therefore, take account of the effort that the child has made as well as the immediate outcome. Thus, it is unfair to penalize children because they have had to hurry to complete work when a longer time span was needed. For example, work during the literacy hour does not always allow time for children to think carefully and experiment with ideas. Assessments should also take account of whether the child was conforming to the 'approved' method (in mathematics, say) or trying to be innovative. Creativity can be interpreted as non-conformity or naughtiness, when in reality it is an expression of a child's desire to explore new ways of doing things. A wilful refusal to obey your directive should not be confused with a child's sincere desire to employ original thinking.

Most children are highly sensitive to an adult's comments, so all feedback must always offer direction and hope to the child, as Clegg and Billington (1994, p. 50) underline: 'Critical feedback has been clearly identified as a feature of effective learning. To make it effective, it has to be positive, and made meaningful by relating it to purpose and intention.' In addition to your own formal assessment of work, it is helpful to invite comments from children about the quality of their work. Although

Teaching principle

Avoid giving the impression that the only reason children do work is to please the teacher.

it takes perseverance and encouragement to involve children in this form of evaluation, it gives them a sense of ownership and a stake in their learning that they would otherwise be denied.

Keeping an assessment file

Files become bulky over the period of a school placement, so after a time it is helpful to separate material relating to lesson planning and assessment from other parts of the file. Similarly, it is useful to keep materials relating to professional development in a different folder. In the lesson-planning folder, it is normally best to put all the lessons for a particular subject in its own subsection, one per subject. Thus, all the literacy lessons are kept in chronological order in the same place in the file, all the mathematics lessons together, and so on. Another folder can be used to store details of your professional development, such as written feedback from tutors, reflective commentaries that you maintain about your progress (daily/weekly), your learning targets for teaching, information from articles about teaching, and so on. You may want to include some information from publications such as *Target Setting and Assessment in the National Literacy Strategy* (QCA 1999) to help you in evaluating children's work and establishing goals.

Assessment comments that relate specifically to an individual lesson can be written directly on to the plan soon after the end of the lesson while events are still fresh in your mind. For example, you may want to make a note about the need to modify the way that children were divided up for activities, owing to the fact that some groups contained children with too widely differing abilities. Again, you may want to annotate the plan to remind yourself that some children require longer to complete a particular task than you first thought. These abbreviated notes should be written in a different colour from the original lesson plan. As part of your annotation, it may be appropriate to use a variety of highlighter colours to remind yourself of key points. For instance, a green highlight can indicate that the children made unexpectedly rapid progress, pink can show confusion about the concept or skill, orange can remind you that rehearsal and further practice is required, and blue can reveal that a part of the lesson was not covered. Any section that is not highlighted indicates that things went according to plan and the children progressed as anticipated, and so on.

Notes about the progress made and the problems encountered by specific children should be written on a separate piece of paper from the plan but, in the short term, kept physically together with it. At the end of each week (say) these more specific comment sheets can be transferred into a separate section in the file on the assumption that by that time you will have taken the necessary action to begin remedying the problem.

Other detailed assessment records, including samples of children's work, mark lists and grades, should be placed in the assessment section rather than with the lesson-planning part. As a consequence, the assessment section becomes the data source for subsequent records and reports. As the mentor or tutor may request evidence about children's progress at any time, it is important to keep the assessment section up to date and organized in an accessible form. For example:

◆ An opening page with your name and the purpose of the section: *Assessment of Children's Learning*
◆ Extracts from the school policy about assessing children's work
◆ Baseline assessments for those children who have been targeted for assessment
◆ Pupil profiling pages, with a section for each child being assessed
◆ Samples of work collected as evidence for assessment
◆ Annotated samples of work with your marking and comments written on them
◆ A photocopy of the appropriate level descriptions from the NC
◆ Levelled pieces of work
◆ Examples of Individual Education Plans (IEPs) where relevant
◆ General comments about children's progress other than the targeted children.

Nearly all teachers and trainee teachers complain, with some justification, about the amount of paperwork that they are required to keep and the time they spend dealing with it, and maintaining assessment records adds to this paper trail. It is certainly true that managing elaborate recording systems and storing large amounts of material can be time-consuming and exhausting. However, effort expended on recording should not be at the expense of lesson preparation and other classroom duties. Wachter (1999, p.63) offers some general tips about strategies for keeping recording under control:

1   Have clearly marked folders, notebooks and Manila envelopes for any papers you need to be able to find again.
2   Sort folders of important papers into files.
3   Store important papers that you need frequently in boxes near where you use them. As far as possible, keep all your paperwork in one place.

It is also important to remember that records about children are confidential, so always use pseudonyms for children in any document that may be seen by others and be careful not to disclose information about a child to anyone other than the teacher or tutor. Generally, if the information is factual (e.g. spelling test scores), there is less need for privacy than if you write a subjective view of a child's personal qualities, application to task or behaviour. If you consider that it is necessary to make a written record of these more intimate details (and this is normally only essential when a child is being specially monitored), it is better not to leave the details in the classroom. If in doubt about the appropriateness of your records and where they should be stored, take advice from the mentor.

This chapter on assessment concludes Part 3, 'Practice'. Part 4 of the book consists of two chapters written specifically for trainee teachers who are approaching the end of their training and actively seeking a first post. Chapter 12 focuses on job applications and interviews; Chapter 13 describes the situation commonly faced by new teachers at the start of the induction year.

Further reading

Clarke, S. (1998) *Targeting Assessment in the Primary Classroom*, London: Hodder and Stoughton.

Buck, D. and Davis, V. (eds) (2001) *Assessing Pupils' Performance Using the P Levels*, London: David Fulton.

PART 4

Progress

CHAPTER 12

Job applications and interviews

Making applications

There is little point in enduring the strains and stresses of a teacher-training course, only to be thwarted when the time comes to find suitable employment. If you are flexible about where you are prepared to work and don't mind applying for a job in less popular areas (notably London and the inner cities) then your search will be much easier. However, bear in mind that if you apply for a job that is a long way from the college, an interview might involve a commitment of up to two days and coincide with time on placement or completing an important assignment for college. Tutors and mentors understand that interviews inevitably require time away, but if you have applied for several jobs and are unsuccessful in your initial attempts to secure a post, you may have to take several absences, with the attendant disruption to your school experience that this incurs. Some trainees prefer to complete their final placement before beginning to search in earnest, though in some cases this strategy entails missing out on suitable positions that may come up during that period of time.

If you are restricted geographically, there are fewer jobs for which to apply, so the earlier you begin the better. It is often the more mature students (frequently with family commitments) who do not possess the flexibility enjoyed by their single counterparts, and although being a bit older is not necessarily a disadvantage, it does not give you an advantage either, especially where the competition is fierce. Applications from mature people need to stress life experiences (such as raising children), stability of character (especially their reliability), long-term commitment to the school (rather than moving on to another post within a few years) and advanced social skills (emphasizing their potential contribution to a team effort). Applications from youthful students can highlight their energy, grasp of technology and 'modern teacher' status. When looking at a vacancy, take careful note of its distance from your home and consider the practical implications of travel. Other than in exceptional circumstances, a journey of about forty-five minutes by car is the maximum to contemplate for a first post. In the process of applying, it is worth bearing in mind the following:

Schools need you as much as you need them

Do not view yourself as a hapless member of the system. You have skills and abilities that schools require if they are to promote high standards. Without any trace of arrogance, consider yourself a highly trained commodity that some fortunate school will be lucky enough to acquire.

Don't wait for the perfect school

Although it is not sensible to apply for every post, especially with the severe constraints on your time during training, it is equally unwise to overlook vacancies because the job specification does not precisely fit your profile. Selection panels are principally looking for the right *person* with potential as much as discovering someone who conforms to the job description. For instance, applicants are quite often appointed to teach children outside the age range for which they were principally trained.

Write as a teacher, not as a student

Be extremely careful that in the letter of application you come across as a newly (or nearly) qualified teacher and not as an experienced student. Schools deal with plenty of trainees. The vacancy is, however, for a teacher, so make sure that you sound like one.

Take account of the people who will read your application

It seems an obvious point to make, but many applicants forget to consider the people who will be making decisions about them. Except in areas where there is an acute teacher shortage and applicants are few, the normal procedure is for the head teacher and one or more governors to consider the applications and draw up a 'long list' of names. The list is then further scrutinized before a final 'shortlist' of about five or six names is compiled. Whereas the head teacher is, of course, viewing applications from a professional perspective, most governors are interested and well-informed lay people who will be impressed by a thoughtful, well written and carefully presented application. Keep in mind that all heads and governors are asking four main questions of a candidate:

- ◆ Can this person be trusted with a class of children?
- ◆ Will this person fit in with other staff?
- ◆ Will this person get on with the parents?
- ◆ Does this person have potential?

Make sure that you fit the bill!

The letter of application

It is essential to present yourself in the best possible light to the head teacher and governors who consider your application. Although a sizeable minority of trainees are appointed to posts in schools where they have been on placement, it is normally the case that your application form is the key evidence that the selection panel possesses on which to base their decision about your suitability. Consequently, the application form assumes considerable significance and should be of the highest quality. If you are asked to hand write the application, use a good quality pen to complete the form rather than a cheap ballpoint pen. Introduce yourself early in the letter and say why you are applying to the school/pool. If you are applying to an individual school, make sure that you find out about its particular characteristics and adjust what you say accordingly. Mention the variety of schools you have experienced and the age ranges you have taught, and describe the breadth of experience that you have gained. It is also important to refer to the curriculum subjects of which you have a practical knowledge, as different training routes have slightly different emphases, so you cannot assume that the person reading your application will know the strengths of yours. It is likely that classrooms of the future will make use of more sophisticated information technology, as well as more classroom assistants, so make sure that you underline your capability in these areas. At some early point in your letter, describe your educational philosophy with reference to classroom contexts. The selection panel will not be impressed by long strings of words and impressive terminology, so avoid the use of author references and expounding complicated theories. Refer briefly to your special interests that are helpful in your role as a teacher, including extra-curricular activities. End with an enthusiastic flourish and make it sound as if you *really* want a job at this particular school.

The application letter should give the panel a clear idea about the sort of person you are, your motivation and potential. If you are invited for interview, the things that you say in your letter will be used as the basis for some of the questions, so it is vital to express your ideas accurately. Be careful that you do not make yourself a hostage to fortune by making assertions or claims that you cannot substantiate or defend. It is also helpful to make a list of key words and phrases that you want to include in the letter, such as:

◆ Commitment
◆ High standards
◆ Achieving potential
◆ Motivation
◆ Individual needs
◆ Job satisfaction
◆ Valuing colleagues.

Some application letters resemble a casual note to a friend. Others are so convoluted and full of jargon that the reader needs a dictionary to understand what is said! It is unwise to swamp the letter with detail but beware of making bland statements (such as 'I believe that children should work independently') without qualifying the statement (e.g. 'Independence needs to be earned and is not an automatic right'). One way and another there needs to be sufficient information to inform the reader about yourself and your capability without cluttering the letter. If you are word-processing, use a good sized font but not an over-large one. If you are writing, take special care about legibility. It is essential to check and double-check the spelling. Some panels will not consider a candidate whose letter contains grammatical or spelling errors.

Example of an application letter

There are many different ways to write an application letter. The following example provides an idea of what a letter *could* look like and not what it *should* look like. The purpose of the letter is to make sure that it reads convincingly and impresses the head teacher and governors who receive it. The subheadings in the example below should be deleted once the letter is ready to send. It is well worth showing the letter to a tutor or teacher and getting their reactions before dispatching it. If you send several letters of application and receive no offers of an interview, ask a few people who have been successful if they are willing to show you a copy of their letters.

Use the head teacher's name (correctly spelt)

Dear Mrs Greenflame

Introduce yourself
I am a trainee teacher currently completing my postgraduate certificate course (primary) at the University of Littletown School of Education. I am applying for the post as Year 4 teacher at Bumble Street Primary, with special interest in curriculum leadership in ICT, commencing next September.

Explain why you are applying
I am particularly interested in this post for four reasons. First, I am keen to work in a large, inner-city school. Second, I have gained a lot of experience teaching key stage 2 children over the past year and found it very rewarding. Third, I have developed a special interest and expertise in ICT (my specialist subject) and wrote an extended dissertation about its use in primary school as part of my studies. Fourth, I gain the impression from the job description and your web site that Bumble Street is the sort of go-ahead school that would help me to develop as a teacher and to which I could make a positive contribution.

Explain your background

Before I began my teacher training, I had already spent time in several primary schools as a volunteer helper and one term as a part-time special needs assistant. I also spent three years working as deputy education officer in a local zoo, which gave me a lot of valuable experience in public speaking and dealing with large groups of children. For six months I went as a volunteer to Kenya to assist in a project providing fresh water to rural communities. My work with children was so satisfying that it convinced me that I should pursue a career in teaching, a decision I do not regret.

Describe your school experiences

Over the period of my training I taught in four different schools. At the start of September I spent one week working alongside the teacher in a Year 5 class in a suburban primary school. During the autumn I jointly taught a Year 2 class with another trainee teacher in a small rural primary school. In the spring term I took the major responsibility for a mixed Year 3 and 4 class in a local junior school. I am currently teaching a Year 6 class in a large inner-city primary school as the final phase of my initial training.

Outline your teaching approach

From my various experiences in school I have become particularly confident in teaching literacy, numeracy and ICT, but I have also enjoyed teaching science and the full range of foundation subjects, and RE. I make every effort to ensure that my teaching is systematic yet sufficiently flexible to accommodate the many spontaneous opportunities that arise during a lesson. I make sure that the children in my class are clear about the rules and limits, but encourage them to take responsibility for their own actions. I am committed to the concept of children achieving a strong measure of independence in learning within agreed rules and procedures. I believe that a classroom should be sufficiently well organized and managed to facilitate effective learning but also a workshop where ideas can be explored and tested. I have discovered that children respond positively to teaching that is interactive and stimulating, and where every child's efforts are valued and appreciated.

Summarize your educational principles

My educational values can easily be summarized. Children should be encouraged to view learning as an adventure and strive to achieve the highest possible standards in all aspects of their work. However, children should be respected as individuals in their own right and not solely in terms of their academic ability. I strive to make my classroom a welcoming place, in which children can operate in a safe, purposeful environment, and where there is a 'can do' and 'can help others to do' mentality.

Specify your particular abilities
If appointed at Bumble Street, I would like to use my expertise in computers for an extra-curricular activity. I am a competent pianist (Grade 6) and although a little rusty would thoroughly enjoy using my musical skills in school. I am also a reasonably good flautist. I represented my hometown of Mudslope in the area swimming gala for three consecutive years and enjoy playing a range of sports.

Emphasize your potential
As a newly qualified teacher I am aware that I have much to learn. I am also convinced that I have a lot to contribute, not least in my specialist subject. I would be keen to share my knowledge and understanding with colleagues and offer support to them in whatever way seemed appropriate. I have always enjoyed good relationship with other adults and I like to think that I am adaptable and co-operative. In this respect, I am fortunate enough to have worked with a variety of excellent learning support assistants and greatly value their expertise and the contribution they make to children's learning. I am also committed to establishing and maintaining good, open relationships with parents and see them as fellow-educators with us.

Conclude briskly
I cannot wait to have a class of my own and helping the children to develop and grow. It has been a lifelong ambition of mine and I am bursting to get started. I hope that I have been able to convey something of my enthusiasm to you through this letter, and eagerly await your response.

Yours sincerely
Rebecca Murray-Crouch

Preparing for interview

Preparation for an interview begins during time on school placement. First, because the sorts of issues and practicalities that you deal with in school will form the basis of your answers. Second, because when you apply for a job it is extremely useful to be able to put the placement school as one of your references (after gaining permission, of course). It is not unknown for the head teacher of the school to which you have applied to contact the school and find out informally what they think of you. This fact should act as a double incentive for you to do well and create a good impression. It is surprisingly common for trainees to apply for a post at one of the schools in which they practised their teaching and some trainee teachers are successful in gaining a job there.

Take time to look very carefully at the school prospectus and get a feel for the sort of place it is and where its priorities lie. Although the panel is looking for someone who has the ability to control the class, who enjoys a good relationship with colleagues and parents and has lots of potential and a willingness to progress, they are also looking for a person who is keen to work in *their* school.

When you look around the school before the interview, keep your eyes open and avoid saying too much or asking intrusive questions. Stay relaxed and cheerful but not casual or flippant. Let your eyes sparkle. Avoid sounding arrogant or patronizing. Instead, remain positive and be courteous but not stiff. Make yourself look and sound like someone who will fit in with the staff and the school's prevailing ethos.

Scrutinize your application letter and remind yourself what you stated and claimed. Use a highlighter to identify key issues. The interview panel will probably follow up some of your points and ask for clarification, so it is worth predicting the sorts of item they might use from the letter and rehearsing your responses. In particular, think carefully about the sort of working environment that you want for the children. Will you divide the class on the basis of ability groups? How will you differentiate tasks within and across groups? Will you foster a spirit of debate and discussion? If so, how will you organize it? Will you stick rigidly to the Literacy Strategy, both in content and format? If so, how will you respond to individual needs and unexpected learning priorities that emerge during sessions? And so on.

If you have fellow students also applying for jobs, it is helpful to establish an informal network with them, interrogating one another, role-playing interviews and sharing experiences.

Interview questions

The panel can vary in size from three to thirteen, but often consists of the head teacher, a senior teacher, a parent governor and another governor. In a religious foundation school, a representative of the church or mosque will normally be included. The head teacher will be interested in appointing someone who will help to maintain academic standards and enjoy a positive working relationship with colleagues and parents. The senior teacher will be concerned about issues to do with staff membership and, if a subject specialism is asked for, your ability to share your knowledge. The governor will probably be looking for someone who will be a credit to the school and has a professional outlook. The parent will focus on teacher–child and teacher–parent relationships. The cleric will want to be convinced that you have high moral standards and will contribute to, rather than damage, the existing ethos. Some interviews require candidates to spend a few minutes talking one-to-one with each member of the panel and/or with a group of children. If you are 'interviewed' by children, be careful not to patronize them or trivialize their questions, and make sure that you come across as an exciting sort of teacher that they would enjoy working with.

Members of the adult panel may have particular concerns that are reflected in their questions. For example:

◆ What do you think is the best way to combat bullying?
◆ What are your views about homework?
◆ What extra-curricular activities would you be willing to support?

And even questions as oddly diverse as:

◆ Do you think children should wear school uniform?
◆ What kind of things make you happy?

However, the sorts of questions that are more commonly encountered include the following.

How do you motivate the children and make lessons enjoyable?

Your answer should reflect your high aspirations to engage with and enthuse every child, as well as acknowledging the challenges of motivating reluctant learners. Stress the steps that can be taken in the short term, such as providing relevant and interesting work and the use of praise and encouragement, but also highlight your long-term strategy of promoting children's pride and ownership in their work and a never-say-die attitude.

How will you develop literacy across the curriculum?

Underline the fact that you view literacy as a life tool, not merely as something for the formal literacy hour. You may want to talk about the opportunities you like to give children for extended writing or refer to some of the ways that you have already enhanced children's literacy through using a variety of writing frames in topic/ thematic work. It is worth identifying occasions when you were successful in promoting dialogue, discussion, discovery reading and writing with a specific purpose, such as in cross-curricular project work.

How will you involve children in setting their own targets?

Whatever inner reservations you may have about the appropriateness of setting targets for learning, they are endemic in society and schools, so emphasize the positive aspects such as the opportunity they offer to establish dialogue and the promotion of high expectations. Explain that involving children in decisions and helping them to think about what they are trying to achieve increases the sense of belonging and clarifies the nature of the challenge for them. You may also want to stress that establishing and achieving targets with the child provides opportunity to celebrate achievement rather than scrutinizing every piece of work for its failings.

How will you ensure that children achieve their potential in learning?

You might mention the importance of careful and systematic observation, talking to children about their progress (conferencing), determining what stage children have reached in their learning through systematic testing, the need to take account of their speed of work and the circumstances under which learning took place. It is worth stressing that it is good to have high but not unreasonable expectations of children and to foster a climate of mutual endeavour and peer support. Emphasize that potential is not a fixed attribute and can be extended through good teaching, which it is your job to provide.

How will you keep track of children's progress?

In particular, the panel may ask you to explain what sorts of record you intend to keep. Remember that the school will already have an assessment and record-keeping system in place, so make sure that you have done your homework and have a reasonable grasp of their approach. Mention the importance of having verifiable evidence, such as samples of children's work, grades and test results, but also the value of regular conferencing with small groups of children to share and appraise their progress.

How will you arrange your room?

You can talk about the way that you intend to have tables separated or grouped, and whether you intend to have a formal arrangement (e.g. tables in lines) or to divide the room into subject areas and establish maths, science corner and literacy corners. In your explanation refer to classroom situations in which you have taught successfully. Underline the importance of health and safety (such as movement around the room and visibility), effective learning and good discipline. As with every issue relating to classroom practice, make sure that your priorities and reasoning are clear in your own mind before you set foot in the interview room.

How will you ensure good order and discipline?

Sound positive but realistic in your answer. Stress that appropriate lessons, enthusiastic teaching and good relationships lie at the heart of effective discipline, and that well motivated children, happy in their work, are less liable to be disruptive. However, make it clear that children who refuse to toe the line will be dealt with firmly. Some lay governors believe that teachers must be authoritarian to exercise discipline. You will need to carefully think through your beliefs before the interview so that on the one hand you do not come across as being feeble, and on the other as an ogre. Use expressions starting with 'I have found that . . .' as part of your reply. Acknowledge the need to take account of agreed school policies on the matter.

What do you see as the principal roles for teaching assistants?

On the basis that it is now quite common to have as many teaching assistants as teachers in a school, your answer should acknowledge that their significance is considerable and likely to grow. Show that you understand the diversity of roles that assistants undertake and the need for a teacher to utilize their many skills. Make a point of saying that assistants must be valued and feel part of the collaborative 'adventure in learning'.

What attitude will you adopt towards parents?

Decide to what extent you see parents as consumers, clients or customers, and check the school prospectus to find out how much parents assist voluntarily in the classroom. It is essential to promote a view that parents are partners in learning rather than soul mates or the enemy or well-intentioned outsiders who should keep their distance. Stress that parents are the 'first' educators of their children and that this principle should be respected and built on. Tell the panel that you believe that all parents want the best for their children and that you do not intend to let them down.

What use will you make of ICT?

Be honest about the limits of your knowledge but don't underestimate how much you know, as it is probably a lot more than many experienced teachers and members of the panel. Emphasize that ICT is going to have an increasingly significant part to play in education and children's lives outside school. Remind the panel that some of today's children will live into the twenty-second century and will need to be flexible and responsive to new ideas and innovations. However, highlight that ICT is a servant, not a master, cannot substitute for sensitive teaching and is more effective where the desire to learn is already strong.

What extra-curricular areas can you contribute?

Give an enthusiastic response to the question but don't commit yourself to anything that, if offered the post, you may live to regret. Additional responsibilities always seem so much more manageable when sitting in the quiet surrounds of an interview room than they do in the intensity of everyday school life.

What is your attitude to inclusion?

The school will already have a policy and may be under pressure to incorporate a wider range of children into mainstream classrooms. It is important to be positive about the right for all children to be valued and receive the best education, but you may want to mention the need for properly trained assistants, appropriate resources and additional staff development for yourself as teacher.

What are your strongest and weakest areas?

You will have completed a Career Entry and Development Profile, so you should be in a good position to speak about the areas for development. Avoid using the word 'weak'. Instead, refer to your inexperience or less well-developed areas and give the strong impression that you are keen to be a good all-rounder and learn quickly. Emphasize your competence and enthusiasm in teaching literacy and mathematics.

What other things matter to you as a teacher?

You may want to say something about developing co-operation, kindness, good habits, self-discipline and creativity. The panel is not appointing you to be a social worker but neither do the members want an automaton that has no interest in children's emotional welfare. If you are applying to teach very young children you may want to refer to the model of teaching from the Foundation Stage Curriculum.

How well has your college course prepared you for the realities of teaching?

This is a surprisingly common question. Try to adopt a positive attitude, even if your course has been less than you hoped for. Talk about the value of classroom experience, the quality of your ICT training and the all-round curriculum development that prepared you for the realities of teaching. Resist the temptation to air any frustrations that you may inwardly hold about the limitations of your training. An interview panel wants to pick winners, not victims.

You may not be asked any of these questions, of course! Even so, it is a valuable exercise to think hard beforehand about what you believe, what you know and what you are still unsure about and willing to learn. The panel will be as interested in what you have *already* achieved as in what you intend to achieve.

Whatever the questions, make sure that you sound like a teacher, not a student. Don't speak of 'my class teacher on teaching practice' or similar phrases, but rather 'When I was teaching seven-year olds' and 'When I teach very young children their initial sounds, I like to' and 'I enjoy incorporating technology into my teaching'. Give the impression of being forward-looking by saying things like: 'I am very keen to promote enquiry-based learning in science, as I have found that when children have the opportunity to engage practically with things that interest them they are more likely to be motivated and to raise questions.' Above all, keep telling yourself that you DO want to be a teacher!

During the interview

Think carefully about the way that you dress and the impression it will create. Aim to look smart but not extravagant. It is worth practising deep breathing beforehand, inhaling to a count of four, holding for a count of four and exhaling slowly through the mouth up to a count of ten with shoulders relaxed. When you enter the room, stand erectly, establish eye contact immediately, smile pleasantly and wait to be asked to sit down. Sit back in the chair with your feet slightly apart and your hands in your lap but try not to resemble a tailor's dummy. Avoid irritating mannerisms, such as tugging at your hair, pulling your ear lobes, slumping in your chair, picking at your socks and waving your hands in the air like windmills. Studies show that a panel forms its impressions within the first couple of minutes, so a good start is essential. Whatever the panel's composition, they will contain experienced and knowledgeable people who will not be impressed by the use of long words or tiresome theories. They will be positively influenced, however, by a thoughtful consideration of issues, dignified but very pleasant manner and quiet enthusiasm.

Throughout the interview, maintain eye contact but don't stare at individual panel members, as this can be perceived as threatening. Listen carefully to the questions, and nod your head slightly as you do so as this gives the impression of intelligent interest. Lots of candidates fail to listen to the question or misinterpret it and give inappropriate answers as a result. Give yourself a few seconds thinking time before answering, but don't leave a long silence, stare at the floor or sigh out loud prior to speaking. Direct your answers to the members of the panel, not to the ceiling, and keep them concise but avoid one-line responses. Instead, try to develop points and, where possible, refer to classroom situations that you have worked in by way of example. It is important to be honest in your answers and true to your convictions, but remember that the panel will be asking themselves whether what you are saying will fit with the school's existing and future priorities, so don't say anything outlandish or crass. It is for this reason that it pays to find out as much as you can about the school before the interview.

Treat every question on its merits. Even if you think that the question is unreasonable, make a serious attempt to give a sensible reply. Don't try to 'read' the acceptability of your comments by the looks on the faces of the panel members. Keep a bright countenance but avoid being flippant. Be honest but upbeat. If they don't like what they hear, you won't get the job. That's the way it goes.

If you are unsure about the answer to a question, admit to it but add a positive comment in which you stress your determination to find out more and take advice. The head teacher will want to appoint a person with potential, not someone that thinks that they are a heavenly gift to teaching! If you provide an answer and a member of the interviewing panel immediately retorts 'Yes, but . . .' then do not panic. Providing you are clear about your beliefs, it is quite in order to restate them strongly and calmly. You may want to add: 'But I see what you mean' or 'I realize that not everyone thinks the way I do, but . . .' or 'I have thought long and hard about this issue and I'm still grappling with it.' One way and another, make every effort to demonstrate that you are a thinking teacher. Panels like candidates who are willing to argue their case courteously but firmly. They are much less keen on those who come across as belligerent, inflexible or vacillating.

Find moments in the interview to introduce some of your favourite topics, such as the fact that you enjoy sport and want to offer your skills in this area. Whatever your passion, don't leave the room until you have told the panel about it. If you are invited to ask questions at the end, don't raise controversial issues or things that are already described in the school prospectus. You may want to ask whether, if appointed, you will have the opportunity to do (whatever is on your heart), as this gives the impression of someone who is wholehearted. Otherwise it is better to decline the invitation and say that everything is clear. When you leave the room, smile, express your thanks and walk out steadily with your head still. If all your instincts tell you that this is definitely not the place for you, it is quite in order to inform the head that you wish to withdraw. However, don't allow nerves to dictate your decision.

Sample teaching

As part of the interview process, you may be asked to teach a lesson to some children or to give a presentation in front of a panel. If so, you will have been informed about this in advance by the school. The amount of time for teaching (normally literacy or mathematics) varies considerably, from a ten minute burst to a full forty-five minutes. Most commonly you will have about twenty minutes to 'strut your stuff'. The panel members are looking for good interactive skills, a confident manner and a positive attitude. It is essential to rehearse your teaching beforehand, either to a group of children, a sympathetic friend or 'inside your head'. Depending on the type of lesson, it is advisable to use the majority of the session for demonstrating that you can engage children from the front, use question-and-answer technique effectively and handle the cut and thrust of direct teaching. You may also want to incorporate some straightforward visual aids, though avoid being over-ambitious. When preparing, use reliable methods that have served you well in the past rather than attempting some dazzling, untried approach.

In your anxiety, be careful that you don't forget elementary principles, such as speaking clearly at a suitable rate, controlling your body language, asking a few thought-provoking questions as well as factual ones, and pausing occasionally to re-establish eye contact with the children. Be lively but not manic. The panel is looking for someone who will enthuse the children, not leave them feeling exhausted!

Depending on the length of the session, the remaining time can be used for an activity (a work sheet or simple table-based practical task, perhaps). You will need to have resources well organized, explain rapidly but thoroughly what has to be done, and ensure that the children can set to work with minimum delay. If you are using an activity sheet it is sensible to have a few spares. It is also worth having a set of sharpened pencils with you to give to children who do not possess one or who break them during the lesson. If you design your own sheet, differentiate by making the first task fairly easy to accomplish, followed by a slightly more challenging one, ending with an open-ended task for more capable workers. Do not include too much detail on a single sheet. It is worth reminding the children that you would like them to try and complete the work but not to rush, as they can keep the sheets and finish them at home if necessary. At the end of your time, conclude with a brief summary, enthuse about their efforts, tell them to pat themselves on the back, then ask them to sit up and look smart. In your eagerness to impress the assessors, don't be unnaturally zealous or run over time. Despite the tension of the situation, keep your face relaxed, smile and look as if you are enjoying the experience (which most candidates do).

Presentations

If you are asked to give a short presentation about (say) your views on catering for the wide range of ability in a class or the incorporation of ICT to enhance learning, it pays to have the minimum of visual aids. If you use a transparency, include as few words on it as possible, probably only a list of your key headings. Introduce the presentation by informing the panel about the structure of your talk and whet their appetite by alluding to your conclusion. For example, on the benefits of whole-class teaching you could start in a similar way to the following (but in your own words):

> Good morning, everyone. In my presentation about the benefits of whole-class teaching, I shall begin by suggesting that there are three distinct approaches that serve three useful purposes. (The transparency or sheet of card is placed into position at this point.) The three approaches are: direct teaching, when the teacher imparts information; question-and-answer sessions when the teacher elicits information from the children; fully interactive teaching, where issues are raised and discussed. I shall further suggest that there are four potential benefits from whole-class teaching. First, that whole-class teaching is efficient in that it allows all children to hear what is said at the same time. Second, it allows children to feel part of a shared endeavour. Third, it enables children to learn from the answers given by others. Fourth, it helps teachers to assess the children's understanding. I will also suggest that although whole-class teaching is a valuable method, it needs to take close account of the differentiated abilities of children. I will conclude by giving an example from my own experience of effective whole-class teaching. (It takes just over one minute to say these words.)

If you employ a visual aid, use a large, bold print type (see Figure 12.1). Keep your talk concise and clear. A lot of people find that it is useful to have a set of small cards for their notes, each card containing a subheading from the visual aid, plus two or three 'prompts' to remind them of the things they intend to say. Do not have too many notes as this distracts from the presentation. Spend about the same amount of

WHOLE CLASS TEACHING

APPROACHES

1 Direct teaching

2 Question-and-answer

3 Fully interactive teaching

POTENTIAL BENEFITS

1 Efficiency

2 Shared endeavour

3 Shared learning

4 Pupil assessment

Figure 12.1 *A visual aid for presentation*

time on each point. Thus, a typical fifteen-minute presentation will consist of a one-minute introduction, two minutes on each of the five main points, three minutes on a classroom example and a summary of about a minute. The panel is not looking for an educational genius, so avoid using too many technical terms or academic arguments. Speak in plain language about classroom and school issues, your beliefs, the contribution you feel you can make to the school, or all three. Try to end your presentation on a positive note.

Problems at interview

Interviews are not usually much fun but they present the chance to share your ideas and beliefs about teaching, so it is wise to view them as an opportunity rather than a punishment. Nevertheless, even the most confident people commonly experience some or all of the following problems:

Drying-up

The anxiety of an interview can lead to an increased heart rate and a dry mouth. Deep breathing and slow exhaling will help to get your body functions under control. Slipping a very small liquorice-based tablet into your mouth a few minutes before the interview will stimulate saliva and keep your mouth moist. Ask your pharmacist for advice.

Not understanding the question

Some interview questions are confusing; others are difficult to understand. If you cannot interpret the question, either ask for the question to be repeated or use a form of words like 'I shall do my best to answer your question but please tell me if I have misunderstood what you say.' Providing you give an interesting reply, the questioner may not bother to correct you, even if you have failed to grasp what they were originally asking.

Digging a hole

Hole digging usually happens because interviewees try to be too sophisticated or controversial and, having realized their error, attempt to backtrack or argue their case too strongly. The best approach is to be open about your uncertainties but to express the things you are sure about with conviction. It is not wise to try and outwit the panel by making smart remarks. Even if you succeed in doing so, they are unlikely to appoint you.

Taking too long to answer

You might love the sound of your own voice but the panel members will not be so enthusiastic. Keep your answers concise and relevant. Use real situations rather than hypothetical ones to support what you say, but beware of sounding too enthusiastic about what happens in another school you have worked in.

Being flummoxed by inappropriate questions

Sometimes you may receive an odd question that makes you wonder if the person is being serious. There are stories about candidates being asked about the size of their golf handicap and their favourite possessions. Keep a straight face and reply courteously, even if you notice that other members of the panel are chuckling quietly to themselves.

Losing the plot

In the intense atmosphere of the interview it is possible to lapse into a state of mental paralysis, where the brain refuses to work and the tongue won't co-operate! If you find that you are becoming distressed, say that you are suddenly feeling hot and ask if it is all right to take off your jacket. During the ensuing moments, you have a chance to refocus and apply yourself afresh. Do not try to gain sympathy or exaggerate your discomfort or you may be perceived as someone who might be a liability on the staff.

After the interview

Sometimes all the candidates sit together and wait to hear the panel's decision but more often the chair of the panel contacts each person by telephone after all the interviews have been completed. Don't be too despondent if you are unsuccessful. It is often the case that there are four or five equally good candidates (of whom you are one) and the final selection hinges on relatively minor points. Occasionally, there is an internal candidate whose knowledge of the school situation gives her or him an almost unassailable advantage. If you can face doing so, it pays to spend an hour during the following few days scrutinizing your performance and the areas for improvement. Many head teachers from the interview school will offer helpful feedback. If you are successful, then congratulations! All the hard work and perseverance has been worthwhile. Turn to the next chapter and start planning for September.

Further reading

Amos, J. (2002) *Be Prepared! Getting Ready for Job Interviews*, Oxford: How To Books.

CHAPTER 13

First appointment

The induction year was introduced in 1999 to provide continuity between pre-service training and fully qualified status. Newly qualified teachers have to successfully complete the year before they can progress in their careers, though failure to pass the induction programme is extremely uncommon. It is not the purpose of this book to provide detailed information about the requirements of the induction year, as advice on the subject can be found in a number of publications (e.g. Bubb 2000, Hayes 2000, Holmes 2000, Liebling 1999). The present chapter discloses the feelings and experiences of newly qualified teachers as they enter their first post. The descriptions were provided by a random selection of NQTs, all of whom were keen to share their stories and anxious that other new teachers should benefit from their experiences. As the extracts reveal, these experiences are varied but share many common features.

In at the deep end

For most new teachers, the first couple of weeks seem to be a mesmerizing concoction of fast-moving events, unexpected demands and an endless number of rapid decisions. Despite these pressures, the pleasure gained from having your own class at last is ample compensation, as the following two extracts show:

Khaled
After finishing in June I did about three weeks supply teaching that paid for my summer holiday. I am now teaching thirty-seven Year 4 children and at first it was a bit like crowd control. Anyway, the induction year has begun and I am glad to have one day off every fortnight to rest and plan. I'm struggling a bit to differentiate the work with such a wide ability spectrum, but the head teacher is really supportive. Generally, I'm really enjoying it. It's a lot less stressful than being a student teacher but more accountable. I'm very glad I did my PGCE, it was a good preparation for knowing what was about to hit me!

Balbinderjit

Well, that's the first week with my own Year 1 class over already. I can't believe it! Everything has been fantastic, far exceeding my expectations. I only had one panic on the first day when the parents were bringing their children in and I was walking around the room thinking: What am I doing? What have I done? Why am I doing this? But I have a wonderful learning support assistant, who I once worked with before, when I was a trainee. She is fabulous. I've been really impressed by the staff support and my head teacher is really pleased with all three of us (NQTs). It's very nice having other people around who haven't got a clue what they're doing! In fact, everybody has been superb and made the whole week easier than it could have been.

I haven't got much time as I'm a lot busier this second week and more than shattered as well. Roll on Saturday! This week has been a lot harder. We're all teaching on autopilot, trying to carry on as normal. But we're there to teach and teach we must do, and put everything else aside. The job is absolutely wonderful and the children are great. I'm enjoying it so much, even though I've already lost my voice!

Not all NQTs enjoy such a positive beginning to their careers, though the majority of them experience a combination of exhilaration and confusion. The start of any new job is bound to be emotionally draining and a bit overwhelming. Feelings are heightened at such times, and a new teacher gains considerable security from knowing that other people are ready and willing to offer support, advice and encouragement. To an extent, the commencement of a new job is dominated by creating order out of chaos. Continuous professional development is supposed to ensure a smooth transition from pre-service training into the first post, but this ideal evaporates in the intensity associated with taking sole responsibility for a class for the first time. The days running up to the start of term are characterized by waves of panic, ecstasy, vulnerability, excitement and anticipation. The extracts from NQTs that form the heart of this chapter present a full range of emotions, from delight to near despair, but also highlight the importance of practical factors, such as knowing where resources are kept and familiarity with school procedures and policies. New teachers rely heavily on colleagues to offer advice about the dominant school culture, practicalities and potential pitfalls.

As you read the descriptions given by the new teachers below, bear in mind that they are made about half way through their first year. Many of the issues are similar to those that trainee teachers have to face on final school placement. The crucial difference is that you are now the one who has to make most of the decisions. Key issues in the extracts are italicized in the text.

Mary – teaching Years 1 and 2 (29 children in the class)
When I first knew I'd got the job I was petrified. I was doing supply work at the end of the summer term in another town, so it was difficult to get here and see the

school at work. By the time I did so, it was too late and the term had ended. So I was quite apprehensive and didn't really settle until I came in during the staff development day. I scrambled around finding backing paper for boards, getting hold of pencils and other resources. They all seemed to have their classrooms sorted out except me!

The classroom was bare and furniture was stacked in a corner, so *I had to start from scratch getting things organized*. I gradually moved stuff around until I'd got the furniture how I wanted it. I still change the position of chairs and tables every month or so. I want to make it easier and safer to move around the room. I think I've finally got it sorted out now.

The first few days were overwhelming, not knowing where things were or who to ask about them. I didn't quite know what to do at first and although people were very helpful, they were busy, too. I was very authoritarian during the first couple of weeks. It was really scary and I was very tense. After a while I sat down and took a good look at myself in the mirror and gave myself a talking to. I then began to relax and things became more normal and my relationship with the class improved.

I was concerned about *time factors*, such as getting to assembly, coping with playground duty and learning the procedures. I didn't want to be last in assembly because I know that on teaching practice everyone looks at you as you walk in and the head tells the children to hurry up.

I also needed to find out about things like *access to the stock cupboard* and who to go to for the key. Not knowing where things were stored was a real problem early on. But you quickly get to sort it out and after a few weeks it's not strange any more.

Dealing with resources is important and it can take ages organizing things. I made the mistake of giving out all the rulers at the start of term and now hardly any of them are left; they're nearly all snapped or broken. The children also lose their pencils and even though they can buy them from the shop in the school, some of them never do and still ask you if you've got a spare pencil they can use. You sometimes have to send a child around the school hunting for a pencil. It all takes up a lot of time.

One of the big differences between being a student and being a qualified teacher is that *you are the one who is solely in charge*. You make all the decisions and there's no-one standing over your shoulder watching what you're doing or telling you what to do. That can be quite difficult at first. Every day is different. Sometimes it all goes smoothly; other times it doesn't. A single positive comment from a child about the work can make all the effort you've put in seem worthwhile. There are peaks and troughs from day to day and you can never be sure how a day will go.

Parents evening in October was a 'getting to know you' time, so it wasn't too bad. I had never done a parents' evening before, so I was a bit nervous, but I enjoyed meeting them and having a general chat. It was useful to get to know something about the children's background and helped me understand them a bit more. The second parents' evening was much more positive, which gave me a real boost. Sometimes you learn things about the children that worry you and you need to liaise with the Social Services. I didn't really know how to go about it but you slowly find out the system.

After the first half-term, things get a bit easier, but the first term was exhausting. You can get very tired and run down. All three NQTs have had time off school. Some things that I was told as a student teacher, I now understand better. For instance, I remember hearing an NQT tell us that you had to start preparing for Christmas straight after half-term. I didn't believe it then, but I do now. We spent ages building up to Christmas, with play rehearsals and different things to practise. It all took a long time.

Being the class teacher means that you can be *more flexible and spontaneous*. It's brilliant to have that freedom. Sometimes I just feel that it's right to pursue something that the children have found interesting or spend more time on a thing because it deserves it, rather than following a lesson plan mechanically, step by step. Incidental lessons can work so much better than the planned ones (though I wouldn't do this if Ofsted were in!). The really good lessons are the spontaneous ones. Children are so pleased to deviate from the normal pattern of things that they get enthusiastic and learn from it. You have to learn to catch the moment because in that way children learn more. You can go off at a tangent and it's okay, providing the overall curriculum balance is right.

We haven't been observed much, but when someone else is in the classroom, the whole atmosphere changes, especially if it's the head teacher. The children behave differently. Some children who would normally answer questions and be enthusiastic just sit there! I'm trying to encourage them to speak up and take part, but they are more reluctant to speak. I'm different too when someone else is in the room. I can't help it.

Teaching can take over at home, too. You can't always sleep properly and it's always on your mind. You have to be careful that you don't strain your body and ruin your health. For instance, it's easy to stay up late to finish a job (such as marking) when you're not really up to it, and get overtired as a result, then become ill. It's not worth it and doesn't help you in the long run. You end up having time off school, so nothing is gained.

You can't help worrying about the job. I've been in tears at home about things that have worried or upset me. I find myself talking about the job all the time to anyone who will listen. I've become a real bore! I find it hard to turn off from being a teacher. I even speak like a teacher to people who have nothing to do with school. I expect them to sit up and listen and not interrupt me! I love Wednesdays, because half the week is over and you feel you're going to survive until Friday. I tend to live for the weekends and holidays. You work out how many weeks you've got to last out until the end of term and count them down.

In staff meetings I tend to sit back and keep out of sight. Everyone else is so much more experienced than I am, so I don't like to say too much. They know what's going on and they've been teaching for years, so they know what they're talking about. The NQTs from last year are much more confident and seem to take things in their stride. We're still learners, so I keep quiet and listen, which is most unusual for me!

In many ways *being an NQT is easier than being a student teacher*. You get to know the children and do things your own way, rather than fitting in with what the teacher does. There's no travel to strange places or lodgings to worry about. I'm free to leave when I want to after school (except when there's a meeting) and do my own thing. Now, after a term and a half, I have sorted out all my routines and so forth, so life is much simpler.

Sabrina – teaching Year 2 (28 children in the class)

I wasn't appointed until 1 September so *I didn't have much time to worry* about the coming term. During the holidays I was thinking about supply work. I had applied for lots of jobs but I didn't get anywhere. I thought that getting my qualification from a well-respected university would have helped me, but it didn't seem to make any difference. I was living in London and applying for jobs in the West Country, but I explained that I was moving down here during the holiday to live locally. It was a real pain in the neck not having a job. Some schools didn't even bother to reply. I also looked in the local bulletin for jobs. Then I saw this job advertised and got it, even though it was for KS1 and I had been trained for KS2. All the content was new because it was KS1, so I just applied my teaching skills to it and did lots of study to find out what I needed to know. The other Year 2 teacher had done all the medium-term curriculum planning, so it was quite easy to use her plans. Without the medium-term plans I wouldn't have accepted the job, because I wouldn't have known what to do. It wasn't so much what I had to do that was the problem but how to go about doing it.

I work one day at a time. There wasn't enough time before I began teaching to think too much about things. Since I started teaching, though, I think about school all the time. It takes over your life. I also worked part-time in a shop on Sundays for the first term, which was a welcome break from school. It has made me stop and do other things; otherwise I would have spent all my time doing schoolwork. As it is, I spend so much time on school work; usually up to nine o'clock each night, then part of Saturday, maybe all morning. Since Christmas the time I spend has been considerably reduced.

When I began, I had a totally empty room. There were no resources, no books, no nothing! I spent the first day scavenging around and trying to build up the room's resources. When I was a student teacher, I was in the receiving teacher's classroom and I was allocated a space within the room to put up displays, and so on. Now it's up to me to decide what to do. I'm aware of being watched to see what I do with my walls and the displays I put up. Sometimes I spend ages on display and sometimes much less time. Usually I take a long time to get a display up and then add to it gradually. I wasn't really sure what I ought to put up but I got ideas from looking at other teacher's work.

Lots of time was spent initially on starting things up. Year 2 pupils work on topics for chunks of time, so although it's hard to get things going, once you have done it it becomes much easier, because they just get on with it. Life is not as frenetic now; it moves at a more manageable pace. I can stop and think about things more than I could last term.

In many ways I compare my teaching with my final teaching practice. It's like a continuation of it. It's different for me because my contract is only for one year and I'm leaving in July, so I don't need to think ahead. When they discuss things to do with next year, it's of no interest to me. I've only got to do this year and I'll be gone, so it feels like being on my final TP. I'm sorry I won't be able to see the children coming through and growing and developing.

As a class teacher, it's good to have your own space. At the end of last term there were two days spare when I could decide the content of the lessons myself. It was absolutely great and I wondered why we didn't do it this way all the time. I also feel that as an NQT I'm being watched a lot of the time. People are seeing how I'm getting on.

When I was still at college, I used to be really keen about things like the Career Entry and Development Profile, but *now I've got my own class I've got better things to do.* I don't ever think about it. I used to think about ways in which I could improve my teaching and how I would go about it by setting targets and so on but it quickly became irrelevant as soon as I began teaching. The CEDP was quite useful for the first term but it became annoying after a time. Once the effects of my final TP wore off the CEDP and target setting etc. became irrelevant. I used a lot of work sheets for mathematics at the start of term. Some of them I took from my old TP files and some I made myself. Now we use published plans and it's much better; it's all there, ready for you to use.

My college course was a good preparation for teaching. It was so all-inclusive that it covered just about everything that you could possibly need to know about being a teacher. It was brilliant. I didn't make a very good start with my training and my first year was a bit of a disaster, so I decided to take a year out. It was the best thing I could have done. I spent a whole year in school as a classroom assistant, just soaking up the atmosphere: administration, homework, special needs English teaching, everything! I absorbed such a lot during that year; then I went back to college and completed my training.

My confidence depends upon the particular context. When I'm comfortable with the situation, my confidence is high; when I'm not, it's low. I do a lot of acting in the classroom. If you didn't act, you wouldn't live long! Sometimes you have to act angry, even when you're not. Sometimes you *are* angry. You have to be consistent and get cross with someone even if you don't feel particularly bothered, or they'll think they can get away with it. I don't have a lot of trouble with behaviour, but I would still like to have gone on a behaviour management course. Unfortunately, all the time has been taken up with numeracy training. I've watched other teachers dealing with naughty children and how they handle them and learned a lot from them.

My first parents' evening wasn't too bad. I didn't feel particularly nervous. I tried to be friendly and chatty. Even though I didn't have that many parents, I was totally exhausted by the end of the evening. The second parents' evening I was more relaxed and I didn't find it as stressful because I knew them already and had met them before. I haven't had any special problems with parents. Some of them I see almost every day. Most of them don't seem that interested. It's not like last year, apparently, when some of the parents of the children were really terrible. It has helped me because I've worked with adults as part of my City and Guilds for adults with learning difficulties.

It's very important as a new teacher to be able to talk about your problems to someone, especially someone in school who knows the situation and understands what you mean. I didn't have too much to do with the other two NQTs at first because they already knew one another by the time I arrived, and they also work in a different key stage from me. Their classrooms are geographically remote from mine, so we don't get that much chance to talk. I know that the other two talk together a lot, especially as they have to do joint planning. I talk to my husband when I get home and unload on him. He knows as much about the children in my class as I do!

Teaching is with you day and night. It doesn't come and go. It's there all the time. You can't leave it behind, ever.

Kerensa – teaching Year 3 (34 children in the class)
Initially, when I first got the job, I was very excited. Then *during the holidays lots of 'What ifs?'* crept in. I started wondering about things, such as what would happen if I couldn't keep the children quiet and lost control.

I tried to prepare in advance of the term but when I first came in there was no-one here to tell me. The first two days of the term were not structured, so I could do what I wanted with the class. This was actually quite hard as I didn't have any plans to use. It was worrying not knowing the school procedures and routines. There was so much to take on board; it was like being a small child again on her first day at school. I felt that everyone else knew what to do except for me.

I had a baptism of fire. By the end of the first week I had six new children and three on the register hadn't turned up. My register looked a terrible mess! Since then, I've had two more new children and one of those has gone already but may be back. I'm very particular about getting trays labelled and pencil containers put on desks, and so on, but my system was ruined by the additional children. Catering for the large numbers of children with special needs has also been a difficulty.

There's a need to *establish yourself very quickly from the start*. I felt that I was a young member of staff, so I had to show myself to be a teacher with authority. I was conscious of doing the same job as all the other teachers in the school, so I felt I had to be just as good as them. One of the main challenges has been organizing my room. On school experience you take over someone else's organization and take it for granted.

I get on well with the other NQT in my key stage but life was hard during the first term. *She and I had to organize the harvest festival service* and that was very difficult. The final rehearsal in the church was rained off, so we just had to do the real service on the morning without rehearsing it. Mind you, I'm glad it's over, as we didn't have to do the Nativity (when everyone was already tired) and we won't have to organize sports day in the summer. Being musical has been very useful. Without that, it would have been quite hard to do the harvest: I organized the songs and Candy taught them some dances. It was good to feel that the expressive arts were being looked at positively.

The whole of the first term was very daunting. At the end of term I asked myself: 'how much have my children improved as a result of my teaching?' and I wasn't really sure. Everything takes so much time and some days are more focused than others. Sometimes you just can't cope with normal teaching, such as when you are feeling ill. It's impossible to maintain excellence all of the time. As a new teacher, I was aware that I would be the target of gossip from parents about who I was. There was a rumour that I was related to another teacher in the school and that this was how I got the job! I was quite scared that parents would find out that I was an NQT and think less of me because of it.

On the first parents' evening, I went for the approach of 'just be confident', but parents asked searching questions that I didn't really know the answer to as I didn't know the children well enough. I did have a few unpleasant parents. There are so many family mix-ups amongst the parents; different dads and children going to one parent and another. I've got a girl in my class who's an aunt to another child! I'd come to the last parents at the end of a long, long evening and I was telling them some good things about their daughter when the father suddenly leaned forward and asked me: 'Are you lying?' It was very unsettling. I was more concerned over the second parents' evening due to my experiences at the first. I used the approach of two minutes about something positive, two on the negatives and ending positively. I'm careful about what I say because I feel a sense of responsibility towards the children in case something I say means that the parents will punish them later.

I know much more about dealing with Social Services now. Parents sometimes share confidences with me and I'm not sure what to do with the information, whether to pass it on or not. I think about individual families and their children. I don't want to do anything that will create problems or cause the child to be taken away from the parent. I've had to learn how to deal with disadvantaged children. Some of them have learning difficulties, but I try not to let their appearance affect my expectations of them.

You can't survive on your own as an NQT. You need other adults around you, to listen to what colleagues are saying; find out who people are and who matters. You can learn a lot about your children's families from other teachers who have had the brothers and sisters in their classes and can tell you about them. Some teachers warn you about particular parents. It's also good to get some reassurance about children's behaviour by talking to other teachers who have taught them and had the same kind of trouble that you have had.

My planning needs to motivate me and not just be words on paper. I do most of my planning over the weekends. But the actual teaching is the best bit. I found that the record-keeping was not up to date, so learning things by word of mouth was very important. The resources that were available (such as photocopiable sheets) are not always useful as they are not your own and may not be quite what you need. It's worth getting your own resources together in advance, especially sheets that you found useful on school experience.

Fitting everything in is difficult and not just ticking over. It's difficult not to forget some things, as there's so much to remember. It has really helped having another NQT in the classroom next door. For instance, it was much easier to fit into the staff room with other NQTs about; otherwise I might have been more nervous.

It has been so nice to have *good relations with the head teacher*. She's been so supportive and helpful. Being observed teaching gave me feedback about the way things are done in the school as much as the quality of my teaching.

Vanda – teaching Years 3 and 4 (32 children in the class)
I was offered a job at the very end of the summer term. I had come for interview some weeks before and failed to get the job, but then the school telephoned me out of the blue and offered me a position in another class. They gave me copies of the schemes of work, which I took away and read. The trouble was that *there was no-one to advise me about their use*, no-one to answer my concerns; so I kept wondering to myself whether I was doing it right as I planned some lessons as best I could on the basis of the information I'd got.

I came in a few days before the start of term to sort out my classroom, which was in a right mess. Furniture was stacked everywhere and I had no pattern of arrangement to use as a guide, unlike when I was on teaching practice and the room was already set out. Most of my preparation work for the term happened during the staff development days prior to the start of term. The trouble was that most teachers were very busy sorting themselves out, so I didn't like to bother them with my questions, though they were very helpful when I did. These days I just ask if I'm unsure about anything.

I didn't really know what I was letting myself in for as a full-time teacher. I felt very concerned and anxious before the start of term, but once it got going I was too busy to have time to worry. *I felt very vulnerable* as I was supposed to know the answer to everything and there was no-one there to tell me. It was quite scary during the first few weeks. For instance, the children all have portfolios. We were told that we had to complete them but I had no idea how to go about it. Everyone else seemed to know what to do except for me! In the end I found out that I had to put in a piece of 'levelled' work in English, a maths investigation and something from science, plus a sample of some other good work from the curriculum. It was difficult to know what to choose.

Dealing with things for the first time was also horrendous. Getting to grips with so much that was new was difficult and scary. I kept worrying 'Am I doing this right? What if I do this wrong?' I didn't know what the consequences would be if I messed things up. It was all very new and there was an awful lot to do during the first term.

Getting to know the children was crucial, especially discovering what standard of work they were capable of doing. Record sheets did not tell you much. As a student, you go into someone else's class and the teacher knows her children. She can tell you all about them. As an NQT I had no information and didn't know how a child might respond in a particular circumstance. Mind you, I quickly found out! There were some written records, but they were of limited use. The job involves a lot of record-keeping and assessing and levelling of work. There's always too much to do and some things just don't get done; so you just have to prioritize.

It's difficult to get things in perspective as an NQT, knowing the things that really matter and the things that don't. Children are not always what they seem and there are some surprises. The chatty, pleasant ones can actually get on your nerves after a time, while some of them you didn't like at first prove to be the best. Children are also different once they leave the classroom, especially in the playground. Their playground behaviour can affect the way they are in lessons.

I had no idea about playground duty. Everyone assumes that you know how to do it. Dealing with fighting is especially difficult. I wasn't sure what to do and hesitated to intervene at first; but when I saw that the supply teacher on duty with me wasn't going to do anything about it, I just went in and sorted it out. I was quite scared, but they did what they were told and I felt better after that. I've had occasions when boys have been fighting and got really angry. I had to sit one boy down away from the others and let him cool off because he was so mad, and it was really scary. I wondered whether it was me that was failing because there were these playground incidents or whether it happens to everyone.

At the first parents' evening I was not able to comment in detail as I was still getting to know the children. I had never written an Individual Education Plan and yet I had eight or nine to do. Parents get a copy of the IEP, together with target sheets for literacy, numeracy and something about behaviour. I made sure that I said some nice things about the children rather than telling parents about the problems. By the time of the second one, I was a lot more honest! Sometimes you see parents in the playground or they will suddenly appear from nowhere. Some of them charge across to talk to you and it can be a bit daunting. I feel that I am being a bit patronizing sometimes when I speak to them but they smile and go off happy. Mind you, some parents are very dodgy and have to be handled carefully.

You need to keep a sense of humour about things, laugh about it all and share with the other NQTs. It's important to have a good break at the weekend and not to work all night. Otherwise, teaching becomes an endless thing and it can be very distressing. You have to accept that things do go wrong and it's not the end of the world. Keep things in proportion. For example, some lessons go wrong. Just say: 'Oh well, never mind; learn from it.' It's helped having another NQT in a parallel class. We plan things together and so I don't feel so isolated.

Quite a lot of your day is spent on things other than going in and teaching. You need to deal with the whole child, outside the classroom as well as in. If you have contact outside the classroom they get to know you better and this affects their class work. Relationships are very much at the heart of everything. I didn't feel part of the staff initially. I didn't say anything at first, but now I feel I can make comments when I want to or keep quiet if I want to. It has been much easier since after Christmas.

Eric – teaching Year 5 (31 children in the class)
I got the job in the June, near the end of my PGCE year. I came into school at the end of that term for a day and picked up loads of plans, but I was told by some of the other teachers not to do anything over the holiday. So I did very little. I was surprised because everyone seemed so laid back about things.

Before the start of the autumn term, I *spent a lot of time trying to scrounge resources* once in school. Everyone else seemed to have their classes sorted out and things in place. I was fortunate because a classroom assistant had covered all my display boards for me, so it was a real help. I didn't get the room the way I wanted it straight away. I tend to change things around quite often to improve access and separate out the naughty children. It helps your control if you can get the furniture arranged so that the troublemakers are separated. It's also important for safety of movement, so that you don't keep tripping over chair legs and children's legs as you move around the room. Sometimes you need to get to a place in the classroom quickly to sort a problem out.

At first you feel overwhelmed by everything. So much happens so quickly and you're not sure what should be done first. For a start, you don't always know where things are stored, so you waste time looking around for them. You get anxious about being on time for things, such as your playground duty.

The actual teaching is much the same as it was on teaching practice, except that there is no-one around to tell you what to do or how to do it. You're on your own basically and have to make all the decisions. I was fortunate in having a classroom assistant for the first day. She knew what was going on more than me and was a big help.

As the class teacher rather than a trainee you have to *deal with parents directly*. When you are on TP, the class teacher is in charge and you have always got her alongside you, so you never have the full responsibility. When you have your own class, you have to deal with all the parents, including the difficult ones. The first parents' evening in October wasn't too bad. It was a chance to meet the parents and see what they were like. I was fine because I can talk. The parents were all really nice. All the children are angelic at that stage in the term so I could say positive things about them. I didn't manage to keep to time, though. I wasn't blunt enough to say that our time was up and move them on and out. Some parents had to wait quite a long time and the evening went on longer than it should have done.

Nothing prepares you entirely for what you find when you begin teaching. Being on school experience, especially as a postgraduate, was manic all the time. It was so intensive it was ridiculous. The constant filling in of forms and keeping thick documents to show that you had met all the TTA standards, finding evidence to show that you could do things and prove that you had satisfied the criteria was mad. It was so time consuming and unnecessary. It hasn't helped me to become a better teacher; it was just exhausting and time-consuming and took away from the real business of teaching.

The advantage of being the class teacher is that you can do things your way. It's entirely different from TP. You can earn respect from the children and parents. You can set up your own system of rewards and rules. When you are in someone else's class on teaching practice, it's sometimes hard to discipline someone else's children in front of them, so you tend to hold back. One of the other differences between being a student teacher and having your own class is that school experience doesn't teach you to be flexible. You have to have all your plans ready and teach exactly what you've got in them. As class teacher you've got to be more flexible and spontaneous. You have to seize the moment and take advantage of sudden opportunities, rather than stick rigidly to the script. You don't follow lesson plans like when you were a trainee teacher. There is no real time to plan in detail. As long as you are well organized you can survive, but the best lessons are often the incidental ones where you can go off at a tangent and follow your instinct. Providing you get the balance of your teaching right over a period of time, it's all right to deviate a bit.

I'm not sure how long it took me *to feel as if I belonged here*. There was no particular turning point, I just gradually fitted in and adjusted. Every day is different. There are highs and lows. It doesn't all run smoothly like it's supposed to. Sometimes there are things outside your control that affect the way the children behave or there are changes in the timetable because of play rehearsals or something similar. As a new teacher, you experience a whole mixture of emotions, from fear to excitement to uncertainty and lots of others. One of the main challenges has been to know where to draw the line and when to stop. You are meeting everything for the first time and it's exhausting. We have all had time off from work.

Things have changed since the head realized that we've got another Ofsted visit due soon. We don't know when it's coming, but we've already started preparing: getting children's work organized, finding examples for levelling against the standards, getting reading records up-to-date and completing marking; that sort of thing. It's all a matter of being well organized. I use a system of leaving myself notes and reminders about things because there's so much to remember. It's easy to panic because you don't know what to do next.

I don't find it easy to switch off. Sometimes I can't sleep properly and I'm thinking about school all the time. A few children really niggle you and you can't get them out of your mind. I wake up at night and find that I'm thinking about them. Even when I first wake up in the morning they are there on my mind.

The first half-term was the worst! It got a bit easier after that and much easier in term two. I'm much more matter-of-fact now than I was before. The next turning point will be after the next parents' evening after this half term (in March). That's when we've got to tell them how their children are getting on and what they are really like in class.

Common experiences of new teachers

All the new teachers found that the first half-term was very demanding. They discovered that it was difficult to step back from the immediacy of teaching and make space to reflect and think. They needed to be highly organized and disciplined and pay careful attention to the way they prioritized their time. It was a challenge to cope with the many new experiences that the situation presented, attempt to get to know the children and establish themselves as teachers in the eyes of parents.

Owing to their inexperience, the new teachers often struggled to distinguish the essential from the important, and the important from the trivial. They were uncertain about what mattered greatly and what could wait, so they tended to give everything equal attention and become exhausted as a result. Once they became more confident, they asked more searching questions and identified what was important and what was not. This helped them to arrange their work more effectively.

A further challenge for the new teachers was the way that they related to colleagues and parents. Being absorbed into the staff team took varying amounts of time but seemed to happen gradually for most of them. Acceptance by colleagues simply could not be hurried. Parental expectations tended to be a little overwhelming, as they assumed that the new teachers would have answers to all their questions and be able to provide guidance and assurance.

The new teachers were agreed that the first term was exhausting, exciting and sometimes harrowing, but eminently worthwhile. Encouragingly, the second term proved to be considerably easier.

Keeping a sense of proportion

In the midst of the stresses and strains of school life, especially during the first term, you may sometimes wonder if you made the right choice of career. However, the upsets are more than compensated for by the fun and fulfilment that teaching offers. This book concludes by offering some genuine instances of where new teachers were faced with situations that meant they had to decide whether to cry or laugh, and decided to laugh! Finding joy in the job is a principle that every new teacher should espouse (Brighouse and Woods 2003).

Incident 1: During the prayer at the end of the day, the new teacher heard a trickling sound and found that it came from an angelic five year-old girl who was quietly relieving herself over the floor, eyes tightly closed and hands clasped together.

Incident 2: A group of children were busy making and trying on costumes and paper hats for a school production when the fire bell went off. They all had to evacuate the building immediately, without taking off their garb, despite the fact that it was pouring with rain outside. The condition of the outfits when they finally got back inside can only be imagined!

Incident 3: In a class of mediocre ability, an exceptionally bright child left just a week before an Ofsted inspection. The very next day a very slow learner with behavioural problems came new to the class after moving into the district. The new teacher did not think that this was a fair exchange!

Incident 4: During playground duty, a child ran up to the new teacher and said that he had bumped heads with another child and now felt dizzy. The other, more experienced teacher who was also on duty, overheard what was said and told the boy to sit still for a few minutes to see if the dizziness went away. Within a short time he said that he felt better and rejoined the football game. On inquiring about health and safety issues, the new teacher was told by her colleague that some of the children thought that if they told a teacher that they had a funny head, the school would contact the parent and they could go home early!

Incident 5: A long awaited new carpet had been fitted in the classroom during the previous afternoon. A seven-year old child sat cross-legged and as good as gold looking intently at the teacher as she read a story, before being violently sick all over the beautiful carpet without a moment's warning!

Have a long and wonderful career.

Further reading

Smith, J. (2002) *The Primary School Year*, London: RoutledgeFalmer.

REFERENCES

Acker, S. (1999) *The Realities of Teachers' Work: Never a Dull Moment*, London: Cassell.

Ainscow, M. and Tweddle, D. A. (1988) *Encouraging Classroom Success*, London: David Fulton.

Alexander, R. (1997) *Policy and Practice in Primary Education*, London: Routledge.

Alsop, S. and Dock, G. (1999) 'The National Curriculum: a decade of reform', in Nicholls, G. (ed.) *Learning to Teach*, London: Kogan Page.

Atkinson, T. (2000) 'Learning to teach: intuitive skills and reasoned objectivity', in Atkinson, T. and Claxton, G. (eds) *The Intuitive Practitioner*, Buckingham: Open University Press.

Ayers, H. and Gray, F. (1998) *Classroom Management*, London: David Fulton.

Barnes, D. (1975) *From Communication to Curriculum*, Harmondsworth: Penguin Education.

Bassey, M. (1987) *Practical Classroom Organisation in the Primary School*, London: Ward Lock.

Beard, J. and Lloyd, B. (1995) *Managing Classroom Collaboration*, London: Cassell.

Bearne, E. (1996) *Differentiation and Diversity in the Primary School*, London: Routledge.

Beetlestone, F. (ed.) (1998) *Creative Children, Imaginative Teaching*, Buckingham: Open University Press.

Bird, J. (1990) 'Developing real-life learning', in Craig, I. (ed.) *Managing the Primary Classroom*, Harlow: Longman.

Bocchino, R. (1999) *Emotional Literacy*, London: Sage.

Bolton, R. (1979) *People Skills*, New York: Simon and Schuster.

Brighouse, T. and Woods, D. (2003) *The Joy of Teaching*, London: RoutledgeFalmer.

Bryans, T. (1989) 'Parental involvement in primary schools: contemporary issues', in Wolfendale, S. (ed.) *Parental Involvement*, London: Cassell.

Bubb, S. (2000) *The Effective Induction of Newly Qualified Teachers*, London: David Fulton.

Calderhead, J. and Lambert, J. (1992) *The Induction of Newly Appointed Teachers*, General Teaching Council, England and Wales/Berkshire: National Foundation for Educational Research.

Calderhead, J. and Shorrock, S. B. (1997) *Understanding Teacher Education*, London: Falmer.

Campbell, A. and Kane, I. (1998) *School-based Teacher Education*, London: David Fulton.

Carlyle, D. E. E. and Woods, P. (2002) *The Emotions of Teacher Stress*, Stoke-on-Trent: Trentham Books.

Clarke, S. (2001) *Unlocking Formative Assessment*, London: Hodder and Stoughton.

Clegg, D. and Billington, S. (1994) *The Effective Primary Classroom*, London: David Fulton.

Clemson, D. and Clemson, W. (1996) *The Really Practical Guide to Primary Assessment*, 2nd edn, Cheltenham: Stanley Thornes.

Costello, P. J. M. (2000) *Thinking Skills and Early Childhood Education*, London: David Fulton.

Cullingford, C. (1995) *The Effective Teacher*, London: Cassell.

Curwin, R. L. and Mendler, A. N. (1988) *Discipline with Dignity*, Virginia: Edward Brothers.

Dean, J. (1992) *Organising Learning in the Primary School Classroom*, London: Routledge.

—— (1999) *Improving the Primary School*, London: Routledge.

DfEE (1998) *The National Literacy Strategy*, London: DfEE Publications.

—— (1999) *The National Numeracy Strategy*, London: DfEE Publications.

—— (2000) *Curriculum Guidance for the Foundation Stage*, London: Qualifications and Curriculum Authority.

DfEE/NACCCE (1999) *All Our Futures: Creativity, Culture and Education*, London: DfEE Publications.

DfEE/QCA (1999) *The National Curriculum: Handbook for Primary Teachers in England*, London: DfEE/QCA.

DfES (2001) *Special Educational Needs Code of Practice*, Annesley: DfES.

Drummond, M. J. (1993) *Assessing Children's Learning*, London: David Fulton.

Edgington, M. (1998) *The Nursery Teacher in Action*, London: Paul Chapman.

Edwards, N. (2000) 'Planning for all abilities: differentiation', in Jacques, K. and Hyland, R. (eds) *Professional Studies, Primary Phase*, Exeter: Learning Matters.

Elliott, J. (1993) 'Making decisions in the classroom', in Eggleston, J. (ed.) *Teacher Decision-making in the Classroom*, London: Routledge & Kegan Paul.

Farrer, F. (2000) *A Quiet Revolution*, London: Rider.

Fisher, J. (1996) *Starting From the Child*, Buckingham: Open University Press.

Fisher, R. (1990) *Teaching Children to Think*, Oxford: Blackwell.

—— (1995) *Teaching Children to Learn*, Cheltenham: Stanley Thornes.

Furlong, J. and Maynard, T. (1995) *Mentoring Student Teachers*, London: Routledge.

Gilbert, I. (2002) *Essential Motivation in the Classroom*, London: RoutledgeFalmer.

Gill, V. (1998) *The Ten Commandments of Good Teaching*, Thousand Oaks, California: Corwin Press.

Gipps, C., McCallum, B. and Hargreaves, E. (2000) *What Makes a Good Primary Teacher?* London: RoutledgeFalmer.

Gootman, M. E. (1997) *The Caring Teacher's Guide to Discipline*, London: Sage.

Griffiths, N. (1998) *A Corner To Learn*, Cheltenham: Stanley Thornes.

Hansen, D. T. (2001) *Exploring the Moral Heart of Teaching*, New York: Teachers College Press.

Hargreaves, A. (1994) *Changing Teachers, Changing Times: Teachers' Work and Culture in the Postmodern Age*, London: Cassell.

Hargreaves, A. and Fullan, M. (1998) *What's Worth Fighting for in Education?* Buckingham: Open University Press.

Harlen, W. (1985) *Teaching and Learning Primary Science*, London: Paul Chapman.

—— (2000) *The Teaching of Science in Primary Schools*, 3rd edn, London: David Fulton.

Harrison, J. (1995) 'A rationale for partnership', in Griffiths, V. and Owen, P. (eds) *Schools in Partnership*, London: Paul Chapman.

Harrop, A. and Williams, T. (1992) 'Rewards and punishments in the primary school: pupils' perceptions and teachers' usage', *Educational Psychology in Practice*, 7, 4, 211–215.

Hayes, D. (1999a) 'A matter of being willing? Mentors' expectations of student primary teachers', *Mentoring and Tutoring*, 7, 1, 67–79.

—— (1999b) *Foundations of Primary Teaching*, 2nd edn, London: David Fulton.

—— (2000) *The Handbook for Newly Qualified Teachers*, London: David Fulton.

—— (2001) 'The impact of mentoring and tutoring on student primary teachers' achievements: a case study', *Mentoring and Tutoring*, 9, 1, 5–21.

Holmes, E. (2000) *Newly Qualified Teachers*, London: The Stationery Office.

Howe, M. J. A. (1999) *A Teacher's Guide to the Psychology of Learning*, Oxford: Blackwell.

Hutchinson, D. (1994) 'Competence-based profiles for ITT and induction: the place of reflection', *British Journal of In-Service Education*, 20, 3, 303–312.

Jones, V. F. and Jones, L. S. (1986) *Comprehensive Classroom Management*, London: Allyn and Bacon.

Katz, L. G. and Chard, S. C. (2000) *Engaging Children's Minds: the Project Approach*, Stamford, Connecticut: Ablex Publishing Corporation.

Kerry, T. (1998) *Questioning and Explaining in Classrooms*, London: Hodder and Stoughton.

Kyriacou, C. (1991) *Essential Teaching Skills*, Cheltenham: Stanley Thornes.

Laar, W., Blatchford, R., Winkley, D., Badman, G. and Howard, R. (1989) *Effective Teaching*, Oxford: National Primary Centre.

Liebling, H. (1999) *Getting Started*, Stafford: Network Educational Press.

Lindsay, G. and Desforges, M. (1998) *Baseline Assessment*, London: David Fulton.

Littledyke, M. (1998) 'Teaching for constructive learning', in Littledyke, M. and Huxford, L. (eds) *Teaching the Primary Curriculum for Constructive Learning*, London: David Fulton.

McCallum, B., Hargreaves, E. and Gipps, C. (2000) 'Learning: the pupils' voice', *Cambridge Journal of Education*, 30, 2, 275–289.

McGee, P. (1998) *Perfect Public Speaking*, London: Arrow Books.

McNamara, S. and Moreton, G. (2001) *Changing Behaviour*, London: David Fulton.

Maynard, T. (2001) 'The student teacher and the school community of practice', *Cambridge Journal of Education*, 31, 1, 39–52.

Merry, R. (1998) *Successful Children, Successful Teaching*, Buckingham: Open University Press.

Mitchell, C. and Weber, S. (1999) *Reinventing Ourselves as Teachers: Beyond Nostalgia*, London: Falmer.

Nias, J. (1989) *Primary Teachers Talking*, London: Routledge.

—— (1997) 'Would schools improve if teachers cared less?' *Education 3–13*, 25, 3, 11–22.

Packard, N. and Race, P. (2000) *2000 Tips for Teachers*, London: Kogan Page/ TES.

Petty, G. (1998) *Teaching Today*, Cheltenham: Stanley Thornes.

Pinder, R. (1987) *Why Don't Teachers Teach Like They Used To?* London: Hilary Shipman.

Pollard, A. (1997) *Reflective Teaching in the Primary School*, London: Routledge.

Pollard, A. (2002) *Reflective Teaching: Effective and Evidence-informed Professional Practice*, New York: Continuum.

Porter, L. (1999) *Young Children's Behaviour*, Sydney: MacLennan and Petty.

Potter, R. (2000) 'An introduction to children's learning', in Jacques, K. and Hyland, R. (eds) *Professional Studies: Primary Phase*, Exeter: Learning Matters.

Proctor, A., Entwistle, M., Judge, B. and McKenzie-Murdoch, S. (1995) *Learning to Teach in the Primary Classroom*, London: Routledge.

QCA (Qualifications and Curriculum Authority) (1999) *Target Setting and Assessment in the National Literacy Strategy*, London: QCA.

Quinn, V. (1997) *Critical Thinking in Young Minds*, London: David Fulton.

Reece, I. and Walker, S. (2000) *Teacher Training and Learning: A Practical Guide*, Sunderland: Business Education Publishers.

Robertson, J. (1996) *Effective Classroom Control*, London: Hodder and Stoughton.

SCAA (Schools Curriculum and Assessment Authority) (1997) *The National Framework for Baseline Assessment*, London: SCAA.

Selley, N. (1999) *The Art of Constructivist Teaching in the Primary School*, London: David Fulton.

Smith, C. J. and Laslett, R. (1993) *Effective Classroom Management: A Teacher's Guide*, London: Routledge.

Spear, M., Gould, K. and Lee, B. (2000) *Who Would Be A Teacher?* Slough: NFER.

Stephenson, J. (1995) 'Significant others: the primary student view of practice in schools', *Educational Studies*, 21, 3, 323–333.

Stern, J. (1995) *Learning to Teach*, London: David Fulton.

TTA (Teacher Training Agency) (2002a) Circular 2/02, *Qualifying to Teach: Professional Standards for Qualified Teacher Status and Requirements for Initial Teacher Training*, London: TTA.

—— (2002b) *Qualifying to Teach: Handbook of Guidance*, London: TTA.

Thody, A., Gray, B. and Bowden, D. (2000) *The Teacher's Survival Guide*, London: Continuum.

Van Gennep, A. (1960) *The Rites of Passage*, London: Routledge & Kegan Paul.

Wachter, J. C. (1999) *Sweating the Small Stuff*, London: Sage/Corwin Press.

Wallace, B. (2000) *Teaching the Very Able Child*, London: David Fulton/ National Association for Able Children in Education.

Wallace, B. and Bentley, R. (eds) (2002) *Teaching Thinking Skills Across the Middle Years*, London: David Fulton/National Association for Able Children in Education.

Waters, M. (1996) *Managing Your Primary Classroom*, London: Collins.

Wilson, S. and Cameron, R. (1996) 'Student teacher perceptions of effective teaching: a developmental perspective', *Journal of Education for Teaching*, 22, 2, 181–195.

Wolfendale, S. and Bastiani, J. (2000) *The Contribution of Parents to School Effectiveness*, London: David Fulton.

Woods, P. (1990) *The Happiest Days? How Pupils Cope With School*, London: Falmer.

Woods, P. and Jeffrey, B. (1996) *Teachable Moments: The Art of Teaching in Primary Schools*, Buckingham: Open University Press.

Wragg, E. C. (1993) *Primary Teaching Skills*, London: Routledge.

NAME INDEX

SUBJECT INDEX

ROUTLEDGE STUDY GUIDES

WORK SMARTER, NOT HARDER!

It's a simple fact - everyone needs a bit of help with their studies. Whether you are studying for academic qualifications (from A-levels to doctorates), undertaking a professional development course or just require good, common sense advice on how to write an essay or put together a coherent and effective report or project, Routledge Study Guides can help you realise your full potential.

Our impressive range of titles covers the following areas:

- Speaking
- Study Technique
- Thinking
- Writing

- Science
- English
- History
- Mathematics
- Politics

- Doctorate
- MBA
- Research

Available at all good bookshops or you can visit the website to browse and buy Routledge Study Guides online at:

www.study-guides.com
www.study-guides.com
www.study-guides.com
www.study-guides.com
www.study-guides.com

ROUTLEDGE